Economic Methodology

ECONOMIC METHODOLOGY

A Bibliography
with References to Works
in the Philosophy of Science,
1860–1988

Compiled by
DEBORAH A. REDMAN

Bibliographies and Indexes in Economics
and Economic History, Number 9

GREENWOOD PRESS
New York • Westport, Connecticut • London

Library of Congress Cataloging-in-Publication Data

Redman, Deborah A.
  Economic methodology : a bibliography with references to works in
the philosophy of science, 1860-1988 / compiled by Deborah A.
Redman.
    p.   cm. — (Bibliographies and indexes in economics and
economic history, ISSN 0749-1786 ; no. 9)
  ISBN 0-313-26859-2 (lib. bdg. : alk. paper)
    1. Economics—Methodology—Bibliography.   2. Science—Philosophy—
Bibliography.   I. Title.   II. Series.
Z7164.E2R43   1989
[HB131]
016.330'.01—dc20   89-17195

British Library Cataloguing in Publication Data is available.

Library of Congress Catalog Card Number: 88-17195
ISBN: 0-313-26859-2
ISSN: 0749-1786

First published in 1989

Greenwood Press, Inc.
88 Post Road West, Westport, Connecticut 06881

Printed in the United States of America

The paper used in this book complies with the
Permanent Paper Standard issued by the National
Information Standards Organization (Z39.48-1984).

10 9 8 7 6 5 4 3 2 1

I often tell my students that they should not publish any methodological notes, papers, or books until after they have done years of substantive research in their field, and attained recognition for their mastery of its technical aspects. The danger of vacuous chatter is great if one engages in methodological discourse without previous work on substantive problems. On the other hand, even a lifetime of scientific research does not generate, let alone guarantee, comprehension of methodological problems. It also takes years of studying philosophy, not limited to just one philosophical school, but catholic in scope. No one should attempt to be a self-made methodologist.

* * *

Fritz Machlup, *Methodology of Economics and Other Social Sciences* (New York: Academic Press, 1978), p. x.

Contents

Introduction

What Is Methodology and Why Is It Important?

The 1980's witnessed a major revival of interest in economic methodology, especially with respect to the tenets of the philosophy of science. With the publication of Mark Blaug's **The Methodology of Economics Or How Economists Explain** in 1980 economic methodology became respectable once again. Daniel Hausman claims that this revived interest is due to the fact that economics has fallen upon hard times:

> When times are hard for economic theory--
> as they are now. . . economists start
> boning up on their philosophy of science,
> because they hope that they will be able
> to trace their difficulties to some
> simple, but definite methodological
> errors. Economists would, ironically,
> like nothing better than to discover
> that they have been methodological
> boneheads! In that case their ailments
> would have a definite cure.[1]

And certainly economists do turn to methodology to find new answers or old mistakes. That alone justifies this volume, which is meant to be a comprehensive bibliography of methodological works since 1860.

Methodology, nonetheless, has never really enjoyed great popularity among economists. Doing methodology, as Sidney Schoeffler so succinctly admits, has the major drawback that the methodologist

> often antagonizes the very people whom
> he respects and admires the most; and
> that he often wins the approval of at
> least some people for whose approval

he does not care. And this somewhat
melancholy situation is even aggravated
by the fact that the methodologist will
usually "pick" on the most creative and
most productive scholars in his field--
since their work is the most important,
it is also the most "worthy" of methodological analysis. There is a distinct
element of intellectual patricide in
methodological work, and this aspect
of it does not help to win it social
approval.[2]

Yet there is need for it, for methodology is criticism
with perspective. And, as Fritz Machlup has noted,
methodological discussion in economics is commonplace.
It occurs every time economists say "such things as 'this
is too abstract,' 'this is more realistic,' 'this is purely
static reasoning,' 'this is not statistically verified,'
'there is no historical evidence for this,' and so on."[3]
Economists' subject matter is constantly in flux; their
problems change as well. This means that the approach
to, i.e., the method of, solving economic problems will
not remain constant and thus will be a continuous source
of controversy. In other words, economists can expect
that methodology is here to stay, and should thus concentrate on bettering their "criticism with perspective."
There is no greater medicine for that than knowing and
understanding what arguments have already been brought
forth.

How This Bibliography Is Organized and Was Compiled

This bibliography has been organized by major areas
of controversy and includes references to the philosophy
of science, which has become strongly intertwined with
economic methodology since T.W. Hutchison introduced
economists to falsification in his **The Significance and
Basic Postulates of Economic Theory** in 1938. This bibliography is divided into 2 parts: one on economic methodology and the other on the philosophy of science. Works by
philosophers of science, however, can be found in the part
on methodology and works by economists in the part on
philosophy of science. For instance, Herbert Simon has
contributed to the pure philosophy of science (see part
II, § 12 miscellaneous) and to economic methodology.
The reason for including extensive references to the
philosophy of science should be clear to anyone who has
kept up with contemporary economic literature, where the
references to Popper, Kuhn, Lakatos, and other contemporary
philosophers of science are innumerable. That can be seen
clearly from sections 5.1. and 7.1. alone, where applications of Kuhnian paradigms and Lakatosian research
programmes to economics are treated.

Because this bibliography contains more than 2,000

entries, it was not possible to annotate all of them. As
a compromise I thus chose to annotate the classics in
economic methodology and almost all of the books: those
published on economic methodology since 1960 (part I,
§ 2) and before 1960 (part I, § 25.1), as well as the
books by Sir Karl Popper (part II, § 2.1), by Paul
Feyerabend (part II, § 8.1.1), and by the German
structuralists (part II, § 9.1). In addition, I have
annotated the works in the first section of part two on
the philosophy of science because I thought most readers
would not be familiar with these works. All other sections
are provided with an introduction to the topic and the
articles collected under that heading.

Part one on methodology is essentially organized by
methodological position and controversy. Sections 6
through 11, for instance, treat controversies: six treats
crises, seven quantification, eight theory (with sub-
sections on causality, prediction, and models), nine
econometrics, ten rationality, and eleven the maximization
hypothesis. In addition, four is organized around the
Friedman controversy, thirteen around knowledge in
economics, fourteen around the is-ought dichotomy, fifteen
around semantics, seventeen around the role of history
and philosophy in economics, eighteen around the role
of ethics and values in economics, twenty around consensus
and dissension among economists, and twenty-one around
the Cambridge controversy. Samuelson, like Friedman, won
his own separate category (§ 5) because of his great
influence upon the discipline. The positions of the
Austrians, the new group of rhetoricians, the institutionalists, the German historical school, and Marxists
are treated in sections 12, 16, 22, 23 and 24 respectively.
The Austrians have been classified by the narrow grouping,
i.e, Shackle, Robbins, et al. are not included. There
is a miscellaneous category, section twenty-five, which
catches the remaining sources.

Part two deals with the philosophy of science. Section
one provides introductory texts and background sources for
the uninitiated. The rest of the sections are organized to
a great extent around the philosophies of science which
economists have incorporated into their economic philosophies. Hence works by and on Karl Popper, Thomas Kuhn,
Imre Lakatos, Paul Feyerabend, and the German structuralists appear as categories. These are not lists of the
entire life works of Popper, Kuhn, etc., but are rather
the works which have relevance for economists and social
scientists. For instance, I include Popper's works on
economics, falsification, rationality, historicism,
prediction in social science, etc. Many of his works
on the natural sciences have bearing on his philosophy
of social sciences by way of his falsification theory,
and thus are listed. But I have left out Kuhn's histories
of physics which do not seem to have a great bearing on
economic methodology.

One can also find a section on holism and the Duhem thesis, which has important implications for testing of theories. Because the debate in the philosophy of science over the role of history parallels the one in economics over history, category 11 came to be. Finally, there is a miscellaneous category which collects further relevant works on the philosophy of science, including the works of the Popper family (e.g., Agassi, Albert, Bartley, Koertge, and Radnitzky) and of the historically minded philosophers of science (Toulmin, Hanson, Fleck, Polanyi, Lauden, Holton, etc.). The works of their critics also appear, e.g., Glymour, who criticizes the "new fuzziness" in the philosophy of science. There are also classics such as the works by Reichenbach and Kant.

Rather than list the works of economics' Nobel Prize recipients separately, I have marked them by placing an asterisk before their names. It is interesting to note that of the Nobel Prize recipients:

1969: Ragnar Frisch & Jan Tinbergen
1970: Paul Samuelson
1971: Simon Kuznets
1972: John R. Hicks & Kenneth J. Arrow
1973: Wassily Leontief
1974: Gunnar Myrdal & Friedrich A. von Hayek
1975: Leonid Kantorovich & Tjalling Koopmans
1976: Milton Friedman
1977: Bertil Ohlin & James Meade
1978: Herbert A. Simon
1979: Theodore W. Schulz & Arthur Lewis
1980: Lawrence R. Klein
1981: James Tobin
1982: George Stigler
1983: Gerard Debreu
1984: Sir Richard Stone
1985: Franco Modigliani
1986: James Buchanan
1987: Robert M. Solow
1988: Maurice Allais

only Kantorovich, the trade theorists Ohlin and Meade, and the economic development theorists Schulz and Lewis have made no contributions to economic methodology.

The bibliography is meant to be as comprehensive as possible, but there are major problems in assembling a bibliography on economic methodology. This bibliography is certainly exhaustive in the sense that the **Journal of Economic Literature** and the **Index of Economic Journals** were systematically searched through under "economic methodology" (036). The **Philosopher's Index** was also worked through systematically (under "economics"). I also benefitted from two computer systems: OCLC and the German equivalent, IBAS. Nonetheless, the bibliographical

research was restricted for several reasons. First, I
could only include sources which I have seen and can read.
Since I have a knowledge of English, French, German,
and Spanish only, I regret that numerous Dutch, Italian,
and Swedish sources could not be included. In some cases
the journal or book simply was not available and hence
could not be included. (Or a journal was only available
for a certain time range.) But because methodology has
gone through popular and very unpopular phases, it presents
a most peculiar research problem: some works which are
of a methodological nature were not listed under "methodology" in the various indices. And there are even reverse
situations. For example, the one that stands out in my
mind is Barro and Grossman's **Money, Employment and
Inflation** (1976), which appeared in the **JEL** listing <u>not</u>
under "theory," but under "history of economic thought
and methodology"! I hope that my own knowledge of both
fields helped to counteract this problem. Very useful
were the existing bibliographies in the works of Blaug,
Caldwell, Hausman, and those in all the books included
in this bibiliography, which were carefully evaluated
and incorporated into this work. (An apology is extended
to anyone whose work has been neglected.)

If "in German" or "in French" appears, this means
that the book has not been translated, to my knowledge.
If an anthology appears in the bibliography, all relevant
works contained in the bibliography have received a
separate entry so that the reader can see the actual
contents of the work. This bibliography contains 2,244
entries; the number of actual sources is smaller as some
sources repeat themselves, appearing, for example, in
the section on "theory" as well as on the "Austrians"
(Morgenstern's article which appears as 8.105 and 12.3.42).
As a final note on the compilation of the bibliography
itself, there are many works on the methodology of social
science in general which simply could not be included
due to space limitations and their peripheral nature.

Finally, I would like to extend a special thanks
to the Bielefeld University librarians: to Gisela Grah,
Dr. Heide Liehl, Barbara Fechtler, Kerstin Kleinebreil,
Sieglinde Kerzel, and Barbara Schipper of the mathematics/
economics section; to Rudolf Wrede of the philosophy
section; and to Erich Grevelding, Waltraud Neudenberger,
Ursula Pape, and Bettina Schein of inter-library loan,
who blithely executed more than 200 requests in the past
2 years. Many thanks also to Michigan State University
librarians who also put through innumerable inter-library
loan requests on my behalf, as well as those at the
libraries at Kiel University and at the Kiel Institut
für Weltwirtschaft.

Notes:

[1] Daniel M. Hausman, "The Limits of Economic Science," in Nicholas Rescher, ed., **The Limits of Lawfulness** (Lanham, MD: University Press of America, 1983), p. 93.

[2] Sidney Schoeffler, **The Failures of Economics: A Diagnostic Study** (Cambridge: Harvard University Press, 1955), p. vii.

[3] Fritz Machlup, "Issues on Methodology: Introductory Remarks," **American Economic Association Papers and Proceedings** 42, No. 2 (May 1952), p. 36.

***

PART ONE

ECONOMIC METHODOLOGY

1

The Classics

1.1 Cairnes, J.E. 1965 (1888). **The Character and Logical Method of Political Economy,** 2nd ed. London: Macmillan and Co.

> This work examines the methods of political economy. In this edition Cairnes considers Jevon's view that mathematics should be used in economics and rejects it. This work is divided into 7 "lectures": introduction; on the mental and physical premises of political economy, and of the logical character of the doctrines thence deduced; on the logical method of political economy; on the logical method of political economy continued; on the solution of an economic problem, and of the degree of perfection of which it is susceptible; of the place and purpose of definition in political economy; of the Malthusian doctrine of population; of the theory of rent.

1.2 *Friedman, Milton. 1953. "The Methodology of Positive Economics." In his **Essays in Positive Economics.** Chicago: University of Chicago Press, 1953, pp. 3-43.

> This is probably the best known work in economic methodology of all times. Friedman argues that prediction is the goal of economists and that the assumptions economists use do not need to be realistic so long as they predict. (Section four of this bibliography is devoted exclusively to the literature on Friedman and the assumptions controversy in economics.)

1.3 Hutchison, T.W. 1965 (1938). **The Significance and Basic Postulates of Economic Theory.** NY: Augustus M. Kelley.

> This classic, first published in 1938, was reprinted

with a new preface in 1960. In the preface Hutchison softens his position on demarcation of 1938 and he retreats from his naturalist position. This work first introduced the economic world to falsification. Hutchison argues that economists must formulate and test empirical generalizations, that statements of pure theory are empty, tautological truths, and that the limitations of ceteris paribus should be acknowledged.

1.4 Keynes, John Neville. 1973 (1917). **The Scope and Method of Political Economy**, 4th ed. NY: Augustus M. Kelley.

This is the classic work on the scope of political economy. It is in this work that "positive" and "normative" science are for the first time used in the modern sense to describe economics. They are also contrasted with an art.

1.5 *Koopmans, Tjalling. 1957. **Three Essays on the State of Economic Science.** NY: McGraw-Hill.

These 3 essays emphasize formal model construction in theory and in empirical research. The 3 essays are on allocation of resources and the price system, the construction of economic knowledge, and the interaction of tools and problems in economics.

1.6 Marshall, Alfred. 1960 (1920). **Principles of Economics,** 9th variorum, with annotations by C.W. Guillebaud. London: Macmillan for the Royal Economic Society; Book I, Vol. 1, "Introduction," and Appendix C, "The Scope and Method of Economics."

For Marshall economics is the science of human behavior rather than the science of wealth. It benefits from the use of theoretical (including mathematical), historical, and statistical techniques. In his Appendix C on "The Scope and Method of Economics" he asserts that "economics" has no near kinship with any physical science" and "is a branch of biology broadly interpreted."

1.7 Menger, Carl. 1969 (1883). **Untersuchungen über die Methode der Sozialwissenschaften and der politischen Ökonomie insbesondere.** Vol. II of his **Gesammelte Werke.** Ed. and with an introduction by F.A. Hayek, 2nd ed. 4 Vols. Tübingen: J.C.B. Mohr; Trans. by Francis J. Nock as **Investigations into the Method of the Social Sciences with Special Reference to Economics.** 1985 (rpt. of 1963). With a new introduction by Lawrence H. White. Ed. by Louis Schneider. NY/London: New York University Press. (Originally published in English as **Problems of Economics and Sociology,** 1963).

Menger's second work, this book is devoted to investigating the methodological mistakes of the German historical school, economics as theoretic science, self-interest, atomism, the historical aspects of economics, the organic analogy, and contrasts and similarities between the social and natural sciences. Menger's methodological works brought birth to the "Austrian school," originally a pejorative appellation used by German historical economists to describe the protheoretic stance of Menger and his followers.

1.8 Mill, John Stuart. 1974 (1874). **Essays on Some Unsettled Questions of Political Economy,** 2nd ed. Clifton, N.Y.: Augustus Kelley; Essay V: "On the Definition of Political Economy; and on the Method of Investigation proper to it" (1836).

This essay is one of the earliest discussions of methodology of economics and it remains one of the the best. Mill believes the premises of economics are well supported empirically and its conclusions follow deductively from its premises. But it is nonetheless a science of "tendencies" and is thus "hypothetical."

1.9 Mill, John Stuart. 1965 (1843). **A System of Logic Ratiocinative and Inductive Being a Connected View of the Principles of Evidence and the Methods of Scientific Investigation.** Vol. VII of the **Collected Works of John Stuart Mill.** Ed. by J. M. Robson and R.F. McRae. Toronto/London: University of Toronto Press/Routledge and Kegan Paul.

This is Mill's principal philosophical work. Deduction, induction, the neutral nature of logic, fallacies, and the logic of the moral sciences are discussed. Chapters VI to X of Book VI, "On the Logic of the Moral Sciences," treat the methodology of the social sciences.

1.10 *Myrdal, Gunnar. 1969. **Objectivity in Social Research.** NY: Pantheon.

This work tries to provide an answer to the problem of how social scientists can be objective. It is in this work that Myrdal recommends that objectivity can be obtained by stating explicitly the value premises underlying one's theoretical work.

1.11 Robbins, Lionel. 1984 (1932). **An Essay on the Nature and Significance of Economic Science,** 3rd ed. Foreword by William Baumol. London: Macmillan.

This is the third edition of Robbin's classic essay; it is a reprint of the 1935 revised edition of the

original 1932 essay with the addition of Robbin's 1980
Richard T. Ely Lecture to the AEA, in which he
reflects on the earlier essay. In this famous essay
Robbins defines economics as "the science which
studies human behavior as a relationship between ends
and scarce means which have alternative uses."

1.12 Robinson, Joan. 1962. **Economic Philosophy.** London:
C.A. Watts and Co.

This classic work treats metaphysics, morals, and
science in its first essay. Then the author discusses
the classical concept of value, neoclassical utility,
the Keynesian revolution, development and underdevelopment, and "the rules of the game."

1.13 Schumpeter, Joseph A. 1954. **History of Economic
Analysis.** NY: Oxford University Press; Part I: "Scope and
Method," pp. 3-47 and his "Science and Ideology." **American
Economic Review** 39, No. 2 (March): 345-59.

These two works are interrelated and hence cited
as one. Schumpeter asserts that parts of economics can
be objective and nonevaluative because economists'
analytical tools are neutral. Ideology is discussed as
a surmountable obstacle. It is also not completely
negative, being related to "vision," the source of
scientific discovery. The "Scope and Method" of his
History of Economic Analysis was never finished.

1.14 von Mises, Ludwig. 1978 (1962). **The Foundation of
Economic Science: An Essay on Method,** 2nd ed. Foreword by
Israel Kirzner. Kansas City: Sheed Andrews and McMeel.

This classic work discusses praxeology, apriorism,
knowledge and economics, certainty and uncertainty,
scope, and positivism. This was von Mises' last book,
and thus his final views as economist-philosopher.

1.15 von Mises, Ludwig. 1960. **Epistemological Problems of
Economics.** Trans. by George Reisman from the German
Grundprobleme der Nationalökonomie (1933). Princeton, N.J.:
D. Van Nostrand Co., Inc.

Here von Mises develops his science of human action.
Such a science cannot be based on logical positivism,
historicism, institutionalism, Marxism, Fabianism,
economic history, econometrics, or statistics. The
aim of this essay is to clear the way for systematic
analyses of human action. Von Mises discusses the
nature and development of the social sciences, scope
of a priori theorems, science and value,
utilitarianism and rationalism, praxeology (which
he first called "sociology"), understanding, and
a subjective theory of value.

1.16 Weber, Max. 1949 (1904). "'Objectivity' in Social Science and Social Policy." In his **The Methodology of the Social Sciences**. Trans. and ed. by Edward A. Shils and Henry A. Finch. Glencoe, Ill.: The Free Press, 1949; Originally appeared as "Die Objektivität sozialwissenschaftlicher und sozialpolitischer Erkenntnis." **Archiv für Sozialwissenschaft und Sozialpolitik** 19 (1904): 24-87.

This is the best known of all of Weber's methodological writings. He asserts that the goal of social science should be understanding. We should empathize with the agents' actions in order to understand them. Hence an element of subjectivism enters into social science. Weber believes social science, nonetheless, can be objective.

***

2

Books Published on Economic Methodology Since 1960

2.1   Adorno, Theodor W., et al. 1976. **The Positivist Dispute in German Sociology.** Trans. of **Der Positivismusstreit in der deutschen Soziologie** (1969) by Glyn Adey and David Frisby. NY: Harper and Row.

This book is the fruit of the 1961 conference of the German Sociological Society in Tübingen on the logic of the social sciences. It contains essays from Adorno, Popper, Dahrendorf, Habermas, H. Albert, and Harold Pilot. Popper presents his "27 theses" here, to which the Frankfurt school (Hegelians/Marxists) were to respond. Popper concludes with a short review of the entire volume; he regrets that both sides talked past other, i.e., did not address each other's issues.

2.2   Albert, Hans. 1972 (1954). **Ökonomische Ideologie und politische Theorie. Das ökonomische Argument in der ordnungspolitischen Debatte,** 2nd ed. Göttingen: Verlag Otto Schwartz & Co.

Albert discusses the rationality principle, values in economics, problems with equilibrium, the assumption of perfect foresight, maximization, consumer sovereignty, power, and ideology in economics. (In German)

2.3   Armstrong, Wallace Edwin. 1960. **Philosophical Reflections of an Economist.** Southampton: Southampton University Press.

This tiny book, actually a 21-page published inaugural lecture, deals with the metaphysical foundations of economics. Armstrong relies heavily on Popper's theory of falsification and metaphysics. He discusses causality, indeterminacy, and uncertainty in physics and economics.

2.4   Arndt, Helmut. 1984. **Economic Theory v. Economic Reality,** rev. Engl. ed. of **Irrwege der politischen Ökonomie: Die Notwendigkeit einer wirtschaftstheoretischen Revolution.** München: C.H. Beck, 1979. Trans. William A. Kirby. East Lansing, MI: Michigan State University Press.

Arndt criticizes textbook explanations which are over-simplifications or incorrect generalizations presented as truths. He also suggests a way to incorporate history into theory and to bring economic theory closer to reality.

2.5   Balogh, Thomas. 1982. **The Irrelevance of Conventional Economics.** London: Weidenfeld and Nicolson.

A book based on lectures, it sketches fashions and failures in economics experienced by the author. He argues that the weaknesses of most economic approaches to applied economics are due to failure or refusal "to recognize the actual nature of economic relationships" (p. 1) because of economics' narrowness and its methods. The work is extremely critical of neoclassical economics.

2.6   Baranzini, Mauro and Roberto Scazzieri, eds. 1986. **Foundations of Economics.** Oxford: Basil Blackwell.

This is a mixed collection of articles by Baranzini, Scazzierei, Hicks, Schmitt, Allais, Bacharack, Helm, Hennings, Georgescu-Roegen, Landesmann, Quadrio-Curzio, Bharadwaj, Bliss, and Pasinetti.

2.7   Barry, Norman P. 1979. **Hayek's Social and Economic Philosophy.** Atlantic Highlands, NJ: Humanities Press.

Barry sketches and discusses Hayek's theories on philosophy, law, politics, and economics, including his views on Popper, Keynes, socialism, liberalism, and conservativism.

2.8   Bell, Daniel and Irving Kristol, eds. 1981. **The Crisis in Economic Theory.** NY: Basic Books.

This work was first published in 1980 as **The Public Interest**'s Special Issue: "The Crisis in Economic Theory." The crisis, the dissolution of the Keynesian consensus, is considered from various viewpoints in economics. 10 essays are contributed by Drucker, Dean, Meltzer, Bell, Willes, Leibenstein, Kirzner, Hahn, Arrow, and Davidson.

2.9   Bensusan-Butt, D.M. 1980. **On Economic Knowledge: A Sceptical Miscellany.** Canberra: Australian National University.

This is a collection of essays written earlier which discuss Keynesian economics, Keynes, economic man, Bentham, knowledge in economics, and Australian economics.

2.10   Black, R.D. Collision, A.W. Coats and Craufurd D.W. Goodwin, eds. 1973. **The Marginal Revolution in Economics: Interpretation and Evaluation.** Papers presented at a conference held at the Villa Serbelloni, Bellagio, Italy, August 22-28, 1971. Durham, N. Carolina: Duke University Press.

These 17 papers were prepared for and given at a symposium in Italy whose theme was "Does marginalism represent a revolution in the history of economic thought?" Participants included: Coats, Blaug, Winch, Black, Meek, Goodwin, Stigler, Shackle, Streissler, Jaffé, de Marchi, Hutchison, Matsuura, Howey.

2.11   Blaug, Mark. 1980(a). **A Methodological Appraisal of Marxian Economics.** Professor Dr. F. de Vries Lectures in Economics, Vol. 3. Amsterdam: North-Holland.

In this slim volume Blaug appraises Marxian economics from the standpoint of Lakatos' theory of scientific research programmes. Blaug shows Marxism fails to be scientific on logical grounds, Marx's prophecies being "ad hoc prophecies." Blaug concludes that Marxism is "a degenerating research programme" which has been degenerating since ca. 1900.

2.12   Blaug, Mark. 1980(b). **The Methodology of Economics Or How Economists Explain.** Cambridge: Cambridge University Press.

In this work Blaug first introduced economists to the philosophy of science with his systematic treatment of the modern philosophy of science (part I). In part II he sketches the history of economic methodology. In part III he appraises neoclassical economics. In part IV he concludes and offers his advice (economists should practice more falsification). This work made methodology once again popular in economics.

2.13   Boland, Lawrence A. 1986. **Methodology for a New Microeconomics.** Boston: Allen and Unwin.

His work focuses on equilibrium. Equilibrium is contrasted with optimization. Its foundations in economics are examined; individualism and calculus are discussed. Limits of equilibrium analysis are discussed; a new microeconomics of non-equilibria is proposed.

2.14   Boland, Lawrence A. 1982. **The Foundations of Economic Method.** London: Allen and Unwin.

Neoclassical economics is his subject and Boland concludes that all of neoclassical economics has one foundation: the problems of induction and of individualism. He then discusses disequilibrium economics, rational expectations, microfoundations, and the problem of time. Finally, conventionalism and the reason why Popper's philosophy of science has been rejected by economists are discussed.

2.15 Boulding, Kenneth. 1970. **Economics As a Science**. NY: McGraw-Hill.

This is a series of essays whose purpose is to introduce the unintiated to "the larger scientific background" (p. v) of economics and to give economists a broader perspective of the discipline (i.e., as a social, ecological, behavioral, political, mathematical, and moral science).

2.16 Brown, Harold I. 1988. **Rationality**. London/NY: Routledge.

The purpose of the work is to describe and criticize the widely used concept of rationality and to propose an alternative model of rationality. Brown argues that science fails to be rational when viewed in light of the classical model, but that the classical model is not accurate. This first part of the book presents a history of the problem of rationality. In the second half Brown develops his own solution to the problem. Although written by a philosopher, the concept of rationality is so central to economics that the work has been included in this section.

2.17 Brunner, Karl, ed. 1979. **Economics and Social Institutions: Insights from the Conferences on Analysis and Ideology**. Boston: Martinus Nijhoff.

This collection is the outgrowth of the Third Annual Interlaken Conference on Analysis and Ideology. The theme is economics as a social science (as envisaged by A. Smith). The contributions cover a wide range of subjects. Most of the authors are economists: Albert, Brunner, Bauer, Buchanan, Gäfgen, Monissen, Pejovich, Jensen, Meckling, Alchian, and Demsetz.

2.18 *Buchanan, James M. 1979. **What Should Economists Do?** Indianapolis: Liberty Press.

This is a collection of previously published and unpublished works on methodology. In addition to more usual works in economic methodology, Buchanan also includes several pieces on public choice theory.

2.19 Caldwell, Bruce J., ed. 1984. **Appraisal and Criticism** in Economics: A Book of Readings. Boston: Allen and Unwin.

> This is an anthology of some of the more interest-
> ing and famous pieces written on economic method-
> ology. .Selections are included from Hutchison,
> Machlup, Friedman, Nagel, Samuelson, Boland, Caldwell,
> Musgrave, Loasby, Cross, Blaug, Reder, Leibenstein,
> Weintraub, Dow, Brown, and Leamer.

2.20 Caldwell, Bruce J. 1982. Beyond Positivism. London:
Allen and Unwin.

> This book is a welcome complement to Blaug's work
> (1980) on the philosophy of science. In part I
> Caldwell surveys the modern philosophy of science
> for economists. In part II he discusses Robbins,
> Hutchison, the assumptions controversy, Friedman and
> Samuelson's methodology. In the final section he
> evaluates the utility of the philosophy of science for
> economists, discusses theory appraisal,
> confirmation, and falsification in economics. He
> concludes by advocating methodological pluralism.

2.21 Campbell, Richmond and Lanning Sowden, eds. 1985.
Paradoxes of Rationality and Cooperation: Prisoner's
Dilemma and Newcomb's Problem. Vancouver: University of
British Columbia Press.

> This is an anthology by philosophers about 2
> paradoxes: the prisoner's dilemma and Newcomb's
> problem. An introduction gives the uninitiated enough
> background to tackle the papers, many of which are now
> ranked as classics in the field.

2.22 Coats, A.W. 1983. Methodological Controversy in
Economics: Historical Essays in Honor of T.W. Hutchison.
Greenwich, CT: Jai Press.

> Coats offers a collection of essays, most of which
> were written in honor or T.W. Hutchison, who retired
> in 1978. The essays are on a variety of topics in
> methodology and history of economic thought.
> Contributors are Coats, Robbins, R.D.C. Black,
> Skinner, O'Brien, Barucci, Grampp, de Marchi,
> Harvey-Phillips, Blaug, and Vickers.

2.23 Cole, Ken, John Cameron and Chris Edwards. 1983. Why
Economists Disagree. London/NY: Longman.

> The authors investigate why economists cannot seem to
> agree, and conclude that there are several reasons for
> this, the inability to prove or disprove empirically
> the hypotheses or theories in economics being one
> reason. The development of economics is seen as the
> outcome of battles between schools of thought which
> are rooted in turn in a political school of thought.

are rooted in turn in a political school of thought.

2.24 Dasgupta, A.K., ed. 1968. **Methodology of Economic Research**. Bombay: Asia Publishing House.

The papers in this volume were presented at a seminar on methodology in India in 1966. The theme: the authors were to describe the method they used in research. The work covers analytical, applied economics, empirical research, and research in economic history.

2.25 Dickson, Harald. 1967. **Variable, Function, Derivative: A Semantic Study in Mathematics and Economics**. Göteborg, Sweden: Scandanavian University Books.

The book is meant for students and teachers of mathematical economics and econometrics and for philosophers. It is a study of the terms variable, function, derivative, partial derivatives, quantity, relation, and differential (especially as used by R.G. D. Allen in his classic **Mathematical Analysis for Economists** (1938)).

2.26 Dolan, Edwin G. 1976. **The Foundations of Modern Austrian Economics**. Kansas City: Sheed and Ward.

The proceedings are from a 1974 conference on Austrian economics. The authors seek to answer "What is the distinctive Austrian contribution to economic theory?" and "What is the direction for modern Austrian economics?" Contributors to the volume are Dolan, Rothbard, Kirzner, Lachmann, O'Driscoll, and Shenoy.

2.27 Dow, Sheila. 1985. **Macroeconomic Thought: A Methodological Approach**. Oxford: Basil Blackwell.

Dow attempts to bridge the gap between methodology and macroeconomic theory. She analyses macroeconomics in terms of concepts rather than issues. She treats the historical development of schools of thought in macroeconomics, microfoundations of macroeconomics, equilibrium, expectations, money, and policy.

2.28 Dyke, Charles. 1981. **Philosophy of Economics**. Englewood Cliffs: Prentice-Hall.

Meant to be an introductory text in the philosophy of economics, Dyke discusses problems with rationality, value, utility, preference, the market, freedom, property, abstraction, and realism in economics.

2.29 Eichner, Alfred S., ed. 1983. **Why Economics Is Not Yet a Science**. With a Preface by Wassily Leontief. London: Macmillan/Sharpe.

The essays in this volume constitute a critique of orthodox economics as an academic discipline. The works especially pick up on Leontief's theme that most economic theories are not supported by empirical evidence. Economics is criticized for being based to a great extent on axiomatic reasoning, for misusing mathematics, and for not testing its hypotheses or theories.

2.30 Elster, Jon. 1979. **Ulysses and the Sirens: Studies in Rationality and Irrationality.** NY/Melbourne: Cambridge University Press.

This work is divided into 4 parts. Part I deals with perfect rationality. Part II discusses imperfect rationality, arising from weakness of will preventing us from using our capacity to obtain perfect rationality. The third section explores problems in rationality. In part IV irrationality is discussed.

2.31 Fischer, Norman. 1979. **Economy and Self: Philosophy and Economics from the Mercantilists to Marx.** No. 24 of the Contributions in Economics and Economic History Series. Westport, CN/London: Greenwood.

The author examines the interconnections between philosophy and economics in the late eighteenth and nineteenth centuries. The themes of the self and individual and holistic explanation in economics are explored.

2.32 Fisher, Robert M. 1986. **The Logic of Economic Discovery: Neoclassical Economics and the Marginal Revolution.** Brighton: Wheatsheaf.

Fisher gives a "rational reconstruction" of neoclassical economic theory using Lakatos' methodology of scientific research programmes. First, he summarizes Lakatos' philosophy of science, emphasizing its merits. He concludes that marginalism had "heuristic power" and that classical economics was a "degenerating programme" and hence discarded. This work is based on Fisher's Ph.D. dissertation at Duke University.

2.33 Fuerle, Richard D. 1986. **The Pure Logic of Choice.** NY: Vantage Press.

In this work Fuerle argues that economics is a deductive and not an inductive science. He explores the foundations of economics and discusses the merit of praxeology as a foundation for economics.

2.34 Furner, Mary O. 1975. **Advocacy and Objectivity: A Crisis in the Professionalization of American Social**

Science 1865–1905. Lexington, KY: University of Kentucky Press.

Furner describes the history of the early development of social sciences, and especially of economics and the American Economic Association. The history clearly shows the strong tie of American economics to Germany and the historical school, the problems that social sciences, especially economics, had in gaining credibility as a science, and the political nature of the discipline.

2.35 Georgescu-Roegen, Nicholas. 1971. **The Entropy Law and the Economic Process.** Cambridge, MA: Harvard University Press.

The work centers around the entropy law in physics, which brought about the downfall of classical physics (which assumed that everything which happens consists of locomotion alone and thus there is no irrevocable change in nature). The author discusses the ramifications of this for economics. This work should be of great interest to anyone exploring the relationship between economics and physics.

2.36 Georgescu-Roegen, Nicholas. 1966. **Analytical Economics: Issues and Problems.** Cambridge, Mass.: Harvard University Press.

This is a collection of 12 previously published articles plus one new, unpublished section (part I, which was later expanded into his **Entropy Law and the Economic Process,** entry 2.35 supra). The articles deal with topics in utility, expectation, production, and economic development.

2.37 Godelier, Maurice. 1972. **Rationality and Irrationality in Economics.** Trans. by Brian Pearce from the French **Rationalité et irrationalité en économie** (1966). London: New Left Books.

Godelier discusses economics and rationality from a Marxian viewpoint. Lange, Hegel, and Marx's contributions are evaluated. Marx's Paris manuscripts are considered. The dialectical method is evaluated. He closes with a consideration of "economic anthropology," the problem of a "general theory" in economics, and he suggests that the concept of rationality be changed in economics.

2.38 Grassl, Wolfgang and Barry Smith, eds. 1986. **Austrian Economics: Historical and Philosophical Background.** London/Sidney: Croom Helm.

The volume is a treatment of the historical and philosophical background of the Menger tradition in

19th- and 20th-century Austria. There are 8 papers from philosophers and economists. The focus is on value and on the philosophical method of the Bretano school.

2.39 Hahn, Frank and Martin Hollis. 1979. **Philosophy and Economic Theory.** Oxford: Oxford University Press.

This is an anthology whose aim is to bring together important writings, mostly from periodicals, for the student or general reader. The volume contains selections from the writings of Friedman, Robbins, Hollis, Nell, von Mises, Simon, Sen, Arrow, Varion, Hammond, and Rawls.

2.40 Hamminga, Bert. 1983. **Neoclassical Theory Structure and Theory Development: An Empirical-Philosophical Case Study Concerning the Theory of International Trade.** Berlin: Springer.

The author (a philosopher) argues that recent works on the philosophy of science make the following mistakes: (1) the author believes that the philosophy of science yields results which can be used by economists to describe and evaluate their work, (2) it is believed that consideration of an economic theory at some point in time reveals its logical structure and **ipso facto** the method by which the theory is constructed, and (3) it is believed that what economists say about themselves is true. Hamminga further argues that Popper, Kuhn, and Lakatos failed in creating a framework capable of describing theory development in economics. This can be seen as history (and not logic) becomes the judge of metatheories (diachronism). He presents an empirical metatheory of theory structure and development in neoclassical economics and applies it to the theory of international trade.

2.41 Hausman, Daniel. 1984. **The Philosophy of Economics: An Anthology.** Cambridge: Cambridge University Press.

This volume is an anthology which includes most of the principal texts on philosophy and methodology of economics. It is aimed at students in economics and philosophy of science, professional philosophers, economists, and citizens. It contains a useful 50-page introduction to the subject. Hausman collects works from J.S. Mill, J.N. Keynes, Weber, Robbins, Knight, Marx, Veblen, Hutchison, Machlup, Friedman, Simon, Myrdal, Schumpeter, Klappholz, Marschak, J.M. Keynes, Lachmann, Dugger, Rosenberg, Hausman, and Blaug.

2.42 Hausman, Daniel. 1981. **Capital, Profits, and Prices: An Essay in the Philosophy of Economics.** NY: Columbia

University Press.

> This is a philosophical inquiry into capital and
> interest theory. Hausman concludes that economics
> does not have a good theory of capital or interest and
> their relation to equilibrium prices. He suggests
> that economic theorists should not exaggerate their
> achievements, but should attempt "to understand them
> correctly and to build upon them" (p. 191). Chapters
> 10 and the "Methodological Postscript" offer further
> conclusions.

2.43 *Hayek, Friedrich A. von. 1979 (1955). **The
Counter-Revolution of Science: Studies in the Abuse of
Reason**, 2nd ed. Indianapolis: Liberty Press.

> This is the famous piece of Hayek's in which he
> develops his thesis of "scientism." Discussed are the
> influence of natural sciences on social sciences,
> the subjective nature of economic data, the
> individualist and "compositive" method of social
> science, historicism, social engineering, and Comtian
> sociology and its relation to Hegel.

2.44 *Hayek, Friedrich A. von. 1978. **New Studies in
Philosophy, Politics, Economics and the History of Ideas.**
London: Routledge and Kegan Paul.

> This volume deals with problems of philosophy,
> politics, and economics. There is also a section on
> the history of ideas. The section on economics deals
> with the Ricardo effect, Keynesian economics and
> inflation and unemployment, and planning.

2.45 Herbst, Jurgen. 1965. **The German Historical School in
American Scholarship.** Ithaca, NY: Cornell University Press.

> Herbst traces the German influence on American
> universities in the 1800's and early 1900's. Americans
> studying in Germany and their impact upon the American
> university after they returned is discussed. The
> influence on economics and on social science in
> general is set out in chapters 6 and 8.

2.46 *Hicks, Sir John. 1979. **Causality in Economics.**
Oxford: Basil Blackwell.

> Hicks discusses the development of ideas of causality
> since the sixteenth century. Then causality and the
> social sciences is discussed, including statics and
> equilibrium, causality in Keynes, lags, and
> probability.

2.47 *Hicks, Sir John. 1974. **The Crisis in Keynesian
Economics.** Oxford: Basil Blackwell.

This is a set of 3 lectures on (1) saving, investment
and the multiplier, (2) money, interest and liquidity,
and (3) wages and inflation. Hicks discusses in part
his classic "Mr. Keynes and the Classics" and the
IS-LM apparatus, which he believes has been
misunderstood by students as "the theory of Keynes."
This misunderstanding has prompted Hicks to
reconstruct Keynes' **General Theory**; that is the
substance of the three essays.

2.48 Hollis, Martin and Edward J. Nell. 1975. **Rational
Economic Man.** London: Cambridge University Press.

The authors argue that neoclassical economic theories
are unsound; they rely on a positivist theory of
knowledge which is also unsound. They argue for a
classical Marxian theory of economics.

2.49 Hook, Sidney, ed. 1967. **Human Values and Economic
Policy.** NY: New York University Press.

This is the proceedings of the 8th annual New York
Institute of Philosophy (1966) which was aimed at
bringing economics and philosophy together, namely
through the evaluation of the value problem in
economics. Contributors are Arrow, Brandt, Samuelson,
Boulding, Nagel, Friedman, Albin, Baier, Johnson,
Kennedy, Kurtz, Ladd, Lowe, van den Haag, Weiss,
Kaysen, Braybrooke, Nathan, Hook, and Wallich.

2.50 Hutchison, T.W. 1981. **The Politics and Philosophy of
Economics: Marxians, Keynesians and Austrians.** NY: New
York University Press.

This is a collection of 9 papers, 6 of which appeared
earlier but were revised for the volume. Hutchison
examines some of the political, philosophical, and
epistemological presuppositions of Marxian, Keynesian,
and Austrian economic theory. The last 2 chapters are
devoted solely to methodological issues.

2.51 Hutchison, T.W. 1978. **On Revolutions and Progress in
Economic Knowledge.** Cambridge: Cambridge University.

This is a series of papers which investigates
revolutions and progress in economics. He focuses
on the 3 or 4 major turning-points in the history
of economics and the sense of progress which resulted.
Ricardian economics, Jevonian economics, and Keynesian
economics are discussed as possible revolutions.

2.52 Hutchison, T.W. 1977(a). **Keynes Versus the
'Keynesians';...?: An Essay in the Thinking of J.M. Keynes
and the Accuracy of Its Interpretation by His Followers.**
With commentaries by Lord Kahn and Sir Austin Robinson.
Hobart Paper No. 11. London: The Institute of Economic

Affairs; Revised and without commentaries as "Keynes **Versus**
the Keynesians" in Hutchison, 1981, pp. 108-54.

This slim paperback has as its focus the
interpretations of Keynes in light of Keynes'
writings. Hutchison concludes that the Keynesian
revolution was not entirely "Keynes-ian" and that
Keynes' name and repute have been used to support
policies which Keynes would never have claimed for his
own. Lord Kahn and Sir Austin Robinson respond.

2.53 Hutchison, T.W. 1977(b). **Knowledge and Ignorance in
Economics**. Chicago: University of Chicago Press.

In 5 essays Hutchison discusses prediction and
economics, the relevance for economics of recent
writings in the philosophy of science by Popper,
Kuhn, Lakatos, and Ravetz, and the "crisis" in
economics. The last section, an appendix, gives actual
examples of failures of economic policy--"economic
knowledge and ignorance in action."

2.54 Hutchison, T.W. 1965 (1938). **The Significance and
Basic Postulates of Economic Theory**. With a new Preface
(1960). NY: Augustus M. Kelley.

This classic, first published in 1938, was reprinted
with a new preface in 1960. In the preface Hutchison
softens his position on demarcation of 1938 and he
retreats from his naturalist position. This work first
introduced the economic world to falsification.

2.55 Hutchison, T.W. 1964. **'Positive' Economics and Policy
Objectives**. London: George Allen and Unwin Ltd.

In part I Hutchison traces the positive-normative
distinction in the history of economic thought and
examines the roles of value-judgement and bias in
economics. In part II he reviews objectives of
economic policies and discusses formulation of these
objectives.

2.56 Jetzer, Jean-Pierre. 1987. **Kritischer Rationalismus
und Nationalökonomie**. Bern/Frankfurt am Main/NY/Paris:
Peter Lang.

In this work Jetzer examines the relationship between
critical rationalism and economics. In the first part
he treats the philosophies of Popper, Albert, Kuhn,
and Lakatos. In part two he considers the economics of
Hicks, Krelle (a German econometrician), and Myrdal.
In the third part the author discusses the lessons
economists can learn from the philosophy of science
and vice versa.

2.57 Jochimsen, Reimut and Helmut Knobel. 1971. **Gegenstand**

und Methoden der Nationalökonomie. Köln: Kiepenhauer und Witsch.

> This collection (in German) contains several translations of English works in methodology, as well as new works. Contributors are Grunberg, Buchanan, Leontief, Schumpeter, Weber, Topitsch, Hansen, Eucken, Lange, Morgenstern, Richter, Samuelson, Novick, Klein, Duesenbery, Machlup, Albert, Boulding, Kloten, Bombach.

2.58 Katouzian, Homa. 1980. **Ideology and Method in Positive Economics.** NY: New York University Press.

> In this book Katouzian discusses political economy, positive economics and neoclassical theory, Popper's influence on economics, paradigms and research programmes, "big science" and economics, value judgements, and mathematics and abstraction in economics.

2.59 Kirzner, Israel M., ed. 1982. **Method, Process, and Austrian Economics: Essays in Honor of Ludwig von Mises.** Lexington, Mass./Toronto: Heath/Lexington Books.

> This is a collection of 19 essays written in honor of Ludwig von Mises' 100th birthday. Contributions are from Kirzner, Buchanan, Vaughn, Lachmann, Boehm, Rizzo, Langlois, Littlechild, White, Loasby, Garrison, Rothbard, O'Driscoll, Pasour, Yeager, and Salerno.

2.60 Kirzner, Israel M. 1976 (1960). **The Economic Point of View: An Essay in the History of Economic Thought**, 2nd ed. Ed. and with an introduction by Lawrence Moss. Kansas City: Universal Press Syndicate.

> The author reacquaints the reader with the Austrian view of the subjectivist basis of economics. Kirzner analyses the science of wealth and welfare, the science of avarice, catallactics and exchange, money, Robbin's definition of economics, macroeconomics, praxeology and human action, rationality, and apriorism. The second edition contains a new introduction. Kirzner argues that economics is a subdiscipline of the broader discipline which von Mises called praxeology, or the science of human action.

2.61 Klamer, Arjo. 1984. **The New Classical Macroeconomics: Conversations with the New Classical Economists and Their Opponents.** Bristol: Harvester Press.

> Klamer interviews (1) Lucas, Sargent, and Townsend of the New Classical School; (2) Tobin, Modigliani, and Solow of the older generation of Neo-Keynesians; (3) Blinder and Taylor of the younger Neo-Keynesians;

(4) Brunner of the Monetarists; (5) D. Gordon and Rapping as nonconventional economists. Then he interprets these interviews with respect to modern macroeconomics. He concludes that rhetorical aspects (rhetoric being the art of persuasion) of economics are the key to understanding economics.

2.62 Klant, J.J. 1984. **The Rules of the Game: The Logical Structure of Economic Theories.** Trans. Ina Swart. Cambridge: Cambridge University Press.

Klant, a Dutch economist, criticizes economic methodology and its pretensions. He examines operationalism, the demarcation problem, apriorism, theory, positivism, and other issues. This is a revised version of his dissertation (in Dutch).

2.63 Krupp, Sherman R., ed. 1966. **The Structure of Economic Science.** Englewood Cliffs, N.J.: Prentice-Hall.

This is a set of papers from economists, philosophers, and a physicist. In part I there is an introduction to methodology and discussion of theory construction and observation, controversy in economics, and the sociology of knowledge. In part II problems with mathematics and econometrics are discussed. Part III provides an investigation into the boundaries of economics, the role of institutions, and the aggregation problem. In part IV values, utility, and welfare are discussed. Contributors are Bronfenbrenner, Margenau, Krupp, Machlup, Nabers, Baumol, Rotwein, Tintner, Boulding, Grunberg, Buchanan, Ward, Lancaster, Rothenberg, Churchman, Brandt.

2.64 Lachmann, Ludwig M. 1977. **Capital, Expectations, and the Market Process: Essays on the Theory of the Market Economy.** Kansas City: Sheed Andrews and McMeel.

This is a collection of Lachmann's papers on Austrian economics. Part I is an introduction which sets Austrian economics in the "crisis" of the 1970's. Part II is a discussion of the significance of Austrian economics, the role of expectations, Shackle's concept of time, von Mises' science of human action, and model constructions. Part III deals with the market process. Part IV treats problems in macroeconomic and capital theory. Part V discusses profits and the market economy. There is also an appendix of Lachmann's writings.

2.65 Lachmann, Ludwig M. 1970. **The Legacy of Max Weber. Three Essays.** London: Heinemann.

This is a 3-essay work on Max Weber. The first essay deals with Weber's theory of action. The second is

concerned with institutions. The third essay deals
with political order and institutions.

2.66 Latsis, Spiro J. 1976. **Method and Appraisal in
Economics.** Cambridge: Cambridge University Press.

This work constitutes the proceedings of the economics
side of the Nafplion Colloquium on Research Programmes
in Physics and Economics held in Greece in September
1974. At the heart of the volume is theory appraisal
in economics. Papers by Blaug, Coats, Latsis, and de
Marchi discuss the extent of applicability of Lakatos'
methodology of scientific research programmes in
economics. Other contributors are Leijonhufvud, Simon,
Hutchison, and Hicks.

2.67 Leibenstein, Harvey. 1976. **Beyond Economic Man: A New
Foundation for Microeconomics.** Cambridge, MA: Harvard
University Press.

The author focuses on microeconomic foundations, and
specifically the "X-efficiency problem." Leibenstein
shows that maximizing and optimizing behavior is at
times inappropriate for understanding some economic
problems. Part I deals with the interdependent
consumer, part II with psychological postulates,
and part III with applications and implications.
An appendix provides a mathematical formalization.

2.68 Leinfellner, Werner and Eckehart Köhler, eds. 1974.
Developments in the Methodology of Social Science.
Dordrecht: D. Reidel.

This is an anthology by philosophers of social
science. General methodology is discussed in part I,
the foundations of social systems in part II, and
problems with social laws and forecasts in part III.
Part IV deals with statistics and hypothesis testing.

2.69 Lekachman, Robert. 1976. **Economists at Bay: Why the
Experts Will Never Solve Your Problems.** NY: McGraw.

This work is highly critical of economists. The author
first sketches "the sad state of economics," then
devotes the next chapter to recent mistakes in
inflation and unemployment management. The third
chapter "explains how innocent young people of good
character and decent mental capacity nevertheless
become economists" (p. xi). The next 2 chapters
treat the role of large corporations and unions. In
Chapter 6 he suggests that the classics be read
because they are still valuable. The final chapter
argues for economics as social science.

2.70 Letwin, William. 1963. **The Origins of Scientific
Economics: English Economic Thought 1660-1776.** London:

Methuen.

> The author discusses the very beginnings of English economics and the struggle to be recognized as a scientific discipline.

2.71 Loasby, Brian J. 1976. **Choice, Complexity and Ignorance: An Enquiry into Economic Theory and the Practice of Decision-Making.** Cambridge: Cambridge University Press.

> This book outlines the implications of complexity and partial ignorance for theory and practical decision-making. Organisational behavior, theories of competition, macroeconomics, and research management are discussed. The debt to Shackle is clear. In chapter 11 he discusses progress in terms of paradigms and programmes.

2.72 Lowe, Adolph. 1977 (1965). **On Economic Knowledge: Toward a Science of Political Economics,** enlarged ed. NY: Sharpe.

> This book is divided into 5 parts. The first deals with the question "Can economics be a science?" The second treats "the logic of economic science." The third develops the "historical trend of economic science" from Smith to Keynes. Part IV develops his theory of political economics and "instrumental analysis." The final section is a postscript on modern political economics. The work is critical of neoclassical economics; Lowe suggests revisions, i.e., that "traditional economics" should be superseded by "political economics."

2.73 Machlup, Fritz. 1978. **Methodology of Economics and Other Social Sciences.** NY: Academic Press.

> This collection of 26 papers does not contain all of Machlup's papers devoted to methodology. Most were published previously, 2 were written especially for the volume, and 1 was translated for the first time into English. Machlup divided the collection into 7 parts: on the nature and significance of methodology; on facts, models, and theories in economics; on verification and operationalism; on ideal types and the interpretation of reality; on comparisons between natural and social sciences; some aspects and applications of economic methodology; and on various methodological positions. This work can be used as an introduction to economic methodology.

2.74 Machlup, Fritz. 1967. **Essays in Economic Semantics.** NY: W. Norton.

> This is a collection of Machlup's essays on semantics

and economics. There is an introduction. The purpose of the second section is to "clarify widely used terms and concepts" in economics (preface). In section 3 marginal utility theory is discussed. In the final section Machlup analyses macroeconomics and development theory.

2.75 Marr, William and Baldev Raj, eds. 1983. **How Economists Explain: A Reader in Methodology.** Lanham, MD: University Press of America.

This reader was put together for students to expose them to various methodological positions. The editors gathered important recent articles on economic methodology and organized them into 9 sections: on the nature of economics; value judgements; economics as hard science; prediction; empiricism; verification; model building; holism; what's right and wrong with economics. Contributors are Machlup, Heilbroner, Ng, Mayer, Coddington, Pope and Pope, Boland, Rotwein, Archibald, McClements, Wilber, Harrison, Simon, Leontief, Heller.

2.76 Mason, Sir John, P. Mathias and J.H. Westcott. 1986. **Predictability in Science and Society.** A Joint Symposium of the Royal Society and the British Academy Held on 20 and 21 March 1986. London: The Royal Society and the British Academy.

These essays are the proceedings of a symposium held by the Royal Society and British Academy on predictability, primarily in economics. Contributors are Sen, Hendry, Lighthill, Mason, Hide, Cohen, Westcott, Burns, Gulland.

2.77 McCloskey, Donald N. 1985. **The Rhetoric of Economics.** Madison: University of Wisconsin Press.

In this work McCloskey argues that "modernism" (the methodological underpinnings of positive economics) does not explain what economists do. Models rely on metaphor. Economists should make use of the literary devices at their disposal. Rhetorics can help them be better writers, teachers, scientists. McCloskey uses the work of Muth, Fogel, Solow, and Becker to illustrate his arguments.

2.78 McKenzie, Richard B. 1983. **The Limits of Economic Science.** Boston: Kluwer-Nijhoff.

These essays focus on the boundaries of economics. McKenzie treats prediction, nonrationality, Austrians and neoclassicism, normative economics, and discusses Einstein's social philosophy.

2.79 Mehta, Jamshed Kaikhusro. 1967. **Rhyme, Rhythm and**

Truth in Economics. NY: Asia Publishing House.

This is a philosophical as opposed to epistemological work. The work is addressed to economists and philosphers "who are interested in knowing how natural and social forces act in unison to affect and shape the life of human beings" (preface).

2.80 Mingat, Alain, Pierre Salmon and Alain Wolfelsperger. 1985. **Méthodologie   économique.**   Paris: Presses Universitaires de France.

The authors begin their volume with a discussion of why methodology embarrasses economists. Then they discuss the object of methodology, the development of scientific knowledge, quantification, the great methodological controversies (Friedman, empiricism, **werfrei** science, etc.), the problem of realism of assumptions, and the methodological foundations of the controversies. The final chapter deals with normative economics. (In French)

2.81 Mini, Piero V. 1974. **Philosophy and Economics.** Gainesville: The University Presses of Florida.

Mini examines the philosophical bases for the theories of classical economics, Keynes, and Marx. The author maintains that differences in theories are due to differences in philosophical perspectives. He treats value theory, the **General Theory**, and Marx's theory of the evolution of history and ideas.

2.82 Mirowski, Philip. 1986. **The Reconstruction of Economic Theory.** Boston: Kluwer-Nijhoff.

This anthology is claimed to be in the "third stream" of economics--i.e., authors neither advocate neoclassical nor Marxian economics. Mirowski and others contend that there is a lack of ingenuity and philosophical sophistication in articles published in conventional journals. The essays discuss the relationship of economics with physics, the price function, property and accounting as theoretical terms, the biological metaphor, and the role of mathematics and abstraction in economics. Contributions are made from Mirowski, Levine, Ellerman, Bausor, Katzner.

Mises: see von Mises (2.121 and 2.122).

2.83 *Myrdal, Gunnar. 1973 (1972). **Against the Stream: Critical Essays on Economics.** NY: Pantheon.

In this work Myrdal is critical of the approaches of modern economics. Some of the topics he treats are crises and cycles in economics, stagflation, values, scientists, world poverty, the need for radical domestic reforms, the scientific nature of social science, twisted terminology and biased ideas, growth and development, economics and politics in international relations, economics of an improved environment, Gandhi as a radical liberal, the future of India, towards a better America, his work **An American Dilemma,** and Marx and "Marxism."

2.84 *Myrdal, Gunnar. 1969. **Objectivity in Social Research.** NY: Pantheon.

This work tries to provide an answer to the problem of how social scientists can be objective. It is in this work that Myrdal recommends that objectivity can be obtained by stating explicitly one's value premises underlying theoretical work.

2.85 Nelson, Richard R. and Sidney G. Winter. 1982. **An Evolutionary Theory of Economic Change.** Cambridge, MA: The Belknap Press of Harvard University Press.

The point of this work is to reconsider the evolutionary viewpoint as a possible framework for a more realistic theory of the firm and industry. They hope to capture the more disorderly character of these processes which is neglected by the orthodox view. Their intellectual debt is to Simon and Schumpeter.

2.86 O'Driscoll, Gerald P., Jr. 1977. **Economics As a Coordination Problem: The Contributions of Friedrich A. Hayek.** Foreword by F.A. Hayek. Kansas City: Sheed Andrew and McMeel.

This work is the first full-length examination of the economic writings of F.A. Hayek. O'Driscoll discusses reasons why economists have not appreciated Hayek since Keynesian economics became popular. He analyses Hayek's contributions to business-cycle theory, the emphasis on microfoundations, the role of institutions and information, his views on socialism and economic efficiency.

2.87 O'Driscoll, Gerald Patrick and Mario Rizzo. 1984. **The Economics of Time and Ignorance.** London: Basil Blackwell.

The authors argue for economic analysis which concentrates upon exchange processes. The book began as an attempt to survey principal features of Austrian economics but became extended to cover subjectivism in general. It is divided into 2 parts: "Framework," which discusses subjectivism, time, uncertainty, and equilibrium and "Applications," which addresses issues on competition, monopoly, capital theory, and monetary theory.

2.88   Pagenstecher, Ulrich. 1987. **Verstehen und Erklären in der Nationalökonomie. Methodenkontroversen 1930–1985.** Nürnberg: Helmut Preussler.

> The author discusses methodological issues in economics since the 1930's. Included are the debate over apriorism between von Mises/Robbins and Hutchison/Harrod/Samuelson; the Friedman controversy; the assumptions controversy; the attacks of economic behaviorists; the perfect information assumption; value judgements in economics. (In German)

2.89   Paul, Ellen Frankel. 1979. **Moral Revolution and Economic Science: The Demise of Laissez-Faire in Nineteenth-Century British Economy.** Westport, CN: Greenwood Press.

> This book explores the proper scope and limitations of government intervention in the economy through the economic, moral, and political writings of the late 18th- and 19th-century British theorists. The focus then is on Smith, Bentham, Ricardo, Mill, Jevons, Wicksteed, Sidgwick, Cairnes, Senior, and Marshall. Their views on the scope of economics in light of laissez-faire are examined.

2.90   Pheby, John. 1988. **Methodology and Economics: A Critical Introduction.** London: Macmillan.

> This is an introduction to some of the philosophies of science that have influenced the work of economists. Pheby treats inductive and deductive arguments in economics, falsification, Kuhn, Lakatos, Laudan, Friedman, Austrian methodology, and Marxian methodology. He is against the naturalistic approach in economics, i.e., the mimicry of the natural sciences. He suggests that there be more cooperation among economists from various schools, including the Austrians and Marxists.

2.91   Pitt, Joseph C, ed. 1981. **Philosophy in Economics. Vol. 16 of The University of Western Ontario Series in Philosophy of Science.** Dordrecht: D. Reidel.

> The 11 papers explore theory and testing in economics. Contributors are Pitt, Green, Hausman, Wolfson, Rosenberg, Strasnick, McClennen, Dacey, Wilde, Good, and Mayo.

2.92   Postan, M.M. 1971. **Fact and Relevance: Essays on Historical Method.** NY/London: Cambridge University Press.

> This is a collection of 14 essays by Postan discussing some aspect of history and social science. The first articles are of a general nature. There are several

articles on macroeconomics and about one-fourth treat economic history. The last 2 discuss Marx and Marxists.

2.93 Rizzo, Mario, ed. 1979. **Time, Uncertainty and Disequilibrium: Exploration of Austrian Themes.** Lexington, Mass./Toronto: Lexington Books/D.C. Heath.

This is a collection of essays on typically Austrian themes, e.g., disequilibrium, subjectivism, time, interest, and uncertainty. The papers (except for 2) are the proceedings of the Conference on Issues in Economic Theory: An Evaluation of Current Austrian Perspectives held in 1978 at New York University. Contributors: Rizzo, Shackle, Littlechild, Hicks, Lachmann, Rothbard, Demsetz, Egger, Kirzner, O'Driscoll, Wagner, Yeager, Ebeling.

2.94 Robbins, Lionel. 1983 (1932). **An Essay on the Nature and Significance of Economic Science,** 3rd ed. Foreword by William Baumol. London: Macmillan.

This is the third edition of Robbin's classic essay; it is a reprint of the 1935 revised edition of the original 1932 essay with the addition of Robbin's 1980 Richard T. Ely Lecture to the AEA in which he reflects on the earlier essay. In this famous essay Robbins defines economics as "the science which studies human behavior as a relationship between ends and scarce means which have alternative uses."

2.95 Robinson, Joan. 1981. **What Are the Questions? and Other Essays.** Armonk, NY: M.E. Sharpe.

This is a collection of some of the author's essays, including "What Are the Questions?". Most are critical of economics.

2.96 Robinson, Joan. 1973. **Economic Heresies: Some Old-Fashioned Questions in Economic Theory,** 2nd ed. NY: Basic Books.

In this series of essays Robinson attempts to find the roots of modern orthodoxy in the neoclassical tradition. She argues that modern orthodoxy is mostly based on the Walrasian tradition, which is narrow in scope, whereas Marshallian economics was much richer. She re-examines some of these old-fashioned (Marshallian) questions in light of today's problems.

2.97 Robinson, Joan. 1962. **Economic Philosophy.** London: C.A. Watts and Co.

This classic work treats metaphysics, morals, and science in the first essay. Then she discusses the classical concepts of value, utility under the classical concepts of value, utility under the neoclassical economists, the Keynesian revolution, development and underdevelopment, and "the rules of the game."

2.98 Rosenberg, Alexander. 1976. **Microeconomic Laws: A Philosophical Analysis.** Pittsburgh: University of Pittsburgh Press.

The author, a philosopher, examines the logical status of microeconomics, the problem of aggregation, microeconomic "laws," the nomological status of microeconomics, and "positive economics" (Robbins). "Economic imperialism" is also discussed.

2.99 Rothbard, Murray N. 1979. **Individualism and the Philosophy of the Social Sciences.** Foreword by Friedrich A. Hayek. Cato Paper No. 4. San Francisco, CA: Cato Institute.

The author treats typically Austrian themes, e.g., scientism, values, the problem of free will, praxeology as the method of the social sciences, and methodological individualism. There is a foreword by Hayek and a suggested reading list.

2.100 Runciman, Walter G. 1972. **A Critique of Max Weber's Philosophy of Social Science.** Cambridge: Cambridge University Press.

In this long essay the author argues that Weber's methodology was wrong on 3 issues: "the difference between theoretical presuppositions and implicit value-judgements; the manner in which 'idiographic' explanations are to be subsumed under causal laws; and the relation of explanation to description" (p. 15) Runciman proposes corrections of these mistakes.

2.101 Samuels, Warren, ed. 1987. **History and Methodology of Economics.** Greenwich, CN/London: Jai Press, 1987.

This is a series of essays which begins with Marx's moral critique of capitalism and theory of social ethics. The next 2 works present an alternative first chapter of Schumpeter's **History of Economic Analysis** (1954): the first is an edited version of Schumpeter's introduction found in the Harvard University achives. The second is a comparison of the version found in the archives with the original publication. Also included are the proceedings of a panel discussion on Keynes by Arjo Klamer which was presented at the 1985 meeting of the History of Economics Society.

2.102 Samuels, Warren J., ed. 1980. **The Methodology of Economic Thought: Critical Papers from the Journal of Economic Issues.** New Brunswick, N.J.: Transaction Books.

This is a collection of articles which were previously published in the **Journal of Economic Issues.**

2.103 Sassower, Raphael. 1985. **Philosophy of Economics, A Critique of Demarcation.** Lanham, MD: University Press of America.

This work is devoted to a critical survey of the standard alternative answers to the question "What gives economics scientific status?" Answers that have been given to this question should be considered in historical context and in a way which allows for comparison between them.

2.104 Sen, Amartya. 1987. **On Ethics and Economics.** Oxford: Basil Blackwell.

Sen investigates economics' relationship to ethics in a series of essays. He concludes that modern economics would benefit from the realization that the two fields are related.

2.105 Shackle, G.L.S. 1972. **Epistemics and Economics: A Critique of Economic Doctrines.** Cambridge: Cambridge University Press.

In book I Shackle describes "general ideas." In book II he discusses the union of "value" with mathematical analysis--the "rise of the rational ideal." In book III he discusses the "dissolution of the rational ideal," in book IV statics, in V diachronism, and in book VI "epistemics versus axiomatics." "Epistemics" is "the theory of thoughts," and economics, according to Shackle, is a branch of epistemics.

2.106 Shackle, G.L.S. 1961. **Decision, Order and Time in Human Affairs.** NY: Cambridge University Press.

These are a series of essays on time, uncertainty, ascendancy, expectations, economic illustrations, and policy, profit, and decision. The second edition includes an extra chapter and a much enlarged bibliography.

2.107 Shrader-Frechette, K.S. 1984. **Science Policy, Ethics, and Economic Methodology: Some Problems of Technology Assessment and Environmental-Impact Analysis.** Dordrecht: D. Reidel.

This work is a philosophical analysis of the methodological, epistemological, and ethical problems facing anyone using economic methods to help formulate public policy, especially with respect to science and technology. The author does not reject current economics. She shows that methodological analysis does however generate better technology assessment and greater awareness of limitations of policy conclusions.

2.108 Silvio, Bianchi, ed. 1981. **Wieviel Mathematik brauchen die Sozialwissenschaften?** With contributions from Edgar Salin, Bruno S. Frey, and S. Bianchi. Bern/Stuttgart: Paul Haupt.

This slim volume consists of 3 essays about how much mathematics social scientists, especially economists, need. The 3 authors see an over-mathematization of the social sciences which is dangerous. They suggest a change in course study; they would like to see more aspects of "political economy" taught at the university. (In German)

2.109 Smyth, R.L., ed. 1962. **Essays in Economic Method: Selected Papers Read to Section F of the British Association for the Advancement of Science, 1860-1913.** Introduction by T.W. Hutchison. London: Duckworth.

This is a collection of essays which were presidential addresses to Section F from 1860 to WWI. Most of the works deal with scope and scientific status of economics and statistics. Hutchison provides an interesting introduction to the essays. The essays are from Senior, Jevons, Ingram, Sidgwick, Cunningham, Nicholson, Bastable, Price, Bonar, Canaan, Bowley, Ashley, and Wicksteed.

2.110 Spadaro, Louis M., ed. 1978. **New Directions in Austrian Economics.** Kansas City: Universal Press Syndicate.

There are 11 previously unpublished papers which were presented at a symposium held in 1976 to commemorate the centennial of the marginalist revolution. All papers explore Austrian themes. Contributors are Spadaro, Egger, Rizzo, Kirzner, Littlechild, Armentano, O'Driscoll, Rothbard, Moss, Garrison.

2.111 Stanfield, J. Ron. 1979. **Economic Thought and Social Change.** Carbondale and Edwardsville: Southern Illinois University Press.

This book is about the state of economics (which is in crisis) in relation to contemporary democratic institutions. Its focus is on social change. Stanfield hopes that the economics profession will become more introspective. The work is highly critical of neoclassical economics.

2.112 Stegmüller, Wolfgang, W. Balzer, and W. Spohn, eds. 1982. **Philosophy of Economics.** Berlin: Springer Verlag.

This volume consists of essays from a colloquium on

"philosophy of economics" held at the University of
Munich in July 1981. The essays are divided into 3
parts: the structuralist view of economic theories,
reconstruction of Marxian theory, and decision theory
as the basis of economic theory. Contributors are
economists and philosophers, namely, Hamminga, Balzer,
Händler, Haslinger, Pearce, Tucci, Kötter, Garcia de
la Sienra, Diederich, Gibbins, Nutzinger, Selten,
Leopold, Sneed, Gottinger, Spohn, Beckmann, Gaertner,
Krüger.

2.113 Stewart, I.M.T. 1979. **Reasoning and Method in
Economics**. Toronto, Canada: McGraw-Hill.

This is an introductory text on the philosophy of
economics aimed at students with no knowledge of
philosophy and only basic knowledge of economics.
Deduction, induction, the hypothetico-deductive
method, prediction and data problems, realism, applied
economics, error, and econometric are treated.

2.114 *Stone, Sir Richard. 1978. **Keynes, Political
Arithmetic and Econometrics: Keynes Lecture in Economics**.
Vol. 44 of the Proceedings of the British Academy. London:
Oxford University Press.

This is a reprint of the 1978 Keynes Lecture in
Economics read to the British Academy in May 1978. Its
theme is Keynes' attitude towards and contributions to
econometrics and mathematics. Stone argues that Keynes
was both critical observer and economist in action. In
his early days as critical observer, Keynes was
hostile to econometrics and mathematics. But later
Stone contends that Keynes' view changed.

2.115 Streissler, Erich W. 1970. **Pitfalls in Econometric
Forecasting**. London: Institute of Economic Affairs.

This work devotes itself to the problems of
econometrics. Streissler describes the "pitfalls" of
macroeconomic models used in forecasting at a level
which can be appreciated by students and businessmen.
There is a glossary of economic terms for the
unintiated and a list of further readings.

2.116 Tarascio, Vincent. 1968. **Pareto's Methodological
Approach to Economics: A Study in the History of Some
Scientific Aspects of Economic Thought**. Chapel Hill:
University of North Carolina Press.

Tarascio examines Pareto's methodology. His ethical
neutrality, the scope and method of economics, and a
constrast between Weber and Marshall are discussed.
This work is based on Tarascio's dissertation at Rice
University.

2.117 Thurow, Lester. 1983. **Dangerous Currents: The State of Economics**. Oxford: Oxford University Press.

This work stresses the link between economics and politics. Thurow is concerned with the failure of the economics profession in providing governments with sound advice at a time when the economy is threatened. Thurow questions supply-side economics, criticizes rational expectations and econometrics, and discusses problems with inflation and unemployment. He makes suggestions for new foundations of economics.

2.118 Tintner, Gerhard. 1968. **Methodology of Mathematical Economics and Econometrics**. Chicago: University of Chicago Press.

This volume is devoted to problems in mathematical economics and econometrics. The work is divided into 4 parts: introduction, mathematical economics, econometrics, and welfare economics and economic policy. (Tintner rates as one of the founders of econometrics.) The work is meant for economists and noneconomists; Tintner hopes to stimulate interest from mathematicians and natural scientists.

2.119 Topitsch, Ernst. 1972. **Logik der Sozialwissenschaften**. Köln: Kiepenheuer & Witsch.

This is a collection of essays (all in German) from social scientists, historians, and philosophers. The work is divided into 8 sections: an introduction; the unity of science; the logic of discovery; the value problem in social science; special methods in social science; formal methods in social science (logistics, mathematics, statistics); special problems of various disciplines; and applications of social research.

2.120 Tuma, Elias H. 1971. **Economic History and the Social Sciences: Problems of Methodology**. London/Berkeley: University of California Press.

The author discusses problems associated with economic history and social sciences. The "new economic history" is discussed, as well as data problems and problems with generalization.

2.121 von Mises, Ludwig. 1978 (1962). **The Ultimate Foundation of Economic Science: An Essay on Method**, 2nd ed. Foreword by Israel Kirzner. Kansas City: Sheed Andrews and McMeel.

This classic work discusses praxeology, apriorism, knowledge and economics, certainty and uncertainty, scope, and positivism. This was von Mises' own last book, and thus his final views as economist-philosopher.

2.122 von Mises, Ludwig. 1960. **Epistemological Problems of Economics.** Trans. by George Reisman from the German **Grundprobleme der Nationalökonomie** (1933). Princeton, N.J.: D. Van Nostrand Co., Inc.

Here von Mises develops his science of human action. Such a science cannot be based on logical positivism, historicism, institutionalism, Marxism, Fabianism, economic history, econometrics, or statistics. The aim of this essay is to clear the way for systematic analyses of human action. Von Mises discusses the nature and development of the social sciences, scope of a priori theorems, science and value, utilitarianism and rationalism, praxeology (which he first called "sociology"), understanding, and a subjective theory of value.

2.123 Ward, Benjamin. 1972. **What's Wrong with Economics?** London: Macmillan.

This is a criticism of neoclassical economics from a Marxian viewpoint which was well-received by the mainstream. Ward treats the problems of economics within a Kuhnian framework.

2.124 Weintraub, E. Roy. 1985. **General Equilibrium Analysis.** Cambridge: Cambridge University Press.

Weintraub analyses equilibrium analysis in terms of the Lakatosian methodology of scientific research programmes.

2.125 White, Lawrence H. 1977. **Methodology of the Austrian School.** Occasional Paper Series No. 1. NY: Center for Libertarian Studies.

This is really not a book, but a 21-page occasional paper which introduces the reader to Austrian methodology. White discusses the methodology of Carl Menger, Friedrich von Wieser, Eugen von Böhm-Bawerk, Ludwig von Mises, Friedrich A. von Hayek, and Ludwig Lachmann.

2.126 Whynes, David K., ed. 1984. **What Is Political Economy? Eight Perspectives.** Oxford/NY: Basil Blackwell.

In Whynes' work political economy is not defined but defended. Hargreaves-Heap and Hollis start the collection of essays with a paper on "the need for political economy." The Austrian, institutionalist, Marxian, and utilitarian approaches to political economy follow. In the last part "themes in political economy" are treated.

2.127 Wiles, Peter and Guy Routh, ed. 1984. **Economics in**

Disarray. Oxford: Basil Blackwell.

This anthology contains 12 previously unpublished papers which are the proceedings of a conference on economic methodology at Oxford in 1982. All contributors are economists. Discussed are the "crisis" in economics, the role of theory and mathematics, monetarism and Duhem's thesis, <u>homo economicus</u>, theory of the firm, the invisible hand theorem, the full-cost principle in the U.S. and U.K., and teaching economics.

2.128 Wiseman, Jack ed. 1983. **Beyond Positive Economics?** London: The British Association for the Advancement of Science.

This is a collection of essays whose aim it is to consider possibilities for a new, "less arrogant" positive economics. Contributors are Wiseman, Shackle, Littlechild, Katouzian, Shearmur, Coats, Loasby, Jefferson, Hey, Earl, Hutchison.

2.129 Wong, Stanley. 1973. **The Foundations of Paul Samuelson's Revealed Preference Theory.** London: Routledge and Kegan Paul.

This work deals with the theory of consumer behavior of Paul Samuelson, i.e., revealed preference theory. Wong argues that Samuelson's "programme of research" is not consistent and that Samuelson does not really solve the problems he set out to solve.

***

3

Scope and Method

Scope and method were the initial problems facing economists as the discipline was formed, the German-Austrian **Methodenstreit** being the example **par excellence.** Of all the works on scope and method, John Neville Keynes' **Scope and Method of Political Economy** (first published in 1890 and revised as the fourth edition in 1917; republished in 1955, 1963, and 1973) rates as a true classic in economic methodology, still well worth a careful reading. Despite the fact that Keynes was writing the first edition at a time when the **Methodenstreit** was fizzling out, Keynes argues for inclusion of methodological discussion in economics because it will lead to an advance in economic knowledge (p. 4). Also unusual for that time is that Keynes argued <u>for</u> the use of mathematical method (with Jevons) because economic phenomena have a "quantitative aspect" which "is of fundamental importance" (p. 252). The passage which is most often cited in this work is his distinction between "positive science," "normative or regulative science," and an "art." The task of the science of political economy is "the establishment of **uniformities**" (p. 35). Machlup's review (in his 1978; originally 1957) is a lovely discussion and introduction to the work in general.

Whereas early discussions on scope concentrate on demarcating the borders of economics from ethics, psychology, sociology, political science, etc., today discussions center on expanding the borders. See, for instance, Hirshleifer's 1985, in which he discusses the "imperialism" of economics. Mathematics has its own peculiar history in terms of scope, one which defies the trend mentioned above. In the beginning, arguments were made to integrate mathematical methods into economics; today many economists, including some mathematical economists, are arguing for narrowing its role in economics. (See §7 below.)

An excellent, short, modern treatise on scope is Deane's 1983, which is "a deliberate echo" of J.N. Keynes' work. She draws a comparison between the methodological crisis of Keynes' day and the present one. Her depiction of the atmosphere in which Keynes was writing (and Marshall his **Principles**, 1890) is quite detailed and holds fascinating parallels for today. She draws the lesson in her conclusion that there is no one kind of economic truth "which holds the key to fruitful analysis of **all** economic problems, no pure economic theory that is immune to changes in social values or current policy problems" (p. 11). Thus scope and method must constantly be redefined. Daniel Hausman's "The Limits of Economic Science" is also recommended.

***

3.1 Barucci, Piero. 1983. "The Scope and Method of Political Economy in the First Histories of Economics." In A. W. Coats. **Methodological Controversy in Economics: Historical Essays in Honor of T.W. Hutchison.** Greenwich, CT: Jai Press, 1983, pp. 125-36.

3.2 Daly, Frederick St. Leger. 1945. "The Scope and Method of Economics." **Canadian Journal of Economics and Political Science** 11, No. 2 (May): 165-76.

3.3 Deane, Phyllis. 1983. "The Scope and Method of Economic Science." **Economic Journal** 93, No. 369 (March): 1-12.

3.4 Edgeworth, F. Y. 1891. "An Introductory Lecture on Political Economy." **Economic Journal** 1 (December): 625-34.

3.5 Evensky, Jerry. 1987. "Expanding the Scope of the Neoclassical Vision." **Review of Social Economy** 45, No. 2 (October): 178-91.

3.6 Gonce, R.A. 1972. "Frank H. Knight on Social Control and the Scope and Method of Economics." **Southern Economic Journal** 38, No. 4 (April): 547-58.

3.7 Grunberg, Emile. 1966. "The Meaning of Scope and External Boundaries of Economics." In Sherman Roy Krupp, ed. **The Structure of Economic Science.** Englewood Cliffs: Prentice-Hall, 1966, pp. 148-65.

3.8 Harrod, Roy F. 1938. "Scope and Method of Economics." **Economic Journal** 48 (September): 383-412.

3.9 Hausman, Daniel. 1983. "The Limits of Economic Science." In **The Limits of Lawfulness: Studies on the Scope and Nature of Scientific Knowledge.** Ed. by Nicholas Rescher. Lanham, MD/London: University Press of America, 1983, pp. 93-100.

3.10 Hirshleifer, Jack. 1985. "The Expanding Domain of Economics." **American Economic Review Special Issue** 75, No. 6 (1985): 53-68.

3.11 Jalladeau, Joel. 1975. "Restrained Or Enlarged Scope of Political Economy? A Few Observations." **Journal of Economic Issues** 9, No. 1 (March): 1-13.

3.12 Kaufmann, Felix. 1933. "On the Subject-Matter and Method of Economic Science." **Economica** 13 (November): 381-401.

3.13 Keynes, John Neville. 1973 (1917). **The Scope and Method of Political Economy**, 4th ed. NY: Augustus M. Kelley.

3.14 Lange, Oskar. 1945. "The Scope and Method of Economics." **Review of Economic Studies** 13, No. 1: 19-32.

3.15 Machlup, Fritz. 1978. "John Neville Keynes' Scope and Method." In his **Methodology of Economics and Other Social Sciences**. NY: Academic Press, 1978, pp. 489-92.

3.16 Marshall, Alfred. 1960 (1920). **Principles of Economics**, 9th variorum, with annotations by C.W. Guillebaud. London: Macmillan for the Royal Economic Society, Appendix C, "The Scope and Method of Economics."

3.17 Robbins, Lionel. 1927. "Mr. Hawtrey on the Scope of Economics." **Economica** 7 (June): 172-78.

3.18 Senior, Nassau. 1860. "Statistical Science." Report of the British Association for the Advancement of Science; Rpt. in R.L. Smyth, ed. **Essays in Economic Method**. London: Gerald Duckworth and Co., 1962, pp. 19-24.

3.19 Sidgwick, Henry. 1885. "The Scope and Method of Economic Science." Report of the British Association for the Advancement of Science. **Journal of the Royal Statistical Society**; Rpt. in R.L. Smyth, ed. **Essays in Economic Method**. London: Gerald Duckworth and Co., 1962, pp. 73-97.

3.20 Suranyi-Unger, Theo. 1960. "Scope and Problems of Economic Philosophy." **Zeitschrift für die gesamte Staatswissenschaft** 116, No. 3: 385-401.

3.21 Wicksteed, P. H. 1914. "The Scope and Method of Political Economy in the Light of the 'Marginal' Theory of Value and of Distribution." **Economic Journal** (March): 1-23; Rpt. in R.L. Smyth, ed. **Essays in Economic Method**. Gerald Duckworth and Co., 1962, pp. 247-72.

***

4

On Milton Friedman's Positive Methodology

No article on methodology has raised more response among economists than Milton Friedman's "The Methodology of Positive Economics," published in 1953. This bibliography contains more than sixty extries dealing with methodological questions raised by his article (not including §4.1, which treats more generally the controversy surrounding assumptions in economic theory).

It is important not to lose sight of the context of Friedman's problem as he was writing: in the 1940's a debate raged on the realism of marginalist assumptions about maximizing behavior of firms. The maximization assumption was attacked for being unrealistic because firms do not really understand marginal-cost pricing. No alternative to the maximizing hypothesis was offered, and it was argued that marginalism does not presuppose that economic agents consciously maximize. This is then the setting from which Friedman's theory of positive economics emerged. Friedman argues that economic assumptions do not need to be realistic so long as they predict. Prediction, according to Friedman, is the main goal of economics. Friedman opposes the criticisms of perfect competition, perfect monopoly, and profit maximization for their lack of realism. This in turn sparked the controversy in the 1960's on the usefulness and admissibility of unrealistic assumptions.

Friedman has been criticized for using "realism" and "assumption" ambiguously. Many economists complain that his methodology (right or wrong) does not describe what economists do. Slowly it has been recognized that the ambiguous and confused terminology which Friedman uses makes a fruitful discussion of his work somewhat difficult, if not futile.

Samuelson nicknamed Friedman's methodology the "Friedman-Twist" or "F-Twist." Wong and Musgrave have

further analysed Samuelson's "F-Twist." The Machlup --
Papandreou -- Nagel -- Archibald -- Simon --Samuelson
discussion of 1963 and the Boland-Frazer/Boland-Hirsch/de
Marchi discussion of the 1980's are quite well known.
Philosophers who have joined the controversy are Agassi,
Giedmin, Hamminga, Klappholz, Machlup, Musgrave, Nagel,
Rosenberg, and Sagal.

***

* *
Friedman, Milton. 1953. "The Methodology of
Positive Economics." In his **Essays in Positive
Economics**. Chicago: University of Chicago Press,
1953, pp. 3-43.

* *

4.1   Agassi, Joseph. 1971. "Tautology and Testability in
Economics." **Philosophy of the Social Sciences** 1: 49-63.

4.2   Archibald, G.C. 1959. "The State of Economic
Science." **British Journal for the Philosophy of Science** 10,
No. 37 (May): 58-69.

4.3   Archibald, G.C., et al. 1963. "Problems of
Methodology: Discussion." **American Economic Association
Papers and Proceedings** 53 (May): 227-36.

4.4   Bear, D.V.T. and Daniel Orr. 1967. "Logic and
Expediency in Economic Theorizing." **Journal of Political
Economy** 75, No. 2 (April): 188-96.

4.5   Boland, Lawrence A. 1987. "Boland on Friedman's
Methodology: A Summation." **Journal of Economic Issues**
21, No. 1 (March): 380-88.

4.6   Boland, Lawrence A. 1984. "Methodology: Reply (An
Essay on the Foundations of Friedman's Methodology)."
American Economic Review 74, No. 4 (September): 795-97.

4.7   Boland, Lawrence A. 1980. "Friedman's Methodology
Vs. Conventional Empiricism: A Reply to Rotwein." **Journal
of Economic Literature** 18 (December): 1555-57.

4.8   Boland, Lawrence A. 1979. "A Critique of Friedman's
Critics." **Journal of Economic Literature** 17, No. 2 (June):
503-22.

4.9   Brady, Michael Emmet. 1986. "A Note on Milton
Friedman's Application of His 'Methodology of Positive
Economics'." **Journal of Economic Issues** 20, No. 3
(September): 845-51.

4.10   Caldwell, Bruce J. 1980. "A Critique of Friedman's
Methodological Instrumentalism." **Southern Economic Journal**
47, No. 2 (October): 366-74.

4.11   Coddington, Alan. 1979. "Friedman's Contribution to Methodological Controversy." **British Review of Economic Issues** 2, No. 4 (May): 1-13.

4.12   Coddington, Alan. 1972. "Positive Economics." **Canadian Journal of Economics** 5, No. 1 (February): 1-15.

4.13   De Alessi, Louis. 1971. "Reversals of Assumptions and Implications." **Journal of Political Economy** 79, No. 4 (August): 867-77.

4.14   De Alessi, Louis. 1965. "Economic Theory As a Language." **Quarterly Journal of Economics** 79, No. 3 (August): 472-77.

4.15   Dennis, Ken G. 1986. "Boland on Friedman: A Rebuttal." **Journal of Economic Issues** 20, No. 3 (September): 633-60.

4.16   Friedman, Milton. 1953. "The Methodology of Positive Economics." In his **Essays in Positive Economics.** Chicago: University of Chicago Press, 1953, pp. 3-43.

4.17   Frazer, William J., Jr. 1984. "Methodology: Reply" (An Essay on the Foundations of Friedman's Methodology). **American Economic Review** 74, No. 4 (September): 793-94.

4.18   Frazer, W. and Lawrence Boland. 1983. "An Essay on the Foundations of Friedman's Methodology." **American Economic Review** 73, No. 1 (March): 129-44.

4.19   Giedymin, Jerzy. 1975. "Antipositivism in Contemporary Philosophy of Social Science and Humanities." **British Journal for the Philosophy of Science** 26: 275-301.

4.20   Hamminga, Bert. 1983. **Neoclassical Theory Structure and Theory Development: An Empirical-Philosophical Case Study Concerning the Theory of International Trade.** Berlin: Springer Verlag.

4.21   Helm, Dieter. 1984. "Predictions and Causes: A Comparison of Friedman and Hicks on Method." **Oxford Economic Papers Supplement** ("Economic Theory and Hicksian Themes," ed. by D.A. Collard, et al.) N.S. 36 (November): 118-34.

4.22   Hillebrand, Konrad. 1982. "Über das Revolutionäre am Monetarismus--ein Streifzug durch erkenntnistheoretische Gelände." **Konjunkturpolitik** 28 (2-3): 170-89.

4.23   Hirsch, Abraham and Neil de Marchi. 1984. "Methodology: A Comment on Frazer and Boland, I" (An Essay on the Foundations of Friedman's Methodology). **American Economic Review** 74, No. 4 (September): 782-88.

4.24   Hoover, Kevin D. 1984. "Methodology: A Comment on Frazer and Boland, II" (An Essay on the Foundations of Friedman's Methodology). **American Economic Review** 74, No. 4 (September): 789–92.

4.25   Katouzian, Homa. 1974. "Scientific Method and Positive Economics." **Scottish Journal of Economics** 21, No. 3 (November): 279–86.

4.26   Klant, J.J. 1974. "Realism of Assumptions in Economic Theory." **Methodology and Science** 7: 141–55.

4.27   Klappholz, Kurt and Joseph Agassi. 1959. "Methodological Prescriptions in Economics." **Economica** 26, No. 101 (February): 60–74.

4.28   Liebhafsky, H.H. and E.E. 1985. "The Instrumentalisms of Dewey and Friedman: Comment." **Journal of Economic Issues** 19, No. 4 (December): 974–83.

4.29   Machlup, Fritz. 1963. "Problems of Methodology: Introductory Remarks." **American Economic Association Papers and Proceedings** 53, No. 2 (May): 204.

4.30   Mason, Will E. 1980–81. "Some Negative Thoughts on Friedman's Positive Economics." **Journal of Post Keynesian Economics** 3 (Winter): 235–55.

4.31   McKenzie, Richard B. 1983. **The Limits of Economic Science**. Boston: Kluwer-Nijhoff, chapter 5; Rev. version of his 1981. "The Necessary Normative Context of Positive Economics." **Journal of Economic Issues** 15 (September): 703–19.

4.32   McLachlan, H. and V.K. Swales. 1987. "Friedman's Methodology: A Comment on Boland" (A Critique of Friedman's Critics). **Journal of Economic Studies** 14, No. 1 (Spring): 1–36.

4.33   Melitz, Jack. 1965. "Friedman and Machlup on the Significance of Testing Economic Assumptions." **Journal of Political Economy** 73, No. 1 (February): 37–60.

4.34   Meyer, Willi. 1978. "Die Methodologie der positiven Ökonomen und ihre Folgen." In **Neuere Entwicklungen in den Wirtschaftswissenschaften**. Ed. by Ernst Helmstädter. New Series Vol. 98 of **Schriften des Vereins für Socialpolitik**. Berlin: Duncker und Humblot, 1978, pp. 19–46.

4.35   Mongin, Philippe. 1987. "L'instrumentalisme dans l'essai de M. Friedman." **Economies et sociétés** 21, No. 10 (October): 73–106.

4.36   Musgrave, Alan. 1981. "'Unreal Assumptions' in Economic Theory: The F-Twist Untwisted." **Kyklos** 34, No. 3:

377-87.

4.37   Nagel,   Ernest.   1963.   "Assumptions   in   Economic
Theory."   **American   Economic   Association   Papers   and
Proceedings** 53, No. 2 (May): 211-19.

4.38   Nooteboom, Bort. 1986. "Plausibility in Economics."
Economics and Philosophy 2, No. 2 (October): 197-224.

4.39   Nurmi, Hannu. 1983. "The F-Twist and the Evaluation
of Political Institutions." **Zeitschrift für Wirtschafts-
und Sozialwissenschaften** 103, No. 2: 143-59.

4.40   Papandreou, Andreas G. 1963. "Theory Construction
and Empirical Meaning in Economics." **American Economic
Association Papers and Proceedings** 53 (May): 205-10.

4.41   Pelloni, Gianluigi. 1987. "A Note on Friedman and
the Neo-Bayesian Approach." **Manchester School of Economic
and Social Studies** 55, No. 4 (December): 407-18.

4.42   Piron,   Robert.   1962.   "On   'The   Methodology   of
Positive   Economics':   Comment."   **Quarterly   Journal   of
Economics** 76: 664-66.

4.43   Rizzo, Mario J. 1978. "Praxeology and Econometrics:
A Critique of Positive Economics." In Louis M. Spadaro, ed.
New Directions in Austrian Economics. Kansas City: Sheed
Andrews and McMeel Inc., 1978, pp. 40-56.

4.44   Rosenberg,   Alexander.   1972.   "Friedman's
'Methodology'   for   Economics: A   Critical   Examination."
Philosophy of the Social Sciences 2: 15-29.

4.45   Rotwein,   Eugene.   1980.   "Friedman's   Critics: A
Critic's Reply to Boland." **Journal of Economic Literature**
18 (December): 1553-55.

4.46   Rotwein,   Eugene.   1959.   "On   'The   Methodology   of
Positive Economics.'" **Quarterly Journal of Economics** 73,
No. 4 (November): 554-75.

4.47   Sagal, Paul T. 1977. "Epistemology of Economics."
Zeitschrift für allgemeine Wissenschaftstheorie 8: 144-62.

4.48   *Samuelson, Paul A. 1965. "Professor Samuelson on
Theory and Realism: Reply." **American Economic Review** 55
(December): 1164-72.

4.49   *Samuelson, Paul A. 1964. "Theory and Realism: A
Reply." **American Economic Review** 54 (September): 736-39.

4.50   *Samuelson, Paul A. 1963. "Problems of Methodology:
Discussion." **American Economic Association Papers and
Proceedings** 53 (May): 231-36.

4.51   Sen, Amartya K. 1980. "Description As Choice." **Oxford University Papers** 32, No. 3 (November): 353-69.

4.52   *Simon, Herbert. 1963. "Problems of Methodology: Discussion." **American Economic Association Papers and Proceedings** 53, No. 2 (May): 229-31.

4.53   Stanley, T.D. 1985. "Positive Economics and Its Instrumental Defence." **Economica** 52, No. 207 (August): 305-19.

4.54   Thygesen, Niels. 1977. "The Scientific Contributions of Milton Friedman." **Scandanavian Journal of Economics** 79, No. 1: 56-98.

4.55   Tietzel, Manfred. 1981. "'Annahmen' in der Wirtschaftstheorie." **Zeitschrift für Wirtschaft und Sozialwissenschaften** 101, No. 3: 237-65.

4.56   Vickrey, William. 1954. "Review of Friedman's 'Essays in Positive Economics'." **American Economic Review** 44 (December): 937-38, and "Correction," 937-38.

4.57   Webb, James. 1987. "Is Friedman's Methodological Instrumentalism a Special Case of Dewey's Instrumental Philosophy? A Comment." **Journal of Economic Issues** 21, No. 1 (March): 393-429.

4.58   Wible, James R. 1987. "Criticism and the Validity of the Special-Case Interpretation of Friedman's Essay: A Reply." **Journal of Economic Issues** 21, No. 1 (March): 430-40.

4.59   Wible, James R. 1984. "The Instrumentalisms of Dewey and Friedman." **Journal of Economic Issues** 18, No. 4 (December): 1049-70.

4.60   Wible, James R. 1982. "Friedman's Positive Economics and Philosophy of Science." **Southern Economic Journal** 49, No. 2 (October): 350-60.

4.61   Wong, Stanley. 1973. "The F-Twist and the Methodology of Paul Samuelson." **American Economic Review** 63 (June): 312-25.

***

4.1   The Assumptions Controversy (Not Limited to Friedman)

4.1.1   Blaug, Mark. 1980. **The Methodology of Economics Or How Economists Explain.** Cambridge: Cambridge University Press, pp. 94-128.

4.1.2   Caldwell, Bruce J. 1982. **Beyond Positivism.** London: George Allen and Unwin, chaps. 6-9.

4.1.3 Hirsch, Abraham. 1980. "The 'Assumptions' Controversy in Historical Perspective." **Journal of Economic Issues** 14, No. 1 (March): 99-118.

4.1.4 Hutchison, T.W. 1966. "Testing Economic Assumptions: A Comment." **Journal of Political Economy** 74, No. 1 (February): 81-83.

4.1.5 Hutchison, T.W. 1965 (1938). **The Significance and Basic Postulates of Economic Theory.** NY: Augustus M. Kelley.

4.1.6 Hutchison, T.W. 1960. "Methodological Prescriptions in Economics: A Reply." **Economica** N.S. 27 (May): 158-61.

4.1.7 Hutchison, T.W. 1956. "Professor Machlup on Verification in Economics." **Southern Economic Journal** 22, No. 4 (April): 476-83; Rpt. in (1) Daniel M. Hausman, ed. **The Philosophy of Economics.** Cambridge: Cambridge University Press, pp. 188-97 and in (2) Bruce Caldwell, ed. **Appraisal and Criticsm in Economics: A Book of Readings.** Boston: Allen and Unwin, 1984, pp. 118-25.

4.1.8 Hutchison, T.W. 1954. "Review of Friedman's **Essays in Positive Economics.**" **Economic Journal** 64 (December): 796-99.

4.1.9 Kästli, René. 1980. "Die Forderung nach Realitätsnähe der Annahmen: ein logischer Widerspruch? Bemerkungen zur Entgegnung von Jürgen v. Kempski." **Zeitschrift für die gesamte Staatswissenschaft** 136, No. 2 (June): 345-46.

4.1.10 Kästili, René. 1978. "Die Forderung nach Realitätsnähe der Annahmen: ein logischer Widerspruch." **Zeitschrift für die gesamte Staatswissenschaft** 134, No. 1 (March): 126-32.

4.1.11 Kaufmann, Felix. 1942. "On the Postulates of Economic Theory." **Social Research** 9: 379-95.

4.1.12 Kaufmann, Felix. 1937. "Do Synthetic Propositions a priori Exist in Economics?" **Economica** N.S. 4 (August): 337-42.

4.1.13 v. Kempski, Jürgen. 1980. "Die Forderung nach Realitätsnähe der Annahmen: ein logischer Widerspruch? Diskussion." **Zeitschrift für die gesamte Staatswissenschaft** 136, No. 2 (June): 342-44.

4.1.14 Klappholz, K. and J. Agassi. 1960. "Methodological Prescriptions in Economics: A Rejoinder." **Economica** 27 (May): 160-61.

4.1.15 Machlup, Fritz. 1964. "Professor Samuelson on Theory and Realism." **American Economic Review** 54 (September):

733-36; Rpt. in (1) his **Methodology of Economics and Other Social Sciences.** NY: Academic Press, 1978, pp. 481-84 and in (2) B. Caldwell, ed. **Appraisal and Criticism in Economics: A Book of Readings.** Boston: Allen and Unwin, 1984, pp. 194-96.

4.1.16 Machlup, Fritz. 1956. "Rejoinder to a Reluctant Ultra-Empiricist." **Southern Economic Journal** 22, No. 4 (April): 483-93; Rpt. in (1) his **Methodology of Economics and Other Social Sciences.** NY: Academic Press, 1978, pp. 493-504 and in (2) B. Caldwell, ed. **Appraisal and Criticism in Economics: A Book of Readings.** Boston: Allen and Unwin, 1984, pp. 125-35 and in (3) Daniel Hausman, ed. **The Philosophy of Economics.** Cambridge: Cambridge University Press, 1984, pp. 198-209.

4.1.17 Machlup, Fritz. 1955. "The Problem of Verification in Economics." **Southern Economic Journal** 22, No. 1 (July): 1-21; Rpt. in (1) his **Methodology of Economics and Other Social Sciences.** NY: Academic Press, 1978, pp. 137-58 and in (2) B. Caldwell, ed. **Appraisal and Criticism in Economics: A Book of Readings.** Boston: Allen and Unwin, 1984, pp. 97-125 and in (3) William Marr and B. Raj, eds. **How Economists Explain: A Reader in Methodology.** Lanham: University Press of America, 1983, pp. 157-83.

4.1.18 Murphy, George G.S. 1969. "On Counterfactual Propositions." **History and Theory** Beiheft 9 (Studies in Quantitative History and the Logic of the Social Sciences): 14-38.

4.1.19 Nagel, Ernest. 1963. "Assumptions in Economic Theory." **American Economic Association Papers and Proceedings** 53, No. 2 (May): 211-19.

4.1.20 Pagenstecher, Ulrich. 1987. **Verstehen und Erklären in der Nationalökonomie. Methodenkontroversen 1930-1985.** Nürnberg: Helmut Preußler, pp. 32-47.

4.1.21 Papandreou, Andreas G. 1963. "Theory Construction and Empirical Meaning in Economics." **American Economic Association Papers and Proceedings** 53: 205-11.

4.1.22 Pope, David and Robin. 1972(a). "In Defense of Predictionism." **Australian Economic Papers** 11, No. 19 (December): 232-38.

4.1.23 Pope, David and Robin. 1972(b). "Predictionists, Assumptionists, and the Relatives of the Assumptionists." **Australian Economic Papers** 11, No. 19 (December): 224-28.

4.1.24 Redman, Barbara J. 1976. "On Economic Theory and Explanation." **Journal of Behavioral Economics** 5 (Summer): 161-76.

4.1.25 Rivett, Kenneth. 1972. "Comment on Pope and Pope."

Australian Economic Papers 11, No. 19 (December): 228-32.

4.1.26 Rivett, Kenneth. 1970. "'Suggest' Or 'Entail'?: The Derivation and Confirmation of Economic Hypotheses." **Australian Economic Papers** 9, No. 15 (December): 127-48.

***

5

Paul Samuelson & Methodology

Samuelson's methodological position is tied to his response to Friedman's article (Samuelson, 1963). There he coins the expression "F-Twist" and develops such a wild methodology that it itself elicited an exclusive literature. In the famous Machlup-Samuelson exchange of 1964, for instance, Machlup shows that Samuelson's methodology drawn to its logical conclusions implies a rejection of theory.

The Garb-Lerner-Massey-Samuelson exchange on methodology of 1965 and the Wong and Musgrave works are all famous discussions of Samuelson's F-Twist.

In Samuelson's 1965(a), he questions whether prediction is really the main goal of science. The view that one goal of science is explanation and understanding has been a message of the philosophy of science since the 1960's.

Samuelson is familiar with some of the philosophy of science literature. That he and Friedman, both Nobel Prize recipients, have developed less-than-satisfactory methodologies of economics should serve as a warning to budding methodologists that methodology is a very difficult subject.

***

5.1 Garb, Gerald. 1965. "Professor Samuelson on Theory and Realism." **American Economic Association Papers and Proceedings** 55 (December): 1151-53.

5.2 Gordon, Donald. 1955. "Professor Samuelson on Operationalism in Economic Theory." **Quarterly Journal of Economics** 69 (May): 305-10.

5.3 Lerner, Abba P. 1965. "Professor Samuelson on Theory

and   Realism: Comment." **American   Economic   Review**   5 (December): 1153–55.

5.4   Machlup,   Fritz.   1964.   "Professor   Samuelson   on   Theory and   Realism." **American   Economic   Review** 54   (September): 733–39; Rpt. in (1) his **Methodology of Economics and Other Social   Sciences.** NY: Academic Press, 1978, pp. 481–84 and in   (2)   B.   Caldwell,   ed. **Appraisal   and   Criticism   in Economics: A Book of Readings.** Boston: Allen and Unwin, 1984, pp. 194–96.

5.5   Massey,   Gerald   J.   1965.   "Professor   Samuelson   on   Theory and   Realism: Comment." **American   Economic   Review**   55 (December): 1155–63.

5.6   Musgrave,   Alan.   1981.   "'Unreal   Assumptions'   in Economic   Theory: The   F–Twist   Untwisted." **Kyklos** 34,   No. 3: 377–87.

5.7   *Samuelson,   Paul   A.   1978.   "Maximizing   and   Biology." **Economic Inquiry** 16, No. 2 (April): 171–83.

5.8   *Samuelson,   Paul   A.   1971.   "Maximimum   Principles   in Analytical   Economics."   (Nobel   Lecture: 1970) **Science** 173 (September   10):   991–97;   Rpt.   in **American   Economic   Review** 62,   No.   3   (June   1972):   249–62   and   in **Synthese** 31   (1975): 323–44.

5.9   *Samuelson,   Paul   A.   1965(a).   "Economic   Forecasting   and Science." **Michigan Quarterly Review** 4 (October): 274–80.

5.10   *Samuelson,   Paul   A.   1965(b).   "Professor   Samuelson   on Theory   and   Realism: Reply." **American   Economic   Review** 55 (December): 1164–72.

5.11   *Samuelson,   Paul   A.   1965(c).   "Some   Notions   on Causality   and   Teleology   in   Economics."   In   Daniel   Lerner, ed. **Cause and Effect.** NY: Free Press, 1965, pp. 99–143.

5.12   *Samuelson,   Paul   A.   1964.   "Theory   and   Realism: A Reply." **American Economic Review** 54 (September): 736–39.

5.13   *Samuelson,   Paul   A.   1963.   "Problems   of   Methodology: Discussion." **American   Economic   Association   Papers   and Proceedings** 53 (May): 231–36.

5.14   *Samuelson,   Paul   A.   1955.   "Operationalism   in   Economic Theory: Comment." **Quarterly   Journal   Economics** 69   (May): 310–14.

5.15   *Samuelson,   Paul   A.   1954(a).   "Introduction: Mathematics   in   Economics––No,   No   Or   Yes,   Yes,   Yes?" **Review of Economic and Statistics** 36, No. 4 (November): 359.

5.16   *Samuelson,   Paul   A.   1954(b).   "Some   Psychological Aspects of Mathematics and Economics." **Review of Economics**

and Statistics 36, No. 4 (November): 380–82.

5.17 *Samuelson, Paul A. 1952. "Economic Theory and Mathematics--An Appraisal." **American Economic Association Papers and Proceedings** 42, No. 2 (May): 56–66.

5.18 Seligman, Benjamin B. 1967. "On the Question of Operationalism: A Review Article (Samuelson's **Collected Papers**). **American Economic Review** 57, No. 1 (March): 146–61.

5.19 Sen, Amartya K. 1980. "Description As Choice." **Oxford Economic Papers** 32, No. 3 (November): 353–69.

5.20 *Simon, Herbert. 1963. "Problems of Methodology: Discussion." **American Economic Association Papers and Proceedings** 53, No. 2 (May): 229–31.

5.21 Tietzel, Manfred. 1981. "'Annahmen' in der Wirtschaftstheorie." **Zeitschrift für Wirtschaft und Sozialwissenschaften** 101, No. 3: 237–65.

5.22 Wong, Stanley. 1978. **The Foundations of Paul Samuelson's Revealed Preference Theory**. London: Routledge and Kegan Paul.

5.23 Wong, Stanley. 1973. "The F-Twist and the Methodology of Paul Samuelson." **American Economic Review** 63 (June): 312–25.

***

6

Crises in Economics

The recent talk of a crisis in economics started in the 1970's with British economists who expressed dissatisfaction with the state and methods of research and teaching in economics. In the 1980's Bell and Kristol's **The Crisis in Economic Theory** appeared. Whereas in Britain the crisis is one of economic methodology (see Hutchison), in the U.S. it is one of theory, i.e., of macroeconomic and econometric theory (see Bell and Kristol, Eichner, Hicks, Ischboldin, and Tobin). Often in the U.S. the "crisis" is called a "revolution" or "counterrevolution."

Many prominent economists have diagnosed economics' ailments and suggested remedies. For instance, Bauer and Walters believe that the profession is in a state of confusion. Blackman bemoans economics' perverse reward system. Hahn is against the overdevelopment of mathematical and econometric theory, while Morgenstern complains that the mathematics used is not solving the problem but is used to show off. Eichner and Leontief believe that economic theory needs a sounder empirical foundation. Phelps-Brown argues that economists' intellectual values are misguided. Simon claims that economic theory is not realistic, that utility- and profit-maximation need to be supplemented by additional behavioral assumptions. Worswick asserts that what economists do is irrelevant.

Crises in economics appear to be cyclical in nature. The current crisis has parallels to the crisis of the 1880's. See Deane, Robinson, Schumpeter, and Stone. Whether "crisis" is not an exaggerated appellation for the current problems in economics is discussed by Hutchison. Both Heller and MacDougall insist, despite the current negativism, on reminding us that there is still much that is right with economics.

***

6.1   Bauer, P.T. and A.A. Walters. 1975. "The State of Economics." **Journal of Law and Economics** 8 (April): 1-23.

6.2   Bell, Daniel and Irving Kristol, eds. 1981. **The Crisis in Economic Theory** NY: Basic Books; Originally publ. as **The Public Interest** (Special Issues: "The Crisis in Economic Theory"): 1980.

6.3   Blackman, James H. 1971. "The Outlook for Economics." **Southern Economic Journal** 37, No. 4 (April): 385-95.

6.4   Coats, A.W, ed. 1983. **Methodological Controversy in Economics: Historical Essays in Honor of T.W. Hutchison.** Greenwich, CT: Jai Press.

6.5   Coats, A.W. 1977. "The Current 'Crisis' in Economics in Historical Perspective." **Nebraska Journal of Economics and Business** 16, No. 3 (Summer): 3-16.

6.6   Dean, James W. 1980. "The Dissolution of the Keynesian Consensus." **The Public Interest** (Special Issue: The Crisis in Economic Theory): 19-34.

6.7   Deane, Phyllis. 1983. "The Scope and Method of Economic Science." **Economic Journal** 93, No. 369 (March): 1-12.

6.8   Drucker, Peter F. 1980. "Toward the Next Economics." **The Public Interest** (Special Issue: The Crisis in Economic Theory): 4-18.

6.9   Eichner, Alfred S. 1983. "Introduction." In his **Why Economics Is Not Yet a Science.** London: Macmillan/Sharpe, 1983, pp. 3-14.

6.10 Gardner, Henry B. 1920. "The Nature of Our Economic Problem." **American Economic Review** 10, No. 21 (March): 1-17.

6.11 Heller, Walter W. 1975. "What's Right with Economics?" **American Economic Review** 65, No. 1 (March): 1-26.

6.12 *Hicks, Sir John. 1974. **The Crisis in Keynesian Economics.** Oxford: Basil Blackwell.

6.13 Hutchison, T.W. 1984. "Our Methodological Crisis." In Peter Wiles and Guy Routh, eds. **Economics in Disarray.** Oxford: Basil Blackwell, 1984, pp. 1-21.

6.14 Ischboldin, Boris. 1960. "A Critique of Economics." **Review of Social Economy** 18: 110-27.

6.15 *Leontief, Wassily. 1982. "Letters: Academic Economics." **Science** 217 (9 July): 104-05; Rpt. in (1) William Marr and Baldev Raj, eds. **How Economists Explain: A**

Reader in Methodology. Lanham: University Press of America, 1983, pp. 331-35 and (2) as the Preface in Alfred S. Eichner, ed. **Why Economics Is Not Yet a Science**. London: Macmillan/Sharpe, 1983, pp. vii-xi.

6.16 *Leontief, Wassily. 1971. "Theoretical Assumptions and Nonobserved Facts." **American Economic Review** 61, No. 1 (March): 1-7.

6.17 Lombardini, Siro. 1985. "At the Roots of the Crisis in Economic Theory." **Economia Internazionale**. Nos. 3/4, 38 (August/ November): 323-50.

6.18 MacDougall, Donald. 1974. "In Praise of Economics." **Economic Journal** 84, No. 336 (December): 773-86.

6.19 Meltzer, Allan H. 1980. "Monetarism and the Crisis in Economics." **The Public Interest** (Special Issue: The Crisis in Economic Theory): 35-45.

6.20 Morgenstern, Oskar. 1972. "Thirteen Critical Points in Contemporary Economic Theory: An Interpretation." **Journal of Economic Literature** 10, No. 4 (December): 1163-89.

6.21 *Myrdal, Gunnar. 1972/1973. "Crises and Cycles in the Development of Economics." **Against the Stream: Critical Essays on Economics**. NY: Pantheon Books, 1972/1973, pp. 1-16.

6.22 Phelps-Brown, Sir E.H. 1972. "The Underdevelopment of Economics." **Economic Journal** 82 (March): 1-10.

6.23 Robinson, Joan. 1972. "The Second Crisis of Economic Theory." **American Economic Review** 62, No. 2 (May): 1-10.

6.24 Schumpeter, Joseph A. 1982 (ca. 1932). "The 'Crisis' in Economics--Fifty Years Ago." **Journal of Economic Literature** 20 (September): 1049-59.

6.25 *Simon, Herbert A. 1986. "The Failure of Armchair Economics." **Challenge** 29, No. 5 (November/December): 18-25.

6.26 *Stone, Richard. 1980. "Political Economy, Economics and Beyond." **Economic Journal** 90 (December): 719-36.

6.27 *Tobin, James. 1984. **Asset Accumulation and Economic Activity: Reflections on Contemporary Macroeconomic Theory**. Oxford: Basil Blackwell.

6.28 Worswick, G.D.N. 1972. "Is Progress in Economic Science Possible?" **Economic Journal** 82 (March): 73-100.

***

7

Mathematics: The Problem of Quantification

The struggle between mathematical and nonmathematical (earlier referred to as "literary") economists was a long and hard one. By the 1960's it was clear that the mathematical economists had won. One of the more famous exchanges was the 1954 debate in the **Review of Economics and Statistics**, in which Samuelson, Duesenberry, Chipman, Tinbergen, Champerowne, Solow, Dorfman, and Koopmans sided for mathematical economics in response to Novick's plea for "literary" economists. Certainly one cannot ignore Shackle's pronouncement that

> Economics is essentially a mathematical subject, for it treats by logic of the relations between quantities (1953, p. 11),

or that

> the list of the greatest economists includes a high proportion who have in some degree been also mathematicians: Cournot, Marshall, Wicksell, Pareto, Edgeworth, Keynes, and Irving Fisher are enough to tell us this (1953, p. 12).

Mathematical technique in economics has grown rapidly since WWII. And, as one might expect when one gets too much of a good thing, protests <u>against</u> the use of mathematics in economics arose once again in the 1970's, and then from mathematical economists. The two paradigm examples are Leontief 1971 and Morgenstern 1976. Mirowski's 1986 should also be mentioned.

As it always is with Keynes, there has been a great debate about what he really thought about mathematics. Phelps argues that he was really against mathematics; Stone claims that he changed his mind in his later years.

Debreu's Nobel Prize lecture provides a good history of mathematical economics with methodological discussion. The same goes for Leontief's 1954. Karl Menger's 1973 is a lovely discussion of the relationship between Austrian marginalism and mathematical economics. There he recommends Dickson's book on the semantics of mathematics, which is a very helpful exposition on problems with clarity of mathematics, using economics as the field of application.

**

7.1 *Allais, Maurice. 1949. "L'emploi des mathématiques en économique." **Metroeconomica** 1 (October): 63-77.

7.2 *Arrow, Kenneth. 1951. "Mathematical Models in the Social Sciences." In Daniel Lerner and Harold D. Lasswell, eds. **The Policy Sciences: Recent Developments in Scope and Method.** Stanford, CA: Stanford University Press, 1951, pp. 129-54.

7.3 Baumol, William J. 1966. "Economic Models and Mathematics." In Sherman Roy Krupp, ed. **The Structure of Economic Science.** Englewood Cliffs: Prentice-Hall, 1966, pp. 88-101.

7.4 Bennett, James T. and Manual H. Johnson. 1979. "Mathematics and Quantification in Economic Literature: Paradigm Or Paradox?" **Journal of Economic Education** (Fall): 40-42.

7.5 Blatt, John. 1983. "How Economists Misuse Mathematics." In Alfred S. Eichner, ed. **Why Economics Is Not Yet a Science.** London: Macmillan/Sharpe, 1983, pp. 166-86.

7.6 Bodenhorn, Diron. 1956. "The Problem of Economic Assumptions in Mathematical Economics." **Journal of Political Economy** 64 (February): 25-32.

7.7 Boulding, Kenneth E. 1948. "Samuelson's Foundation's: The Role of Mathematics in Economics." **Journal of Political Economy** 56 (June): 187-99.

7.8 Brems, Hans. 1975. "Marshall on Mathematics." **Journal of Law and Economics** 18, No. 2 (October): 583-85.

7.9 Candler, John. 1926. "Quantitative Analysis and the Evolution of Economic Science." **American Economic Review** 16 (September): 426-33.

7.10 Champerowne, D.G. 1954. "On the Use and Misuse of Mathematics in Presenting Economic Theory." **Review of Economics and Statistics** 36, No. 4 (November): 369-72.

7.11 Chipman, John S. 1954. "Empirical Testing and Mathematical Models." **Review of Economics and Statistics** 36, No. 4 (November): 363-65.

7.12 Clark, J.M. 1947. "Mathematical Economists and Others: A Plea for Communicability." **Econometrica** 15, No. 2 (April): 75-78.

7.13 *Debreu, Gerard. 1984. "Economic Theory in the Mathematical Mode." (Nobel Prize Lecture, 1983) **American Economic Review** 74, No. 3 (June): 267-78; Rpt. in **Scandanavian Journal of Economics** 86, No. 4 (1984): 393-410.

7.14 Dickinson, Z.C. 1924. "Quantitative Methods in Psychological Economics." **American Economic Association Papers and Proceedings** 14 (March): 117-26.

7.15 Dickson, Harald. 1967. **Variable, Function, Derivative: A Semantic Study in Mathematics.** Göteborg, Sweden: Scandanavian University Books.

7.16 Dorfman, Robert. 1954. "A Catechism: Mathematics in Social Science." **Review of Economics and Statistics** 36, No. 4 (November): 374-77.

7.17 Duesenberry, James S. 1954. "The Methodological Basis of Economic Theory." **Review of Economics and Statistics** 36, No. 4 (November): 361-63.

7.18 Edgeworth, F.Y. 1899. "Professor Seligman on the Mathematical Method in Political Economy." **Economic Journal** 9 (June): 286-315.

7.19 Enke, Stephen. 1955. "More on the Misuse of Mathematics in Economics: A Rejoinder." **Review of Economics and Statistics** 37 (May): 131-33.

7.20 Fisher, Irving, et al. 1932. "Quantitative Economics." **American Economic Association Papers and Proceedings** 22 (March): 16-24.

7.21 Fisher, Irving. 1898. "Cournot and Mathematical Economics." **Quarterly Journal of Economics** 12 (January): 119-38.

7.22 *Frisch, Ragnar. 1950. "L'emploi des models pour l'elaboration d'une politique économique rationnelle." **Revue d'économie politique** 61 (September-October): 474-98.

7.23 Georgescu-Roegen, Nicholas. 1966. **Analytical Economics: Issues and Problems.** Cambridge, Mass.: Harvard University Press.

7.24 Gottinger, Hans-Werner. 1970. "Methodologische Entwicklungen in der Messtheorie." **Jahrbücher für**

Nationalökonomie und Statistik 184, No. 2 (May): 126–58.

7.25 Gruchy, Allan G. and Fritz Machlup. 1952. "Issues in Methodology: Discussion." **American Economic Association Papers and Proceedings** 42, No. 2 (May): 67–73.

7.26 Harbinger, A.C. 1952. "Pitfalls in Mathematical Model-Building." **American Economic Review** 42: 855–65.

7.27 Henderson, James P. 1985. "The Whewell Group of Mathematical Economists." **Manchester School of Economic and Social Studies** 53, No. 4 (December): 404–31.

7.28 Hildenbrand, Werner. 1982. "The Role of Mathematics in Economics." In L. Jonathan Cohen, et al., eds. **Logic, Methodology and Philosophy of Science VI**. Amsterdam: North-Holland, 1982, pp. 63–76.

7.29 Ischboldin, Boris. 1960. "A Critique of Econometrics." **Review of Social Economy** 18: 110–27.

7.30 Katzner, Donald W. 1979–80. "On Not Quantifying the Nonquantifiable: Reply." **Journal of Post Keynesian Economics** 2, No. 2 (Winter): 270–73.

7.31 Katzner, Donald W. 1978–79. "On Not Quantifying the Non-Quantifiable." **Journal of Post Keynesian Economics** 1, No. 2 (Winter): 113–28.

7.32 *Klein, Lawrence R. 1954. "The Contributions of Mathematics in Economics." **Review of Economics and Statistics** 36, No. 4 (November): 359–61.

7.33 *Koopmans, Tjalling C. 1954. "On the Use of Mathematics in Economics." **Review of Economics and Statistics** 36, No. 4 (November): 377–79.

7.34 Lancaster, Kelvin. 1962. "The Scope of Qualitative Economics." **Review of Economic Studies** 29 (February): 99–123.

7.35 *Leontief, Wassily. 1982. "Letters: Academic Economics." **Science** 217 (9 July): 104–05; Rpt. in (1) William Marr and Baldev Raj, eds. **How Economists Explain: A Reader in Methodology**. Lanham, MD: University Press of America, 1983, pp. 331–35 and (2) as the Preface in Alfred S. Eichner, ed. **Why Economics Is Not Yet a Science**. London: Macmillan/Sharpe, 1983, pp. vii–xi.

7.36 *Leontief, Wassily. 1971. "Theoretical Asumptions and Nonobserved Facts." **American Economic Review** 61, No. 1 (March): 1–7.

7.37 *Leontief, Wassily. 1961. "The Problem of Quality and Quantity in Economics." In Daniel Lerner, ed. **Quantity and Quality**. NY: The Free Press of Glencoe, 1961, pp. 117–28.

7.38 Loeffel, Hans. 1971. "Die Mathematik in der modernen Gesellschaft." **Schweizerische   Zeitschrift   für Volkswirtschaft und Statistik** 107, No. 4 (December): 831-42.

7.39 Menger, Karl. 1973. "Austrian Marginalism and Mathematical Economics." In J.R. Hicks and W. Weber, eds. **Carl Menger and the Austrian School of Economics.** Oxford: Oxford University Press, 1973, pp. 38-60.

7.40 Mills, Frederick C., et al. 1928. "The Present Status and Future Prospects of Quantitative Economics." **American Economic Association Papers and Proceedings** 18 (March): 28-45.

7.41 Mirowski, Philip. 1987. "Shall I Compare Thee to a Minkowski-Ricardo-Leontief-Metzler Matrix of the Masak-Hicks Type? Or, Rhetoric, Mathematics, and the Nature of Neoclassical Economic Theory." **Economics and Philosophy** 3, No. 1 (April): 67-95.

7.42 Mirowski, Philip. 1986. "Mathematical Formalism and Economic Explanation." In his **The Reconstruction of Economic Theory.** Boston: Kluwer-Nijhoff, 1986, pp. 179-240.

7.43 Mitchell, Wesley C. 1925. "Quantitative Analysis in Economic Theory." **American Economic Review** 15, No. 1 (March): 1-12.

7.44 Morgenstern, Oskar. 1976. "Limits to the Uses of Mathematics in Economics." In his **Selected Economic Writings of Oskar Morgenstern.** Ed. by Andrew Schotter. NY: New York University Press, 1976, pp. 441-58.

7.45 Morishima, Michio. 1984. "The Good and Bad Uses of Mathematics." In Peter Wiles and Guy Routh, eds. **Economics in Disarray.** Oxford: Basil Blackwell, 1984, pp. 51-73.

7.46 Niebyl, Karl H. 1940. "Modern Mathematics and Some Problems of Quantity, Quality, and Motion in Economic Analysis." **Philosophy of Science** 7 (January): 103-20.

7.47 Novick, David. 1954. "Mathematics: Logic, Quantity, and Method." **Review of Economics and Statistics** 36, No. 4 (November): 357-58.

7.48 Paloma, Giuseppe. 1976. "Les héretiques dans l'économie mathématique." **Economie appliquée** 29: 353-407.

7.49 Phelps, Michael G. 1980. "Laments, Ancient and Modern: Keynes on Mathematical and Econometric Methodology." **Journal of Post Keynesian Economics** 2, No. 4 (Summer): 482-93.

7.50 Pigou, A.C. 1941. "Newspaper Reviewers, Economics and

Mathematics." **Economic Journal** 51 (June-September): 276-80.

7.51 Robertson, Ross M. 1949. "Mathematical Economics Before Cournot." **Journal of Political Economy** 57: 524-27.

7.52 Rotwein, Eugene. 1966. "Mathematical Economics: The Empirical View and an Appeal for Pluralism." In Sherman Roy Krupp, ed. **The Structure of Economic Science.** Englewood Cliffs, 1966, pp. 102-13.

7.53 Rutherford, Malcolm. 1987. "Wesley Mitchell: Institutions and Quantitative Methods." **Eastern Economic Journal** 13, No. 1 (January-March): 63-73.

7.54 *Samuelson, Paul A. 1954(a). "Introduction: Mathematics in Economics--No, No Or Yes, Yes, Yes?" **Review of Economics and Statistics** 36, No. 4 (November): 359.

7.55 *Samuelson, Paul A. 1954(b). "Some Psychological Aspects of Mathematics and Economics." **Review of Economics and Statistics** 36, No. 4 (November): 380-82.

7.56 *Samuelson, Paul A. 1952. "Economic Theory and Mathematics--An Appraisal." **American Economic Association Papers and Proceedings** 42, No. 2 (May): 56-66.

7.57 Schabas, Margaret. 1985. "Some Reactions to Jevon's Mathematical Program: The Case of Cairnes and Mill." **History of Political Economy** 17, No. 3 (Fall): 337-53.

7.58 Schoeffler, Sidney. 1956. "Mathematics in Economics: Some Dangers." **Review of Economics and Statistics** 38 (February): 88-90.

7.59 Schulz, Henry. 1927. "Mathematical Economics and the Quantitative Method." **Journal of Political Economy** 35 (October): 702-06.

7.60 Schumpeter, Joseph A. 1952 (1906). "Über die mathematische Methode der theoretischen Ökonomie." **Zeitschrift für Volkswirtschaft, Sozialpolitik und Verwaltung** 15 (1906): 30-49; Rpt. in his **Aufsätze zur ökonomischen Theorie.** Tübingen: J.C.B. Mohr, 1952, pp. 529-48.

7.61 Shackle, G.L.S. 1953. "Economics and Sincerity." **Oxford Economics Papers** N.S. 5 (March): 1-12.

7.62 Silvio, Bianchi, ed. 1981. **Wieviel Mathematik brauchen die Sozialwissenschaften?** With contributions from Edgar Salin, Bruno S. Frey, and S. Bianchi. Bern/Stuttgart: Paul Haupt.

7.63 *Solow, Robert. 1954. "The Survival of Mathematical Economics." **Review of Economics and Statistics** 36, No. 4 (November): 372-74.

7.64 Spengler, Joseph. 1961. "Quantification in Economics: Its History." In Daniel Lerner, ed. **Quantity and Quality.** NY: The Free Press of Glencoe, 1961, pp. 129-211.

7.65 *Stigler, George. 1955. "Mathematics in Economics: Further Comment, II." **Review of Economics and Statistics** 37 (August): 299-300.

7.66 *Stigler, George. 1950. "The Mathematical Method in Economics." In his **Five Lectures on Economic Problems.** NY: Macmillan, 1969 (rpt. of 1949).

7.67 *Stone, Sir Richard. 1978. **Keynes, Political Arithmetic and Econometrics: Keynes Lecture in Economics.** Vol. 44 of the Proceedings of the British Academy. London: Oxford University Press.

7.68 *Stone, Sir Richard. 1964. "Mathematics in the Social Sciences." **Scientific American** 211, No. 3 (September): 168-82.

7.69 *Tinbergen, Jan. 1954. "The Functions of Mathematical Treatment." **Review of Economics and Statistics** 36, No. 4 (November): 365-69.

7.70 *Tinbergen, Jan. 1949. "Möglichkeiten und Grenzen der Anwendung des mathematischen Verfahrens in der Wirtschaftswissenschaft." **Zeitschrift für die gesamte Staatswissenschaft** 105, No. 4: 638-52.

7.71 Tintner, Gerhard. 1968. **Methodology of Mathematical Economics and Econometrics.** Chicago: University of Chicago Press.

7.72 Vining, Rutledge. 1951. "Economic Theory and Quantitative Research: A Broad Interpretation of the Mitchell Position." **American Economic Association Papers and Proceedings** 41, No. 2 (May): 106-18.

7.73 Vining, Rutledge. 1950. "Methodological Issues in Quantitative Economics: Variations Upon a Theme by Frank H. Knight." **American Economic Review** 40 (June): 267-84.

7.74 Weisser, Gerhard. 1968. "Quantifizierbares und Nichtquantizierbares in den Sozialwissenschaften." **WWI-Mitteilungen** 21; Rpt. in Siegfried Katterle, W. Mudra, and L. Neumann, eds. **Beiträge zur Gesellschaftspolitik.** Göttingen: Otto Schwartz, pp. 602-25.

7.75 Wilson, E. B. 1955. "Mathematics in Economics: Further Comment, I." **Review of Economics and Statistics** 37 (August): 297-98.

7.76 Working, Holbrook. 1927. "The Use of the Quantitative Method in the Study of Economic Theory" (round table discussion). **American Economic Association Papers and Proceedings** 17 (March): 18-24.

***

8

Theory

This is a hard category to discuss collectively as so
many theoretical areas are included under this heading.
Problems with causality, prediction, and models have been
given separate sections: § § § 8.1, 8.2, and 8.3
respectively.

Perhaps the most famous single piece on theory is the
Clapham-Pigou exchange on "empty economic boxes" (see
entries 8.31, 8.32, 8.117, and 8.122). Clapham initiated
the controversy by attacking the concepts of increasing and
diminishing rates of return in industry for being unhelpful
because economists cannot really classify industries into
the respective box. Hence these analytical tools are
useless--merely "empty boxes" which ought to be abolished.
Pigou replies that analytical tools are indispensable and
that complete realism in economics is not possible. Later
Robertson (1924) took up the debate with Pigou. The idea of
empty boxes, i.e., useless analytical tools, has dotted the
literature since then.

The amount written on Keynes and his methodology is
voluminous: see, e.g., Akerlof, Bensusan-Butt,
Brown-Colier, Clower, Guthrie, Hansen, Hicks (1980-81),
Leijonhufvud, Littleboy, Lucas and Sargent (1978), Solow,
and Worswick (1983). Hicks' work on IS-LM, in which he
explains why he is dissatisfied with the IS-LM apparatus
which he helped to create, is already a classic.
Leijonhufvud (1983(a)) also discusses problems with IS-LM.

Rational expectations enters the methodological realm
because it calls for a change in method, i.e., how
expectations are treated. See Bausor, Leijonhufvud, Lucas
and Sargent (1978), Maddock, Wible, and Willes.

On microeconomic topics one should see Boland (1986),
Hausman (1984), Kloten, Leibenstein (1979) and (1976),
Machlup 1978(b), A. Nelson, Pfouts, Rappaport, Rosenberg

(1980), 1976(a) and (b), and (1974), Shubik, and Wolfson. Equilibrium and general equilibrium analysis have also generated a considerable literature: Amir and Baumberger, Arrow (1974), Coddington, Hahn, Hausman (1981), Katzner, Krupp, Malinvaud, Milgate, Morgenstern (1976), Petri, Prezeau, Rosenberg (1986), Shapiro, and Weintraub (1985(a) and (b)).

Finally, one of the most important contributions is the clarification of key economic concepts. See Amir and Baumberger, Arrow (1980), Chipman, Clower and Leijonhufvud, Finger (1971b), Hicks, Leijonhufvud, Malinvaud, Milgate, and Prezeau. Clower and Leijonhufvud's discussion of Say's law should be read by all economists and students of economics. The same goes for Chipman and Malinvaud's treatment of equilibrium in economics.

In the section on causality, Sir John Hick's recent work, **Causality in Economics**, is one focal point. Reviews of this work are made by Davidson, Addison et al., Hutchison, and Sims. In § 8.2 on prediction, the Morgenstern--Grunberg & Modigliani--Cyert & Grunberg exchange is famous. The third section, § 8.3 on model-building, spills over into mathematics and econometrics.

***

8.1   Akerlof, George. 1979. "The Case Against Conservative Macroeconomics: An Inaugural Lecture." **Economica** 46 (August): 219-37.

8.2   Alchian, Armen. 1950. "Uncertainty, Evolution and Economic Theory." **Journal of Political Economy** 58, No. 3 (June): 211-21.

8.3   Amir, Schmuel and Jörg Baumberger. 1979. "On the Meaning of Equilibrium and Disequilibrium in Economic Systems." **Economie appliquée** 32, Nos. 2-3: 339-65.

8.4   Archibald, G.C. 1963. "Reply to Chicago." **Review of Economic Studies** 30: 68-71.

8.5   Archibald, G.C. 1961. "Chamberlin **versus** Chicago." **Review of Economic Studies** 29: 2-28.

8.6   Arndt, Helmut. 1984. **Economic Theory v. Economic Reality**, rev. Engl. ed. of **Irrwege der politischen Ökonomie: Die Notwendigkeit einer wirtschaftlichen Revolution** (1979). Trans. by William A. Kirby. East Lansing, MI: Michigan State University Press.

8.7   *Arrow, Kenneth J. 1980. "Real and Nominal Values in Economics." **The Public Interest** (Special Issue: The Crisis in Economic Theory): 139-50.

8.8   *Arrow, Kenneth J. 1974. "General Economic Equilibrium: Purpose, Analytic Techniques, Collective Choice." **American Economic Review** 64, No. 3 (June): 253–72.

8.9   Basmann, R.L. 1975. "Modern Logic and the Suppositious Weakness of the Empirical Foundations of Economic Science." **Schweizerische Zeitschrift für Volkswirtschaft und Statistik** 111, No. 2 (April): 153–76.

8.10   Bausor, Randall. 1985. "Conceptual Evolution in Economics: The Case of Rational Expectations." **Eastern Economic Journal** 11, No. 4 (1985): 297–308.

8.11   Bear, D.V.T. and Daniel Orr. 1967. "Logic and Expediency in Economic Theorizing." **Journal of Political Economy** 75, No. 2 (April): 188–96.

8.12   Bensusan-Butt, D.M. 1980. "Keynes's General Theory: Then and Now." In his **On Economic Knowledge: A Sceptical Miscellany**. Canberra: Australian National University, 1980, pp. 25–40.

8.13   Bernadelli, Harro. 1961. "The Origins of Modern Economic Theory." **Economic Record** 37 (September): 320–38.

8.14   Boland, Lawrence A. 1986. **Methodology for a New Microeconomics**. Boston: Allen and Unwin.

8.15   Boland, Lawrence A. 1983. "On the Best Strategy for Doing Philosophy of Economics" (review of Hausman's **Capital, Profits, and Prices**). **British Journal for the Philosophy of Science** (December): 387–92.

8.16   Boland, Lawrence A. 1977. "Testability in Economic Science." **South African Journal of Economics** 45 (March): 93–105.

8.17   Boland, Lawrence A. 1970. "Axiomatic Analysis and Economic Understanding." **Australian Economic Papers** 9, No. 14 (June): 62–75.

8.18   Bombach, Gottfried. 1960. "Kreislauftheorie und volkswirtschaftliche Gesamtrechnung." **Jahrbuch für Sozialwissenschaft** 11: 217–42 and 331–50; Rpt. in Reimut Jochimsen and Helmut Knobel. **Gegenstand und Methoden der Nationalökonomie**. Köln: Kiepenheuer & Witsch, 1971, pp. 356–71.

8.19   Boulding, Kenneth E. 1956. "Some Contributions of Economics to the General Theory of Value." **Philosophy of Science** 23 (January): 1–14.

8.20   Boulding, Kenneth E. 1955. "In Defence of Statics." **Quarterly Journal of Economics** 69, No. 4 (November): 485–502.

8.21   Boulding, Kenneth E. 1952. "Implications for General Economic Or More Realistic Theories of the Firm." **American Economic Association Papers and Proceedings** 42, No. 2 (May): 37-44.

8.22   Brainard, W.C. and R.N. Cooper. 1975. "Empirical Monetary Macroeconomics: What Have We Learned in the Last 25 Years?" **American Economic Association Papers and Proceedings** 65, No. 2 (May): 167-75.

8.23   Brand, Peter. 1980. "Manipulation-Proofness: A Concept for Widening the Scope of Arrowian Welfare Economics Both Practically and Intellectually." **Theory and Decision** 12 (December): 325-58.

8.24   Brown-Collier, Elba K. 1985. "Methodology and the Practice of Economics: A Critique of Patinkin's Interpretation of Keynes." **Eastern Economic Journal** 11, No. 4 (October-December): 373-83.

8.25   Brunner, Karl, ed. 1969. "'Assumptions' and the Cognitive Quality of Theories." **Synthese** 20, No. 4 (December): 501-25.

8.26   *Buchanan, James M. 1958. "**Ceteris Paribus**: Some Notes on Methodology." **Southern Economic Journal** 24, No. 3 (January): 259-70.

8.27   Canaan, Edwin. 1902. "The Practical Utility of Economic Science." Report of the British Association for the Advancement of Science. **Economic Journal** (December); Rpt. as "The Practical Usefulness of Economic Theory" in R.L. Smyth, ed. **Essays in Economic Method**. London: Gerald Duckworth and Co., 1962, pp. 187-99.

8.28   Chalk, Alfred. 1970. "Concepts of Change and the Role of Predictability in Economics." **History of Political Economy** 2: 97-117.

8.29   Chase, Richard X. 1981. "The Development of Contemporary Mainstream Macroeconomics: Vision, Ideology, and Theory." **Revista Internazionale di Scienze Economiche e Commerciali** 6; Rpt. in Alfred S. Eichner, ed. **Why Economics Is Not Yet a Science**. London: Macmillan/Sharpe, 1983, pp. 126-65.

8.30   Chipman, J. 1965. "The Nature and Meaning of Equilibrium in Economic Theory." In Don Martindale, ed. **Functionalism in the Social Sciences: The Strength and Limits of Functionalism in Anthropology, Economics, Political Science and Sociology**. Philadelphia: American Academy of Political and Social Science, 1965, pp. 35-64.

8.31   Clapham, J.H. 1922(a). "Of Empty Economic Boxes." **Economic Journal** 32 (September): 305-14.

8.32   Clapham, J.H. 1922(b). "A Rejoinder" (Pigou, 1922). **Economic Journal** 32 (December): 560-63.

8.33   Clark, A.F. 1977. "Testability in Economic Science: A Comment." **South African Journal of Economics** 45: 106-107.

8.34   Clower, Robert. 1975. "Reflections on the Keynesian Perplex." **Zeitschrift für Nationalökonomie** 35: 1-24.

8.35   Clower, Robert. 1974. "Reflections on Science. . . and Economics." **Intermountain Economic Review** 5: 1-12.

8.36   Clower, Robert and Axel Leijonhufvud. 1973. "Say's Principle, What It Means and Doesn't Mean: Part I." **Intermountain Economic Review** 4, No. 2 (Fall): 1-16. (Part II never appeared); Rpt. in Axel Leijonhufvud. **Information and Coordination: Essays in Macroeconomic Theory.** NY/Oxford: Oxford University Press, 1981, pp. 79-101.

8.37   Coddington, Alan. 1975. "The Rationale of General Equilibrium Theory." **Economic Inquiry** 13, No. 4 (December): 539-58.

8.38   Covick, O.E. 1974. "The Quantity Theory of Drink—A Restatement." **Australian Economic Papers** 13, No. 3 (December): 171-77.

8.39   Cyert, Richard M. and Garrel Pottinger. 1979. "Towards a Better Microeconomic Theory." **Philosophy of Science** 46: 204-22.

8.40   Dacey, Raymond. 1981. "Some Implications of 'Theory Absorption' for Economic Theory and the Economics of Information." In Joseph Pitt, ed. **Philosophy in Economics.** Dordrecht: D. Reidel, 1981, pp. 111-36.

8.41   Dasgupta, A.K. 1985. **Epochs of Economic Theory.** Oxford: Basil Blackwell.

8.42   De Marchi, Neil. 1970. "The Empirical Content and Longevity of Ricardian Economics." **Economica** 37 (August): 257-76.

8.43   Dorfman, Robert. 1954. "The Nature and Significance of Input-Output." **Review of Economics and Statistics** 36, No. 2 (May): 121-33.

8.44   Dow, Sheila. 1985. **Macroeconomic Thought: A Methodological Approach.** Oxford: Basil Blackwell.

8.45   Dumez, Hervé. 1985. "Walras, Marshall: stratégies scientifiques comparées." **Revue d'économie politique** 95, No. 2 (March-April): 168-73.

8.46   Ellig, Jerome R. 1986. "Do We Walk with Walras?" **Atlantic Economic Journal** 14, No. 2 (July): 82.

8.47   Fabian, Robert G. 1971. "Cultural Influences on Economic Theory." **Journal of Economic Issues** 5, No. 3 (September): 46-59.

8.48   Field, A.J. 1979. "On the Explanation of Rules Using Rational Choice Models." **Journal of Economic Issues** 13, No. 1 (March): 49-72.

8.49   Field, James A. 1917. "The Place of Economic Theory in Graduate Work." **Journal of Political Economy** 25 (January): 48-57.

8.50   Finger, J.M. 1971(a). "The Correspondence Principle: A Superfluous Tool of Economic Analysis." **Journal of Economic Issues** 5, No. 1 (March): 47-56.

8.51   Finger, J.M. 1971(b). "Is Equilibrium an Operational Concept?" **Economic Journal** 81 (September): 609-12.

8.52   Fishburn, Peter C. 1970. "Utility Theory with Inexact Preferences and Degrees of Preference." **Synthese** 21 (June): 204-21.

8.53   Fogel, Robert William. 1965. "The Reunification of Economic History with Economic Theory." **American Economic Association Papers and Proceedings** 60, No. 2 (May): 92-98.

8.54   Frazer, William J., Jr. 1978. "Evolutionary Economics, Rational Expectations, and Monetary Policy." **Journal of Economic Issues** 12, No. 2 (June): 343-72.

8.55   *Friedman, Milton. 1946. "Lange on Price Flexibility and Employment: A Methodological Criticism." **American Economic Review** 36 (September): 613-31.

8.56   Fusfeld, Daniel R. 1980. "The Conceptual Framework of Modern Economics." **Journal of Economic Issues** 14, No. 1 (March): 1-52.

8.57   Garb, Gerald. 1964. "The Problem of Causality in Economics." **Kyklos** 17: 594-609.

8.58   Garrison, Roger W. 1978. "Austrian Macroeconomics: A Diagrammatical Exposition." In Louis M. Spadaro, ed. **New Directions in Austrian Economics.** Kansas City: Sheed Andrews and McMeel, Inc., 1978, pp. 167-204.

8.59   Georgescu-Roegen, Nicholas. 1974. "Dynamic Models and Economic Growth." **Economie appliquée** 27, No. 4: 529-63.

8.60   Greenwald, William I. 1957. "Common Irrelevancies in Contemporary Theorizing by Economists." **Kyklos** 10, No. 3: 302-14.

8.61   Guthrie, William G. 1984. "Selective Rediscovery of

Economic Ideas: What Keynes Found in Malthus." **Southern Economic Journal** 50, No. 3 (January): 771-80.

8.62   Haberler, Gottfried. 1936. "Mr. Keynes' Theory of the 'Multiplier': A Methodological Criticism." **Zeitschrift für Nationalökonomie** 7 (August): 299-305.

8.63   Händler, Ernst W. 1982. "The Evolution of Economic Theories: A Formal Approach." **Erkenntnis** 18, No. 1 (July): 65-96.

8.64   Hahn, Frank H. 1983. "On General Equilibrium and Stability." In E.C. Brown and Robert Solow, eds. **Paul Samuelson and Modern Economic Theory.** NY: McGraw-Hill, 1983, pp. 31-55.

8.65   Hahn, Frank. 1980. "General Equilibrium Theory." **The Public Interest** (Special Issue: The Crisis in Economic Theory): 123-38.

8.66   Hahn, Frank. 1973. "The Winter of Our Discontent." **Economica** 40, No. 159 (August): 322-30.

8.67   Hahn, Frank. 1970. "Some Adjustment Problems." **Econometrica** 38, No. 1 (January): 1-17.

8.68   Hansen, Alvin Harvey. 1966. "Keynes After Thirty Years (with Special Reference to the United States)." **Weltwirtschaftliches Archiv** 97 (1966 II): 213-32.

8.69   Hausman, Daniel. 1984. "Defending Microeconomic Theory." **Philosophical Forum** 15 (Summer): 392-404.

8.70   Hausman, Daniel. 1981. "Are General Equilibrium Theories Explanatory." In Joseph Pitt. **Philosophy in Economics.** Dordrecht: D. Reidel: 1981, pp. 17-32.

8.71   *Hicks, Sir John. 1980-81. "IS-LM: An Explanation." **Journal of Post Keynesian Economics** 3, No. 2 (Winter): 139-54; Rpt. in Jean-Paul Fitoussi, ed. **Modern Macroeconomic Theory.** Oxford: Basil Blackwell, 1983, pp. 49-63.

8.72   *Hicks, Sir John. 1975. "Revival of Political Economy. The Old and the New." **Economic Record** 51: 365-67.

8.73   Hutchinson, William K. 1978. "Stabilization Policies for Mature Economies: Comment." **Journal of Economic Issues** 12, No. 2 (June): 401-04.

8.74   Katzner, D.W. 1985. "Alternatives to Equilibrium Analysis." **Eastern Economic Journal** 11, No. 4 (October-December): 404-21.

8.75   Klant, J.J. 1984. **The Rules of the Game: The Logical Structure of Economic Theories.** Trans. Ina Swart.

Cambridge: Cambridge University Press.

8.76   Klant, J.J. 1972. "A Note on Giffen's Paradox and Falsifiability." **Weltwirtschaftliches Archiv** 108: 669-72.

8.77   *Klein, Lawrence R. 1947. "Macro-Economics As Guide to Economic Policy." **Econometrica** 15 (April): 111-51.

8.78   Kloten, Norbert. 1958. "Mikro- und Makroanalyse als Grundlage   wirtschaftspolitischer   Entscheidungen. **Zeitschrift für die gesamte Staatswissenschaft** 114: 28-46; Rpt. in Reimut Jochimsen and Helmut Knobel, eds. **Gegenstand und Methoden der Nationalökonomie.** Köln: Kiepenheuer & Witsch, 1971, pp. 337-53.

8.79   Knight, Frank. 1961. "Methodology in Economics: Parts I and II." **Southern Economic Journal** 27, No. 3 (January): 185-93 and 27, No. 4 (April): 273-82.

8.80   Knight, Frank. 1946. "New Frontiers in Economics: Immutable Law in Economics: Its Reality and Limitations." **American Economic Association Papers and Proceedings** 36: 93-111.

8.81   Kohn, Meir. 1986. "Monetary Analysis, the Equilibrium Method, and Keynes's 'General Theory.'" **Journal of Political Economy** 94, No. 5 (December): 1191-1224.

8.82   *Koopmans, Tjalling C. 1947. "Measurement Without Theory" (Review of Burns and Mitchell's **Measuring Business Cycles,** 1946) **Review of Economics and Statistics** 29, No. 3 (August): 161-72.

8.83   Krupp, Sherman Roy. 1965. "Equilibrium Theory in Economics and in Functional Analysis As Types of Explanation." In Don Martindale, ed. **Functionalism in the Social Sciences: The Strength and Limits of Functionalism in Anthropology, Economics, Political Science and Sociology.** Philadelphia: American Academy of Political and Social Science, 1965, pp. 65-83.

8.84   Lancaster, Kelvin. 1966. "Economic Aggregation and Additivity." In Sherman Roy Krupp, ed. **The Structure of Economic Science.** Englewood Cliffs: Prentice-Hall, 1966, pp. 201-15.

8.85   Lancaster, Kelvin. 1962. "The Scope of Qualitative Economics." **Review of Economic Studies** 29: 99-123.

8.86   Leibenstein, Harvey. 1979. "A Branch of Economics Is Missing: Micro-Macro Theory." **Journal of Economic Literature** 17, (June): 477-502.

8.87   Leibenstein, Harvey. 1976. **Beyond Economic Man: A New Foundation for Microeconomics.** Cambridge, MA: Harvard University Press.

8.88   Leijonhufvud, Axel. 1983(a). "What Was the Matter with IS-LM?" In Jean-Paul Fitoussi, ed. **Modern Macroeconomic Theory.** Oxford: Basil Blackwell, 1983, pp. 64-90.

8.89   Leijonhufvud, Axel. 1983(b). "What Would Keynes Have Thought of Rational Expectations?" In David Worswick and James Trevitheck, eds. **Keynes and the Modern World: Proceedings of the Keynes Centenary Conference, King's College, Cambridge.** Cambridge: Cambridge University Press, 1983, pp. 179-205.

8.90   *Leontief, Wassily. 1982. "Letters: Academic Economics." **Science** 217 (9 July): 104-05; Rpt. (1) in William Marr and Baldev Raj, eds. **How Economists Explain: A Reader in Methodology.** Lanham: University Press of America, 1983, pp. 331-35 and (2) as the Preface in Alfred S. Eichner, ed. **Why Economics Is Not Yet a Science.** London: Macmillan/Sharpe, 1983, pp. vii-xi.

8.91   *Leontief, Wassily. 1937. "Implicit Theorizing: A Methodological Criticism of the Neo-Cambridge School." **Quarterly Journal of Economics** 51: 337-51.

8.92   Littleboy, Bruce and Ghanshyam Mehta. 1985. "Keynes and Scientific Methodology: Whither and Whence." **Indian Economic Journal** 33, No. 1 (July-September): 66-76.

8.93   Lucas, Robert E., Jr. 1976. "Econometric Policy Evaluation: A Critique." In Karl Brunner and Allan H. Meltzer, eds. **The Phillips Curve and Labor Markets.** Vol. 1 of the **Carnegie-Rochester Conference Series on Public Policy.** (A supplement series to the Journal of Monetary Economics). Amsterdam: North-Holland, 1976, pp. 19-46.

8.94   Lucas, Robert E. and Thomas J. Sargent. 1978. "After Keynesian Macroeconomics." In **After the Phillips Curve: Persistence of High Inflation and High Unemployment.** The Federal Reserve Bank of Boston. Boston Conference Series No. 19. Boston: Federal Reserve Bank of Boston, 1978, pp. 49-72, and "Discussion" (B. Friedman), pp. 73-80; "Response to Friedman," pp. 81-82; and "Rebuttal," p. 83.

8.95   Machlup, Fritz. 1978(a). **Methodology of Economics and Other Social Sciences.** NY: Academic Press.

8.96   Machlup, Fritz. 1978(b). "A Note on Models in Microeconomics." In his 1978(a), pp. 75-100.

8.97   Maddock, Rodney. 1984. "Rational Expectations Macrotheory: A Lakatosian Case Study in Program Adjustment." **History of Political Economy** 16, No. 2 (Summer): 291-309.

8.98   Malinvaud, E. 1982. "The Equilbrium Concept in

Economics." In L. Jonathan Cohen, et al., eds. **Logic, Methodology and Philosophy of Science VI.** Amsterdam: North-Holland, 1982, pp. 585-94.

8.99   Marschak, Jacob. 1946. "Neumann's and Morgenstern's New Approach to Static Economics." **Journal of Political Economy** 54, No. 2 (April): 97-115.

8.100   Marsden, David. 1984. "Homo Economicus and the Labour Market." In Peter Wiles and Guy Routh, eds. **Economics in Disarray.** Oxford: Basil Blackwell, 1984, pp. 121-53.

8.101   Menger, Karl. 1979(a). "Remarks on the Law of Diminishing Returns: A Study in Meta-Economics." In his **Selected Papers in Logic and Foundations, Didactics, Economics.** Dordrecht/London: Reidel, 1979, pp. 279-302.

8.102   Menger, Karl. 1979(b). "The Role of Uncertainty in Economics." In his **Selected Papers in Logic and Foundations, Didactics, Economics.** Dordrecht/London: Reidel, 1979, pp. 259-78.

8.103   Milgate, Murray. 1979. "On the Origin of the Notion of 'Intertemporal Equilibrium.'" **Economica** 46: 1-10.

8.104   Mitchell, Wesley C. 1916. "The Role of Money in Economic Theory." **American Economic Association Papers and Proceedings** 6 (March): 140-61.

8.105   Morgenstern, Oskar. 1972. "Thirteen Critical Points in Contemporary Economic Theory: An Interpretation." **Journal of Economic Literature** 10, No. 4 (December): 1163-1189.

8.106   Morgenstern, Oskar. 1976 (1935). "Perfect Foresight and Economic Equilibrium." Trans. Frank Knight. In **Selected Economic Writings of Oskar Morgenstern.** Ed. Andrew Schotter. NY: New York University Press, 1976, pp. 169-83.

8.107   Morgenstern, Oskar. 1953. "When Is a Problem of Economic Policy Solvable?" In Valentin F. Wagner and Fritz Marbach, eds. **Wirtschaftstheorie und Wirtschaftspolitik. Festschrift für Alfred Amonn zum 70. Geburtstag.** Bern: Francke, 1953, pp. 241-49.

8.108   Morgenstern, Oskar. 1934. **Die Grenzen der Wirtschaftspolitik.** Vienna: Julius Springer Verlag; Trans. by Vera Smith as **The Limits of Economics.** London: W. Hodge and Co., 1937.

8.109   Morgenstern, Oskar. 1928. **Wirtschaftsprognose, eine Untersuchung ihrer Voraussetzungen und Möglichkeiten.** Vienna: Julius Springer.

8.110   Nelson, Alan. 1984. "Some Issues Surrounding the

Reduction of Macroeconomics to Microeconomics." **Philosophy of Science** 1 (December): 573-94.

8.111 Nelson, Richard and Sidney G. Winter. 1974. "Neoclassical vs. Evolutionary Theory of Economic Growth: Critique and Prospectus." **Economic Journal** 84 (December): 886-905.

8.112 O'Driscoll, Gerald P., Jr. 1982. "Monopoly in Theory and Practice." In Israel M. Kirzner, ed. **Method, Process, and Austrian Economics: Essays in Honor of Ludwig von Mises.** Lexington, Mass./Toronto: Heath/Lexington Books, 1982, pp. 189-213.

8.113 Perroux, Francois. 1950. "Economic Space: Theory and Applications."   **Quarterly   Journal   of   Economics**   64 (February): 89-104.

8.114 Petri, Fabio. 1978. "The Difference Between Long-Period and Short-Period General Equilibrium and the Capital Theory Controversy." **Australian Economic Papers** 17, No. 31 (December): 246-60.

8.115 Pfouts, Ralph W. 1984. "Method and Applied Microeconomics." **Atlantic Economic Journal** 12, No. 3 (September): 16-19.

8.116 Pigou, A. 1922. "Empty Economic Boxes: A Reply." **Economic Journal** 32 (December): 458-65.

8.117 Pikler, Andrew G. 1954/1955. "Utility Theories in Field Physics and Mathematical Economics, Part I and II." **British Journal for the Philosophy of Science** 5 (May 1954): 47-58 and 5 (February 1955): 303-18.

8.118 Prezeau, Carl. 1981. "L'équilibre social et l'équilibre général reconsidérés." **Economie appliquée** 34, No. 1: 29-60.

8.119 Puu, Tonu. 1967. "Some Reflections on the Relation Between Economic Theory and Empirical Reality." **Swedish Journal of Economics** 69, No. 2 (June): 86-114.

8.120 Rappaport, Steven. 1986. "The Modal View and Defending Microeconomics." In **PSA 1986**, Vol. 1. Arthur Fire and Peter Machamer, eds. East Lansing, MI: Philosophy of Science Association, 1986, pp. 289-97.

8.121 Robertson, D. 1924. "Those Empty Boxes," followed by A.C. Pigou's comment and Robertson's rejoinder. **Economic Journal** 34 (March): 16-31.

8.122 Rosenberg, Alexander. 1986. "The Explanatory Role of Existence Proofs." **Ethics** 97 (October): 177-86.

8.123 Rosenberg, Alexander. 1985. "Prospects for the

Elimination of Tastes from Economics and Ethics." **Social Philosophy and Policy** 2 (Spring): 48-68.

8.124 Rosenberg, Alexander. 1980. "A Skeptical History of Microeconomic Theory." **Theory and Decision** 12, No. 1 (March): 79-93; Slightly rev. in Joseph C. Pitt, ed. **Philosophy in Economics.** Dordrecht: D. Reidel, 1981, pp. 47-61.

8.125 Rosenberg, Alexander. 1979. "Can Economic Theory Explain Everything?" **Philosophy of the Social Sciences** 9 (December): 509-29.

8.126 Rosenberg, Alexander. 1976(a). **Microeconomic Laws: A Philosophical Analysis.** Pittsburgh: University of Pittsburgh Press.

8.127 Rosenberg, Alexander. 1976(b). "On the Interanimation of Micro- and Macroeconomics." **Philosophy of the Social Sciences** 6: 35-53.

8.128 Rosenberg, Alexander. 1974. "Partial Interpretation and Microeconomics." In Werner Leinfellner and Eckehart Köhler, eds. **Developments in the Methodology of Social Science.** Dordrecht: D. Reidel, 1974, pp. 93-109.

8.129 Rothbard, Murray N. 1978. "Austrian Definitions of the Supply of Money." In Louis M. Spadaro, ed. **New Directions in Austrian Economics.** Kansas City: Sheed Andrews and McMeel, 1978, pp. 143-56.

8.130 Rugina, Anghel N. 1987. "The Third Revolution in Economic Thinking: A New Methodology of Orientation, Clarification and Development of New Knowledge." **Revista Internazionale di Scienze Economiche e Commerciali** 34, No. 6 (June): 487-512.

8.131 Rugina, Anghel N. 1986(a). "Principia Oeconomica: New and Old Foundations of Economic Analysis." **International Journal of Social Economics** 13, Nos. 7/8: 1-67.

8.132 Rugina, Anghel N. 1986(b). "New Frontiers of a **Principia Oeconomica:** The Development of an Orientation Table and Its Significance." **Revista Internazionale di Szienze Economiche e Commerciali** 33, No. 2 (February): 105-22.

8.133 *Samuelson, Paul A. 1971. "Maximum Principles in Analytical Economics." (Nobel Lecture: 1970) **Science** 173 (September 10): 991-97; Rpt. in **American Economic Review** 62, No. 3 (June 1972): 249-62 and in **Synthese** 31 (1975): 323-44.

8.134 Schleicher, Stefan. 1982. "Endogeneity, Exogeneity and Economic Policy-Empirical Evidence on the Econometrics of New Classical Macroeconomics." **Empirica** 2: 93-111.

8.135   Sen, Amartya. 1974. "On Some Debates in Capital Theory." **Economica** 41 (August): 328-35.

8.136   Shapiro, Nina. 1978. "Keynes and the Equilibrium Economics." **Australian Economic Papers** 17, No. 31 (December): 207-23.

8.137   Sheffrin, Steven. 1978. "Stabilization Policies for Mature Economies: Comment." **Journal of Economic Issues** 12, No. 2 (June): 393-97.

8.138   Shubik, Martin. 1970. "A Curmudgeon's Guide to Microeconomics." **Journal of Economic Literature** 8, No. 1 (March): 405-34.

8.139   Shupak, Mark B. 1962. "The Predictive Accuracy of Empirical Demand Analysis." **Economic Journal** 72 (September): 550-75.

8.140   Silberberg, Eugene. 1974. "A Revision of Comparative Statics Methodology, Or How to Do Comparative Statics on the Back of an Envelope." **Journal of Economic Theory** 7, No. 2: 159-72.

8.141   Simon, Julian L. 1982. "Linguistic Confusion in Economics: Utility, Causality, Product Differentiation, and the Supply of Natural Resources." **Kyklos** 35, No. 4: 673-701.

8.142   Simpson, Jerry P. 1967. "Government Transfers, Interest and Subsidies in the National Income Accounts." **Journal of Economic Issues** 1, No. 3 (September): 211-18.

8.143   Sims, Christopher A. 1980. "Macroeconomics and Reality." **Econometrica** 48, No. 1 (January): 1-48.

8.144   Smith, V. Kerry and Clifford S. Russell. 1975. "The Selection of Macro Policy Instruments Over Time." **Australian Economic Papers** 14, No. 24 (June): 120-27.

8.145   *Solow, R.M. 1984. "Mr. Hicks and the Classics." **Oxford Economic Papers Supplement** ("Economic Theory and Hicksian Themes," ed. by D.A. Collard, et al.) N.S. 36 (November): 13-25.

8.146   *Stigler, George. 1963. "Archibald Versus Chicago." **Review of Economic Studies** 30: 63-64.

8.147   *Stigler, George and Gary Becker. 1977. "De Gustibus Non Est Disputandum." **American Economic Review** 67, No.2 (March): 76-90.

8.148   *Stone, Richard. 1964. "The **A Priori** and the Empirical in Economics." **British Journal for the Philosophy** of Science 15, No. 58 (August): 115-22.

8.149 Tarascio, Vincent J. and Bruce Caldwell. 1979. "Theory Choice in Economics: Philosophy and Practice." **Journal of Economic Issues** 13 (December): 983-1006.

8.150 Thurow, Lester C. 1977. "Economics 1977." **Daedalus** (Fall): 79-94.

8.151 *Tobin, James. 1985. "Neoclassical Theory in America: J.B. Clark and Fisher." **American Economic Review Special Issue** 75, No. 6 (December): 28-38.

8.152 Toumanoff, Peter G. 1984. "A Positive Analysis of the Theory of Market Failure." **Kyklos** 37, No. 4: 529-41.

8.153 Veblen, Thorstein. 1909. "The Limitations of Marginal Utility." **Journal of Political Economy** 17 (November): 620-36.

8.154 Velupillai, K. 1973. "A Note on the Origin of the 'Correspondence Principle.'" **Swedish Journal of Economics** 75, No. 3 September): 302-04.

8.155 Vickers, Douglas. 1985. "On Relational Structures and Non-equilibrium in Economic Theory." **Eastern Economic Journal** 11, No. 4 (October-December): 384-404.

8.156 Walker, Donald A. 1970. "Léon Walras in the Light of His Correspondence and Related Papers." **Journal of Political Economy** 78 (July-August): 685-701.

8.157 Weintraub, E. Roy. 1985(a). "Appraising General Equilibrium Analysis." **Economics and Philosophy** 1, No. 1 (April): 23-37.

8.158 Weintraub, E. Roy. 1985(b). "Joan Robinson's Critique of Equilibrium: An Appraisal." **American Economic Association Papers and Proceedings** 75, No. 2 (May): 146-49.

8.159 Wible, James R. 1984-85. "An Epistemic Critique of Rational Expectations and the Neoclassical Macroeconomic Research Program." **Journal of Post Keynesian Economics** 7, No. 2 (Winter): 269-81.

8.160 Wilber, Charles K. 1979. "Empirical Verification and Theory Selection: The Keynesian-Monetarist Debate." **Journal of Economic Issues** 13 (December): 973-81.

8.161 Willes, Mark H. 1980. "'Rational Expectations' As a Counterrevolution." **The Public Interest** (Special Issue: The Crisis in Economic Theory): 81-96.

8.162 Winthrop, Henry. 1945. "Conceptual Difficulties in Modern Economic Theory." **Philosophy of Science** 12 (January): 30-39 (on limitations of marginal analysis).

8.163 Wolfson, R.J. 1981. "New Consumer Theory and the Relations Between Goods." In Joseph C. Pitt, ed. **Philosophy in Economics.** Dordrecht: D. Reidel, 1981, pp. 33-46.

8.164 Worswick, David and James Trevitheck. 1983. **Keynes and the Modern World: Proceedings of the Keynes Centenary Conference, King's College, Cambridge.** Cambridge: Cambridge University Press.

***

8.1 On Causality

8.1.1 Addison, John T., John Burton, and Thomas S. Torrance. 1981. "Causation, Social Science and Sir John Hicks." **Oxford Economic Papers** 36, No. 1 (March): 1-11.

8.1.2 Davidson, Paul. 1980. "Causality in Economics: A Review" (of Hick's **Causality in Economics**) **Journal of Post Keynesian Economics** 2, No. 4 (Summer): 576-84.

8.1.3 Fisher, Franklin M. 1969. "Causation and Specification in Economic Theory and Econometrics." **Synthese** 20: 489-500.

8.1.4 Garb, Gerald. 1971. "The Concept of Causality in Economics: Comment." **Kyklos** 24, No. 4: 767-68.

8.1.5 Garb, Gerald. 1964. "The Problem of Causality in Economics." **Kyklos** 17: 594-609.

8.1.6 Granger, C.W.J. 1980. "Testing for Causality: A Personal Viewpoint." **Journal of Economic Dynamics and Social Control** 2: 329-52.

8.1.7 Hausman, Daniel. 1983. "Are There Causal Relations Among Dependent Variables?" **Philosophy of Science** 50, No. 1 (March): 58-81.

8.1.8 Helm, Dieter. 1984. "Predictions and Causes: A Comparison of Friedman and Hicks on Method." **Oxford Economic Papers Supplement** ("Economic Theory and Hicksian Themes," ed. by D.A. Collard, et al.) N.S. 36 (November): 118-34.

8.1.9 *Hicks, Sir John. 1984. "The 'New Causality': An Explanation." **Oxford Economic Papers** 36, No. 1 (March): 12-15.

8.1.10 *Hicks, Sir John. 1979. **Causality in Economics.** Oxford: Basil Blackwell.

8.1.11 Hutchison, T.W. 1980. "Review of Hick's **Causality in Economics.**" **Zeitschrift für Nationalökonomie** 40: pp. 251-52.

8.1.12 McClelland, Peter D. 1975. **Causal Explanation and Model Building in History, Economics and the New Economic History**. Ithaca, NY: Cornell University Press.

8.1.13 Orcutt, Guy H. 1952. "Actions, Consequences, and Causal Relations." **Review of Economics and Statistics** 34 (November): 305-13.

8.1.14 *Samuelson, Paul A. 1965. "Some Notions on Causality and Teleology in Economics." In Daniel Lerner, ed. **Cause and Effect**. NY: Free Press, 1965, pp. 99-143.

8.1.15 *Simon, Herbert A. 1952. "On the Definition of the Causal Relations." **Journal of Philosophy** 49: 517-28.

8.1.16 Simon, Julian L. 1971. "The Concept of Causality in Economics: Reply." **Kyklos** 24, No. 4: 769-70.

8.1.17 Simon, Julian L. 1970. "The Concept of Causality in Economics." **Kyklos** 23, No. 2: 226-54.

8.1.18 Sims, Christopher A. 1981. "What Kind of Science Is Economics? A Review Article on Causality in Economics by John R. Hicks." **Journal of Political Economy** 89, No. 3 (June): 578-83.

8.1.19 Termini, Valeria. 1984. "A Note on Hick's 'Contemporaneous Causality.'" **Cambridge Journal of Economics** 8, No. 1: 87-92.

8.1.20 Zellner, Arnold. 1979. "Causality and Econometrics." In Karl Brunner and Allan Meltzer, eds. **Three Aspects of Policy and Policymaking**. Vol. 10 of the **Carnegie-Rochester Conference Series on Public Policy** (A Supplemental Series to the Journal of Monetary Economics). Amsterdam: North-Holland, 1979, pp. 9-54.

***

8.2   On Prediction

8.2.1 Albert, Hans. 1972. "Theorie und Prognose in den Sozialwissenschaften." In Ernst Topitsch, ed. **Logik der Sozialwissenschaften**. Köln: Kiepenheuer und Witsch, 1972, pp. 126-37.

8.2.2 Alchian, Armen. 1950. "Uncertainty, Evolution and Economic Theory." **Journal of Political Economy** 58, No. 3 (June): 211-21.

8.2.3 Boulding, K.E. 1953. "Projection, Prediction, and Precariousness." **Review of Economics and Statistics** 35, No. 4 (November): 257-60.

8.2.4 Burns, Sir Terence. 1986. "The Interpretation and

Use of Economic Predictions (with discussion)." In Mason,
Mathias, and Westcott, 1986, pp. 103-25.

8.2.5 Chalk, Alfred. 1970. "Concepts of Change and the
Role Predictability in Economics." **History of Political
Economy** 2: 97-117.

8.2.6 Cyert, Richard M. and Emile Grunberg. 1963.
"Assumption, Prediction and Explanation in Economics." In
Richard M. Cyert and James G. March, eds. **A Behavioral
Theory of the Firm**. Englewood Cliffs, N.J.: Prentice-Hall,
1963, pp. 298-311.

8.2.7 Dacey, Raymond. 1975. "The Effects of Theory and
Data in Economic Prediction." **Kyklos** 28: 407-11.

8.2.8 Fourastie, Jean. 1954. "Predicting Economic Changes
in Our Time." **Diogenes** 5 (Winter): 14-38.

8.2.9 Grunberg, Emile and Franco Modigliani. 1954. "The
Predictability of Social Events." **Journal of Political
Economy** 62, No. 6 (December): 465-78.

8.2.10 Hahn, L. Albert. 1953. "Über Wirtschaftsprognosen."
**Schweizerische Zeitschrift für Volkswirtschaft und
Statistik** 89: 405-13.

8.2.11 Heilbroner, Robert. 1970. "On the Limits of Economic
Prediction." **Diogenes** 70 (Summer): 27-40.

8.2.12 Heiner, Ronald A. 1983. "The Origin of Predictable
Behavior." **American Economic Review** 73, No. 4 (September):
560-95.

8.2.13 Hendry, D.F. 1986. "The Role of Prediction in
Evaluating Econometric Models" (with discussion). In Mason,
Mathias, and Westcott, 1986, pp. 25-34.

8.2.14 Hotelling, Harold. 1942-43. "Problems of
Prediction." **American Journal of Sociology** 48: 61-76.

8.2.15 Hutchison, T.W. 1967. "Review of Popper's **Elend des
Historizismus**." **Zeitschrift für Nationalökonomie** 27:
503-04.

8.2.16 Hutchison, T.W. 1964. "Review of Popper's
Conjectures and Refutations." **Economica** 31 (May): 217-19.

8.2.17 Marget, A.W. 1929. "Morgenstern on the Methodology
of Economic Forecasting." **Journal of Political Economy** 37,
No. 3 (June): 312-39.

8.2.18 Marschak, Jacob. 1947. "Economic Structure, Path,
Policy, and Prediction." **American Economic Association
Papers and Proceedings** 37: 81-84.

8.2.19 Mason, Sir John, P. Mathias, and J.H. Westcott. 1986. **Predictability in Science and Society. A Joint Symposium of the Royal Society and the British Academy Held on 20 and 21 March 1986.** London: The Royal Society and the British Academy.

8.2.20 Morgenstern, Oskar. 1928. **Wirtschaftsprognose, eine Untersuchung ihrer Voraussetzungen und Möglichkeiten.** Vienna: Julius Springer.

8.2.21 Schöpf, Anton. 1966. **Das Prognoseproblem in der Nationalökonomie. Versuch einer Gesamtbetrachtung.** Vol. 2 of **Beiträge zur ganzheitlichen Wirtschafts- und Gesellschaftslehre.** Berlin: Duncker & Humblot.

8.2.22 Sen, A. K. 1986. "Prediction and Economic Theory" (with discussion). In Mason, Mathias, and Westcott, 1986, pp. 3-23.

8.2.23 Solo, Robert. 1955. "Prediction, Projection, and Social Prognosis." **Journal of Philosophy** 52 (August): 459-63.

8.2.24 Wild, Jürgen. 1970. "Probleme der theoretischen Deduktion von Prognosen." **Zeitschrift für die gesamte Staatswissenschaft** 126, No. 4 (October): 553-76.

8.2.25 Zweig, Ferdinand. 1950. **Economic Ideas: A Study of Historical Perspectives.** NY: Prentice-Hall, pp. 25-33.

8.3   On Models

8.3.1 *Arrow, Kenneth. 1951. "Mathematical Models in the Social Sciences." In Daniel Lerner and Harold Lasswell, eds. **The Policy Sciences: Recent Developments in Scope and Method.** Stanford, CA: Stanford University Press, 1951, pp. 129-54.

8.3.2 Baumol, William J. 1966. "Economic Models and Mathematics." In Sherman Roy Krupp, ed. **The Structure of Economic Science.** Englewood Cliffs, NJ: Prentice-Hall, 1966, pp. 88-101.

8.3.3 Bell, Daniel. 1980. "Models and Reality in Economic Discourse." **The Public Interest** (Special Issue: The Crisis in Economic Theory): 46-80.

8.3.4 Boland, L. A. 1969. "Economic Understanding and Understanding Economics." **South African Journal of Economics** 37 (June): 144-60.

8.3.5 Gibbard, Allan and Hal R. Varion. 1978. "Economic Models." **Journal of Philosophy** 75, No. 11 (November): 664-77.

8.3.6 Kregel, Jan. 1976. "Economic Methodology in the Face

of Uncertainty: The Modeling Methods of Keynes and the Post-Keynesians." **Economic Journal** 86 (June): 209-25.

8.3.7 McClelland, Peter D. 1975. **Causal Explanation and Model Building in History, Economics and the New Economic History.** Ithaca, NY: Cornell University Press.

8.3.8 McClements, L.D. 1973. "Some Aspects of Model Building." **Journal of Agricultural Economics** 24: 103-20; Rpt. in William L. Marr and Baldev Raj, eds. **How Economists Explain: A Reader in Methodology.** Lanham: University Press of America, 1983, pp. 203-27.

8.3.9 Rosenberg, Alexander. 1978. "The Puzzle of Economic Modelling." **Journal of Philosophy** 75, No. 11 (November): 679-83.

(See the next section on econometrics for more on modelling.)

***

9

Methodological Problems in Econometrics

If we mark the beginning of econometrics in the founding of the Econometric Society in 1930, econometrics is about sixty years old. Since 1930 the field has expanded immensely. Originally it was hoped that this branch of economics would provide the testing ground for competing economics theories. (Keynes (1939), by the way, strongly objected to this optimistic view of the founding fathers.) Realizing these goals turned out to be far more complicated than originally expected.

Today it is clear that econometric work has never settled a dispute over theory among or between the Keynesian, post-Keynesian, new Keynesian, monetarist, new classical, or Marxist economists. This is only one reason why econometrics is in "crisis" today. Besides this, there are still considerable problems getting good economic data. (Morgenstern's work is a classic on problems with data in economics.) Streissler discusses problems with prediction. Leamer's "Let's Take the Con Out of Econometrics," which appeared in 1983, aroused considerable controversy: he condemns econometricians for being overly confident and not careful enough with their methods. Glymour, a philosopher of science, reviewed Leamer's article (1985), and Leamer responded (1985).

The latest problem to plague the profession is called the "Lucas critique" (for Professor Robert Lucas of the University of Chicago who formulated it) and concerns macroeconomic models. Lucas claims that if government policy changes, the model used to predict the effects of a change in policy will fail. The reason for this: the parameters of the model (and not just those directly related to policy) will change and invalidate the entire model, completely frustrating enlightened forecasting. It is hoped that this problem can be partially resolved by modelling more carefully the expectations which lie behind the parameters.

***

9.1 Armstrong, J.   Scott.   1978.   "Forecasting   with
Econometric Methods: Folklore Versus Fact." **Journal of
Business** 51, No. 4: 549-64.

9.2 "The Art of Crunching Numbers." 1987. **The Economist** (9
May): 70-71.

9.3 Bentzel, R. B. Hansen. 1954. "On Recursiveness and
Interdependency in Economic Models." **Review of Economic
Studies** 22: 153-68.

9.4 Black, F. 1982. "The Trouble with Econometric Models."
Financial Analysts Journal 38 (March/April): 29-37.

9.5 Boland, Lawrence A. 1977. "Model Specification and
Stochasticism in Economic Methodology." **South African
Journal of Economics** 45 (June): 182-89.

9.6 Boland, Lawrence A. 1968. "The Identification Problem
and the Validity of Economic Models." **South African Journal
of Economics** 36 (September): 236-40.

9.7 Bowley, A.L. 1906. "The Importance of Scientific
Method in Statistical Research." Report of the British
Association for the Advancement of Science. **Journal of the
Royal Statistical Society** 1906; Rpt. in R.L. Smyth, ed.
Essays in Economic Method. London: Gerald Duckworth and
Co., 1962, pp. 200-22.

9.8 Cargill, Thomas F. 1974. "Early Applications of
Spectral Methods to Economic Time Series." **History of
Political Economy** 6, No. 1: 1-16.

9.9 Chakravarty, Sukhamoy. 1935. "Methodology and
Economics." **Journal of Quantitative Economics** 1, No. 1
(January): 1-9.

9.10 Christ, Carl F. 1985. "Early Progress in Estimating
Quantitative Economic Relationships in America." **American
Economic Review Special Issue** 75, No. 6 (December): 39-52.

9.11 Christ, Carl F. 1967. "Econometrics in Economics: Some
Achievements and Challenges." **Australian Economic Papers** 6
(December): 155-70.

9.12 Feige, Edgar L. 1975. "The Consequences of Journal
Editorial Policies and a Suggestion for Revision." **Journal
of Political Economy** 83, No. 6: 1291-96.

9.13 Fels, Rendigs. 1951. "Methodology of Research on the
Business Cycle." **Southern Economic Journal**   17 (April):
397-408.

9.14 Fisher, Franklin M. 1969. "Causation and Specification in Economic Theory and Econometrics." **Synthese** 20: 489-500.

9.15 Fogel, Robert William. 1965. "The Reunification of Economic History with Economic Theory." **American Economic Association Papers and Proceedings** 60, No. 2 (May): 92-98.

9.16 *Frisch, Ragnar. 1981. "From Utopian Theory to Practical Applications: The Case of Econometrics" (Nobel Prize Lecture: 1969). **American Economic Review Special Issue** 71 (December): 1-16.

9.17 Glymour, Clark. 1985. "Interpreting Leamer." **Economics and Philosophy** 1: 290-94.

9.18 Grayson, Henry. 1948. "The Econometric Approach: A Critical Analysis." **Journal of Political Economy** 56: 253-57.

9.19 Haavelmo, Trygve. 1958. "The Role of Econometrician in the Advancement of Economic Theory." **Econometrica** 26, No. 3 (July): 351-57.

9.20 Haavelmo, Trygve. 1944. "The Probability Approach in Econometrics." **Econometrica Supplement** 12 (July): 1-115.

9.21 Hendry, David F. 1980. "Econometrics: Alchemy Or Science?" **Economica** 47 (November): 387-406.

9.22 Ischboldin, Boris. 1960. "A Critique of Econometrics." **Review of Social Economy** 18 (September): 110-27.

9.23 Johnston, J. 1967. "Econometrics: Achievements and Prospects." **Three Banks Review** 73 (March): 3-22.

9.24 Keynes, John M. 1939. "Professor Tinbergen's Method." **Economic Journal** 49: 558-68.

9.25 *Klein, Lawrence. 1985. **Economic Theory and Econometrics.** Ed. by Jaime Marquez. Oxford: Basil Blackwell.

9.26 *Klein, Lawrence. 1947. "The Use of Econometric Models As a Guide to Economic Policy." **Econometrica** 15, No. 2 (April): 111-51.

9.27 *Koopmans, Tjalling C. 1949. "Identification Problems in Economic Model Construction." **Econometrica** 17, No. 2 (April): 125-44.

9.28 *Koopmans, Tjalling C. 1941. "The Logic of Econometric Business Cycle Research." **Journal of Political Economy** 49, No. 2 (April): 157-81.

9.29 Leamer, Edward E. 1985. "Self-Interpretation." **Economics and Philosophy** 1: 295-302.

9.30 Leamer, Edward E. 1983. "Let's Take the Con Out of Econometrics." **American Economic Review** 73, No. 1 (March): 31-43.

9.31 *Leontief, Wassily W. 1971. "Theoretical Assumptions and Nonobserved Facts." **American Economic Review** 61, No. 1 (March): 1-7.

9.32 *Leontief, Wassily. 1954. "Mathematics in Economics." **Bulletin of the Mathematical Society** 60: 215-33.

9.33 Lucas, Robert E. 1976. "Econometric Policy Evaluation: A Critique." In Karl Brunner and Allan H. Meltzer, eds. **The Phillips Curve and Labor Markets.** Vol. 1 of the **Carnegie-Rochester Conference Series on Public Policy.** (A supplement series to the Journal of Monetary Economics) Amsterdam: North-Holland, 1976, pp. 19-46.

9.34 Marschak, Jacob. 1969. "On Econometric Tools." **Synthese** 20: 483-88.

9.35 Mayer, Thomas. 1980. "Economics As a Hard Science: Realistic Goal Or Wishful Thinking?" **Economic Inquiry** 18 (April): 165-78.

9.36 Mayer, Thomas. 1975. "Selecting Economic Hypotheses by Goodness of Fit." **Economic Journal** 85 (December): 877-83.

9.37 McClelland, Peter D. 1973. "Model-Building in the New Economic History." In Allen G. Bogue, ed. **Emerging Theoretical Models in Social and Political History.** London: Sage, 1973, pp. 13-34.

9.38 Meissner, Werner and Herman Wold. 1974. "The Foundation of Science on Cognitive Mini-Models, with Applications to the German **Methodenstreit** and the Advent of Econometrics." In Werner Leinfellner and Eckehart Köhler, eds. 1974. **Developments in the Methodology of Social Science.** Dordrecht: D. Reidel, 1974, pp. 111-46.

9.39 Ménard, Claude. 1980. "Three Forms of Resistance to Statistics: Say, Cournot, Walras." **History of Political Economy** 12, No. 4: 524-41.

9.40 Moore, Henry L. 1908. "The Statistical Complement of Pure Economics." **Quarterly Journal of Economics** 23 (November): 1-33.

9.41 Morgenstern, Oskar. 1963. **On the Accuracy of Economic Observations,** 2nd completely rev. ed. NY: Princeton University Press.

9.42 Niehans, Jürg. 1981. "Economics: History, Doctrine, Science, Art." **Kyklos** 34, No. 2: 165-77.

9.43 O'Brien, D.P. 1974. "Whither Economics? An Inaugural Lecture." Durham: University of Durham.

9.44 Orcutt, Guy H. 1952. "Actions, Consequences and Causal Relations." **Review of Economics and Statistics** 34: 305-13.

9.45 Persons, Warren M. 1925. "Statistics and Economic Theory." **Review of Economics and Statistics** 7 (July): 179-97.

9.46 Poirier, Dale J. 1988. "Frequentist and Subjectivist Perspectives on the Problems of Model Building in Economics." **Journal of Economic Perspectives** 2, No. 1 (Winter): 121-44 and discussion, pp. 145-70.

9.47 Rhodes, George. 1976. "Derived Demand for a Cognitive Econometric Game and Policy-making with Econometric Models." **Schweizerische Zeitschrift für Volkswirtschaft und Statistik** 112, No. 2 (June): 175-90.

9.48 Rizzo, Mario J. 1978. "Praxeology and Econometrics: A Critique of Positivist Economics." In Louis M. Spadaro, ed., **New Directions in Austrian Economics.** Kansas City: Sheed Andrews and McMeel., Inc. 1978, pp. 40-56.

9.49 Rowley, Robin and Omar Hamouda. 1987. "Troublesome Probability and Economics." **Journal of Post Keynesian Economics** 10, No. 1 (Fall): 44-64.

9.50 *Samuelson, Paul. 1965. "Economic Forecasting and Science." **Michigan Quarterly Review** 4 (October): 274-80.

9.51 Schleicher, Stephan. 1982. "Endogeneity, Exogeneity and Economic Policy--Empirical Evidence on the Econometrics of New Classical Macroeconomics." **Empirica** 2: 93-111.

9.52 Schumpeter, Joseph Alois. 1933. "The Common Sense of Econometrics." **Econometrica** 1: 5-12.

9.53 Shupak, Mark B. 1962. "The Predictive Accuracy of Empirical Demand Analysis." **Economic Journal** 72 (September): 550-575.

9.54 *Simon, Herbert A. 1955. "Causality and Econometrics: A Comment." **Econometrica** 23 (April): 193-97.

9.55 Simpson, James R. and Lonnie L. Jones. 1975. "Note: The Progress of the Econometric Movement." **History of Political Economy** 7, No. 2 (Summer): 273-75.

9.56 Stigler, Stephen M. 1986. **The History of Statistics: The Measurement of Uncertainty Before 1900.** Cambridge, Mass./London: Harvard University/Belknap Press.

9.57 *Stone, Sir Richard. 1970. **Keynes, Political Arithmetic and Econometrics: Keynes Lecture in Economics.**

Vol. 44 of the Proceedings of the British Academy. London: Oxford University Press.

9.58 Streissler, Erich W. 1970. **Pitfalls in Econometric Forecasting**. London: Institute of Economic Affairs.

9.59 Strotz, Robert H. 1960. "Interdependence As a Specification Error." **Econometrica** 28, No. 2 (April): 428-42.

9.60 Sukhamoy, Chakravarty. 1935. "Methodology and Economics." **Journal of Quantitative Economics** 1, No. 1 (January): 1-9.

9.61 Swamy, P.A.V.D., R.K. Conway, and P. von zur Muehlen. 1985. "The Foundations of Econometrics--Are There Any?" **Econometric Reviews** 4, No. 1: 1-61 and "discussion," pp. 62-119.

9.62 *Tinbergen, Jan. 1981. "The Use of Models: Experience and Prospects" (Nobel Prize Lecture: 1969). **American Economic Review Special Issue** 71 (December): 17-22.

9.63 Tintner, Gerhard. 1968. **Methodology of Mathematical Economics and Econometrics**. Chicago: University of Chicago Press.

9.64 Tintner, Gerhard. 1966. "Some Thoughts About the State of Econometrics." In Sherman Roy Krupp, ed. **The Structure of Economic Science**. Englewood Cliffs: Prentice-Hall, 1966, pp. 114-28.

9.65 Tintner, Gerhard. 1953. "The Definition of Econometrics." **Econometrica** 21, No. 1 (January): 31-40.

9.66 Tuma, Elias H. 1971. **Economic History and the Social Sciences: Problems of Methodology**. London/Berkeley: University of California Press, chapter 9 (on the New Economic History).

9.67 Wang, Tong-eng. 1973. "Quantitative Analysis of the Progress of the Econometric Movement: An Exploration." **History of Political Economy** 5, No. 1 (Spring): 151-64.

9.68 White, William H. 1967. "The Trustworthiness of 'Reliable' Econometric Evidence." **Zeitschrift für Nationalökonomie** 27 (April): 19-38.

9.69 Wold, H. 1954. "Causality and Econometrics." **Econometrica** 22, No. 2 (April): 162-77.

9.70 Wolfson, Robert. 1970. "Points of View, Scientific Theories and Econometric Models." **Philosophy of Science** 37: 249-60.

9.71 Woodman, Harold D. 1972. "Economic History and

Economic   Theory: The   New   Economic   History   in   America."
Journal of Interdisciplinary History 3: 323-50.

9.72 Zellner, Arnold. 1979. "Causality and Econometrics."
In Karl Brunner and Allan H. Meltzer, eds. **Three Aspects
of   Policy   and   Policymaking.**   Vol.   10   of   the
Carnegie-Rochester Conference Series on Public Policy (A
Supplemental Series to the Journal of Monetary Economics).
Amsterdam: North-Holland, 1979, pp. 9-54.

***

10

Rationality

The rationality postulate, the hypothesis that individuals chose and act rationally, has always posed problems for economists. Machlup defends it as a useful fiction. Shackle is one of the hardest critics of the hypothesis in its extreme form.

The form the rationality postulate takes is related to an information assumption: whether the agents are assumed to have and use full information (the extreme form, sometimes called unbounded rationality) or incomplete information (often called bounded rationality). Advocates of the latter form often rely on the expected-utility approach. Tisdell provides a useful discussion of the various definitions of rationality used by economists and philosophers.

Game theory analyzes behavior of rational members of a group and shows that rationality enables behavior to be determined in accordance with a probability distribution. The prisoner's dilemma shows clearly how individual rationality conflicts with a socially optimal (i.e., Pareto optimal) outcome: when the players act according to their own self-interest, the outcome is socially inferior. See the anthology edited by Campbell and Sowdon and the article by Baier, where the ethical and philosophical ramifications of the prisoner's dilemma are discussed.

***

10.1 Albert, Hans. 1972 (1954). **Ökonomische Ideologie und politische Theorie. Das ökonomische Argument in der ordnungspolitischen Debatte**, 2nd ed. Göttingen: Verlag Otto Schwartz & Co.

10.2 Axelsson, Runo. 1973. "The Economic Postulate of Rationality--Some Methodological Views." **Swedish Journal of Economics** 75 (September): 289-95.

10.3 Baier, Kurt. 1977. "Rationaltiy and Morality."
Erkenntnis 11: 197-223.

10.4 Barnes, Barry and David Bloor. 1982. "Relativism,
Rationalism and the Sociology of Knowledge." In Martin
Hollis and Steven Lukes, eds. **Rationality and Relativism.**
Oxford: Basil Blackwell, 1982, pp. 21-47.

10.5 Beardsley, Monroe Curtis. 1944. "'Rationality' in
Conduct: Walras and Pareto." **Ethics** 54 (January): 79-95.

10.6 Becker, Gary. 1962. "Irrational Behavior and Economic
Theory." **Journal of Political Economy** 70, No. 1 (February):
1-13.

10.7 Benn, S.I. and G. W. Mortimore, eds. 1976.
Rationality and the Social Sciences. London: Routledge and
Kegan Paul.

10.8 Blair, Douglas H. and Robert A. Pollack. 1983.
"Rational Collective Choice." **Scientific American** 249, No.
2 (August): 76-83.

10.9 Brown, Harold I. 1988. **Rationality.** London/NY:
Routledge.

10.10 Caldwell, Bruce J. 1982. **Beyond Positivism.** London:
Allen and Unwin.

10.11 Campbell, Richmond/Lanning Sowden, eds. 1985.
**Paradoxes of Rationality and Cooperation: Prisoner's
Dilemma and Newcomb's Problem.** Vancouver: University of
British Columbia Press.

10.12 Diesing, Paul. 1950. "The Nature and Limitations of
Economic Rationality." **Ethics** 61 (October): 12-26.

10.13 Elster, Jon. 1979. **Ulysses and the Sirens: Studies in
Rationality.** NY/Melbourne: Cambridge University Press.

10.14 Godelier, Maurice. 1972. **Rationality and
Irrationality in Economics.** Trans. by Brian Pearce from the
French **Rationalité et irrationalité en économie** (1966).
London: New Left Books.

10.15 Grofman, Bernard. 1974. "Rational Choice Models and
Self-Fulfilling and Self-Defeating Prophecies." In Werner
Leinfellner and Eckehart Köhler, eds. **Developments in the
Methodology of Social Science.** Dordrecht: D. Reidel, pp.
381-83.

10.16 Guitton, Henri. 1987. "The Rational and the
Non-Rational in Economics." **International Journal of Social
Economics** 14, Nos. 3/4/5: 33-36.

10.17 Harsanyi, John C. 1977. "Morality and the Theory of Rational Behavior." **Social Research** 44, No. 4 (Winter): 623-56.

10.18 Hollis, Martin and Edward J. Nell. 1975. **Rational Economic Man**. London: Cambridge University Press.

10.19 Hutchison, T.W. 1937. "Expectation and Rational Conduct." **Zeitschrift für Nationalökonomie** 8, No. 5: 636-53.

10.20 Kirzner, Israel. 1962. "Rational Action and Economic Theory." **Journal of Political Economy** 70 (August): 380-85.

10.21 *Klein, Lawrence R. 1946. "Macro-Economics and the Theory of Rational Behavior." **Econometrica** 14 (April): 93-108.

10.22 Kötter, Rudolf. 1980. **Empirismus und Rationalismus in der Ökonomie**. Dissertation Erlangen-Nürnberg, 1980.

10.23 Kristol, Irving. 1980. "Rationalism in Economics." **The Public Interest** (Special Issue: The Crisis in Economic Theory): 201-218.

10.24 Lallement, Jérome. 1987. "Popper et le principe de rationalité." **Economies et sociétés** 21, No. 10 (October): 25-40.

10.25 Lange, Oskar. 1964. "Das Prinzip der wirtschaftlichen Rationalität. Ökonomie und Praxeologie." **Zeitschrift für die gesamte Staatswissenschaft** 120: 193-242.

10.26 Latsis, Spiro. 1983. "The Role and Status of the Rationality Principle in the Social Sciences." In Robert S. Cohen and Marx W. Wartofsky, eds. **Epistemology, Methodology, and the Social Sciences**. Vol. 71 of **Boston Studies in the Philosophy of Science**. Dordrecht: D. Reidel, 1983, pp. 123-51.

10.27 Machan, Tibor R. 1981. "The Non-Rational Domain and the Limits of Economic Analysis: Comment on McKenzie." **Southern Economic Journal** 47 (April): 1123-27.

10.28 Machlup, Fritz. 1978. **Methodology of Economics and Other Social Sciences** NY: Academic Press.

10.29 MacKay, Alfred F. 1980. **Arrow's Theorem: The Paradox of Social Choice. A Case Study in the Philosophy of Economics**. New Haven, Conn. Yale University Press.

10.30 Marschak, Jacob. 1950. "Rational Behavior, Uncertain Prospects, and Measurable Utility." **Econometrica** 18: 111-41.

10.31 McKenzie, Richard B. 1979. "The Non-Rational Domain

and the Limits of Economics." **Southern Economic Journal** 46, No. 1 (July): 145-57.

10.32 Mitchell, Wesley C. 1910. "The Rationality of Economic Activity, Pt. I & II." **Journal of Political Economy** 18 (February): 97-113 and (March): 197-216.

10.33 Mongin, Philippe. 1984. "Modèle rationnel ou modèle économique de la rationalité?" **Revue économique** 35, No. 1 (January): 9-63.

10.34 Mortimore, G.W. and J. B. Maund. 1976. "Rationality in Belief." In S.I. Benn and G.W. Mortimore, 1976, pp. 11-33.

10.35 Rothschild, K.W. 1946. "The Meaning of Rationality: A Note on Professor Lange's Article." **Review of Economic Studies** 14, No. 1: 50-52.

10.36 Schumpeter, Joseph A. 1984 (ca. 1940). "The Meaning of Rationality in the Social Sciences." **Zeitschrift für die gesamte Staatswissenschaft** 140: 577-93.

10.37 Sen, Amartya. 1987. **On Ethics and Economics**. Oxford: Basil Blackwell.

10.38 Sen, Amartya. 1977. "Rational Fools: A Critique of the Behavioral Foundations of Economic Theory." **Philosophy and Public Affairs** 6, No. 4 (Summer): 317-44; Rpt. in his **Choice, Welfare and Measurement**. Oxford: Basil Blackwell, 1982, pp. 84-106.

10.39 Shackle, G.L.S. 1972. **Epistemics and Economics: A Critique of Economic Doctrines**. Cambridge: Cambridge University Press.

10.40 *Simon, Herbert A. 1979. "Rational Decision Making in Business Organizations" (Nobel Lecture, 1978). **American Economic Review** 69 (September): 493-513; Rpt. in William Marr and Baldev Raj, eds. **How Economists Explain: A Reader in Methodology**. Lanham, MD: University Press of America, 1983, pp. 281-315.

10.41 *Simon, Herbert A. 1978. "Rationality As Process and As Product of Thought." **American Economic Association Papers and Proceedings** 68, No. 2 (May): 1-16.

10.42 *Simon, Herbert A. 1977. "The Logic of Rational Decision." In his **Models of Discovery**. Dordrecht: Reidel, 1977, pp. 137-53.

10.43 *Simon, Herbert A. 1976. "From Substantive to Procedural Rationality." In Spiro Latsis. **Method and Appraisal in Economics**. Cambridge: Cambridge University Press, 1976, pp. 129-48.

10.44 Tisdell, Clem. 1975. "Concepts of Rationality in Economics." **Philosophy of the Social Sciences** 5: 259-72.

10.45 Tversky, Amos and Daniel Kahneman. 1981. "The Framing of Decisions and the Rationality of Choice." **Science** (30 January): 211: 453-58.

10.46 Watts, M. 1981. "The Non-Rational Domain and the Limits of Economic Analysis: Comment on McKenzie." **Southern Economic Journal** 47 (April): 1120-1122.

10.47 Wisman, Jon D. 1987. "Human Interests, Modes of Rationality and the Social Foundations of Economic Science." **International Journal of Social Economics** 14, Nos. 7/8/9: 88-98.

***

11

Maximization

Sections 10 and 11 can be viewed as sister sections, as the rationality postulate and the neoclassical maximization hypothesis are interrelated. The maximization hypothesis assumes a certain kind of rational behavior on the part of individuals.

The maximization hypothesis has from the very beginning of economics been a source of contention. It is the view of man implied by the hypothesis which has stirred controversy: "economic man" acts in his self-interest, is motivated by avarice. Machlup's "The Universal Bogey" is still one of the best pieces ever written on misunderstandings of the maximization hypothesis. He recognizes the limits of the assumption, claims that it is nonetheless a "necessary fiction."

Recently attempts have been made by numerous economists and psychologists to relax or supplement the hypothesis. Herbert Simon, for instance, has advanced the thesis that businessmen do not maximize profits, they "satisfice." Leibenstein, Nelson and Winter, and Kahneman and Tversky (pschologists) all offer alternative models to the maximization hypothesis.

In a recent exchange in the **American Economic View,** Boland (1981) claims that it is useless to criticize the maximization hypothesis because it is an untestable "metaphysical statement." Caldwell denies this, and Boland (1983) replies in turn to Caldwell. They both agree that the maximization hypothesis cannot be tested, but continue to disagree about the meaning of "criticism."

***

11.1 Archibald, G.C. 1965. "The Qualitative Content of Maximizing Models." **Journal of Political Economy** 73 (February): 27-36.

11.2 Boland, Lawrence A. 1983. "The Neoclassical Maximization Hypothesis: Reply." **American Economic Review** 73, No. 4 (September): 828-30.

11.3 Boland, Lawrence. 1981. "On the Futility of Criticizing the Neoclassical Maximization Hypothesis." **American Economic Review** 71, No. 5 (December): 1031-36.

11.4 Brennan, Geoffrey and *James Buchanan. 1983. "Predictive Power and the Choice Among Regimes." **Economic Journal** 93, No. 369: 89-105.

11.5 Caldwell, Bruce J. 1983. "The Neoclassical Maximization Hypothesis: Comment." **American Economic Review** 73 (September): 824-27.

11.6 Cyert, Richard M. and Garrel Pottinger. 1979. "Towards a Better Microeconomic Theory." **Philosophy of Science** 46: 204-22.

11.7 Grammp, William D. 1951. "The Moral Hero and the Economic Man." **Ethics** 61 (January): 136-50.

11.8 Heiner, Ronald A. 1983. "The Origin of Predictable Behavior." **American Economic Review** 73, No. 4 (September): 560-95.

11.9 Hollis, Martin. 1983. "Rational Preferences." **Philosophical Forum** 14, Nos. 3-4 (Spring-Summer): 246-62.

11.10 Kahneman, Daniel and Amos Tversky. 1982. "The Psychology of Preferences." **Scientific American** 246: 162-73.

11.11 Leibenstein, Harvey. 1985. "On Relaxing the Maximization Postulate." **Journal of Behavioral Economics** 14: 2-16.

11.12 "Leibenstein on the Maximization Postulate." 1986. **Journal of Behavioral Economics** 15 (Winter).

11.13 Machlup, Fritz. 1978. "The Universal Bogey: Economic Man." In his **Methodology of Economics and Other Social Sciences**. NY: Academic Press, 1978, pp. 283-301.

11.14 Mongin, Philippe. 1986. "Are 'All-and-Some' Statements Falsifiable After All? The Example of Utility Theory." **Economics and Philosophy** 2, No. 2 (October): 185-95.

11.15 Nelson, Richard R. and Sidney G. Winter. 1982. **An Evolutionary Theory of Economic Change**. Cambridge, MA: The Belknap Press of Harvard University Press.

11.16 *Samuelson, Paul A. 1978. "Maximizing and Biology."

Economic Inquiry 16, No. 2 (April): 171-83.

11.17 *Samuelson, Paul A. 1971. "Maximum Principles in Analytical Economics." (Nobel Lecture: 1970) **Science** 173 (September 10): 991-97; Rpt. in **Synthese** 31 (1975): 323-44 and **American Economic Review** 62, No. 3 (June): 249-62.

11.18 Williams, Edward E. and M. Chapman Findlay, III. 1981. "A Reconsideration of the Rationality Postulate: 'Right Hemisphere Thinking' in Economics." **American Journal of Economics and Sociology** 40, No. 1 (January): 17-36.

(See also sources in the previous section on rationality.)

***

12

Austrian Methodology

The Austrians are prolific writers on methodological topics. The methodological works of the first-, second-, and third-generation Austrians have been listed separately below. Many of these works are classics or near-classics. The remaining section collects works about the Austrians and by modern Austrians.

The "Austrians," as an economic school of thought, are the intellectual descendants of Carl Menger (1840-1921). Menger's first work, **Principles of Economics (Grundsätze der Volkswirtschaftslehre)** appeared in 1871 and marked the birth of the school. His second work, **Investigations into the Method of the Social Sciences with Special Reference to Economics (Untersuchungen über die Methode der Sozialwissenschaften und der politischen Ökonomie insbesondere)** published in 1883, was an attack on the German historical school's rejection of theory. The members of the German historical school pejoratively referred to Menger and his followers as the "Austrians": and so the school came to be. Von Wieser (1851-1926) and Böhm-Bawerk (1851-1941) further refined Menger's thinking.

The second generation, von Mises (1881-1973) and Joseph Schumpeter (1883-1950) are probably better known by today's economic students than the first generation. All of the third generation emigrated to the U.S.: Haberler (1901-), Machlup (1902-1983), Morgenstern (1902-1977), and Hayek (1899-   ). (Hayek originally emigrated to England where he taught at the London School of Economics; later he held a position at the University of Chicago, but Hayek does have British citizenship.)

What is distinctive about the Austrian views on the economy? Menger emphasized subjective utility (forerunner of marginalism) and the atomistic method (what is today called methodological individualism). Austrians in general stress that knowledge is not perfect. Hence, the role of expectations and time become very important.

On methodology there is seemingly very little agreement. Nonetheless one can say that they emphasize the purposefulness of human action and are very suspicious of empirical proofs because they do not trust prediction. They believe that prediction of patterns or trends only is possible.

***

12.1   Methodological Works by First-Generation Austrians: Carl Menger and Friedrich von Wieser

C a r l   M e n g e r :

12.1.1   1968-70. **Gesammelte Werke.** Ed. and with an introduction by F. A. Hayek, 2nd. ed., 4 Vols. Tübingen: J.C.B. Mohr.

Vol. II: **Untersuchungen über die Methode der Sozialwissenschaften und der politischen Ökonomie insbesondere** 1969 (1883); Trans. by Francis J. Nock as **Investigations into the Method of the Social Sciences with Special Reference to Economics.** 1985 (rpt. of 1963). With a new introduction by Lawrence H. White. Ed. by Louis Schneider. NY/London: New York University Press.

Vol. III: **Kleinere Schriften zur Methode und Geschichte der Volkswirtschaftslehre** 1970.

***

F r i e d r i c h   F r e i h e r r   v o n   W i e s e r :

12.1.2   1911. "Das Wesen und der Hauptinhalt der theoretischen Nationalökonomie. Kritische Glossen zu Schumpeters gleichnamigem Werk." **Jahrbuch für Gesetzgebung, Verwaltung und Volkswirtschaft im deutschen Reich** 35, 2: 395-417.

12.1.3   1891. "The Austrian School and the Theory of Value." **Economic Journal** 1: 108-21.

12.1.4   1884. **Über den Ursprung und die Hauptgesetze des wirtschaftlichen Werthes.** Wien: Alfred Hölder.

***

12.2   Methodological Works by Second-Generation Austrians: Ludwig von Mises and Joseph Schumpeter

L u d w i g   v o n   M i s e s :

12.2.1   1978 (posthumously). **The Ultimate Foundation of**

Economic Science, 2nd ed. Kansas City: Sheed Andrews and McMeel.

12.2.2   1960. **Epistemological Problems of Economics.** Trans. George Reisman from the German **Grundprobleme der Nationalökonomie.** 1933. Princeton, N.J.: D. Van Nostrand Co., Inc.

12.2.3   1949. **Human Action. A Treatise on Economics.** New Haven, Conn.: Yale University Press.

***

J o s e p h   A l o i s   S c h u m p e t e r:

12.2.4   1984 (ca. 1940). "The Meaning of Rationality in the Social Sciences." **Zeitschrift für die gesamte Staatswissenschaft** 140, No. 4 (December): 577-93.

12.2.5   1982 (ca. 1931). "The 'Crisis' in Economics--Fifty Years Ago." **Journal of Economic Literature** 20 (September): 1049-59.

12.2.6   1954. **History of Economic Analysis.** NY: Oxford University Press.

12.2.7   1949. "Science and Ideology." **American Economic Review** 39, No. 2 (March): 345-59.

12.2.8   1970 (rpt. of 1908). **Das Wesen und der Hauptinhalt der theoretischen Nationalökonomie.** Berlin: Duncker und Humblot.

12.2.9   1906. "Über die mathematische Methode der theoretischen Ökonomie." **Zeitschrift für Volkswirtschaft, Sozialpolitik und Verwaltung** 15: 30-49; Rpt. in his **Aufsätze zur ökonomischen Theorie.** Tübingen: J.C.B. Mohr, 1952, pp. 529-48.

***

12.3   Methodological Works by Third-Generation Austrians: Haberler, Hayek, Machlup, and Morgenstern

G o t t f r i e d   v o n   H a b e r l e r:

12.3.1   1936. "Mr. Keynes' Theory of the 'Multiplier': A Methodological Criticism." **Zeitschrift für Nationalökonomie** 7 (August): 299-305.

***

*F r i e d r i c h   A.   v o n   H a y e k:

12.3.2   1979 (1955). **The Counter-Revolution of Science: Studies in the Abuse of Reason,** 2nd ed. Indianapolis:

Liberty Press.

12.3.3   1978. **New Studies in Philosophy, Politics, Economics and the History of Ideas.** London: Routledge and Kegan Paul.

12.3.4   1973. "The Place of Menger's **Grundsätze** in the History of Economic Thought." In Hicks and Weber, 1973, pp. 1-14.

12.3.5   1955. "Degrees of Explanation." **British Journal for the Philosophy of Science** 7, No. 23 (November): 209-25.

12.3.6   1945. "The Use of Knowledge in Society." **American Economic Review** 35, No. 4 (September): 519-30.

12.3.7   1943. "The Facts of the Social Sciences." **Ethics** 54, No. 1 (October): 1-13.

12.3.8   1942-43. "Scientism and the Study of Society." **Economica** N.S. 9, 10, & 11 (later incorporated into his 1979 above):

    Part I: 9 (August 1942): 267-91
    Part II: 10 (February 1943): 34-63
    Part III: 11 (February 1944): 27-39.

12.3.9   1937. "Economics and Knowledge." **Economica** 4, Nos. 13-16 (February): 33-54.

12.3.10   1933. "The Trend of Economics Thinking." **Economica** 13 (May): 121-37.

***

Fritz   Machlup:

12.3.11   1978(a). "Adolph Löwe's Instrumental Analysis." In his 1978(m), pp. 505-12.

12.3.12   1978(b). "Are the Social Sciences Really Inferior?" In his 1978(m), pp. 345-67.

12.3.13   1978(c). "Fact and Theory in Economics." In his 1978(m), pp. 101-30.

12.3.14   1978(d). "Friedrich Hayek on Scientific and Scientistic Attitudes." In his 1978(m), pp. 513-34.

12.3.15   1978(e). "Gunnar Myrdal on Concealed Value Judgements." In his 1978(m), 475-80.

12.3.16   1978(f). "The Ideal Type: A Bad Name for a Good Construct." In his 1978(m), pp. 211-22.

12.3.17   1978(g). "Ideal Types, Reality, and Construction."

In his 1978(m), pp. 223-66.

12.3.18 1978(h). "If Matter Could Talk." In his 1978(m),
pp. 309-32.

12.3.19 1978(i). "The Inferiority Complex of the Social
Sciences." In his 1978(m), pp. 333-44.

12.3.20 1978(j). "John Neville Keynes' Scope and Method."
In his 1978(m), pp. 489-92.

12.3.21 1978(k).   "Joseph   Schumpeter's   Economic
Methodology." In his 1978(m), pp. 461-74.

12.3.22 1978(1). "Homo Oeconomicus and His Classmates." In
his 1978(m), pp. 267-82.

12.3.23 1978(m). **Methodology of Economics and Other Social
Sciences.** NY: Academic Press.

12.3.24 1978(n). "A Note on Models in Microeconomics." In
his 1978(m), pp. 75-100.

12.3.25 1978(o). "Operationalism and Pure Theory in
Economics." In his 1978(m), pp. 189-203; Rpt. from Sherman
Roy Krupp, ed. **The Structure of Scientific Economics.**
Englewood-Cliffs: Prentice-Hall, 1966, pp. 53-67.

12.3.26 1978(p). "Operational Concepts and Mental
Constructs in Model and Theory Formation." In his 1978(m),
pp. 159-88.

12.3.27 1978(q). "Paul Samuelson on Theory and Realism."
In his 1978(m), pp. 481-84.

12.3.28 1978(r). "Positive and Normative Economics."
In his 1978(m), pp. 425-50.

12.3.29 1978(s). "The Problem of Verification in
Economics." In his 1978(m), pp. 137-58.

12.3.30 1978(t).   "Spiro   Latsis   on   Situational
Determinism." In his 1978(m), pp. 521-34; Rpt. from the
British Journal for the Philosophy of Science 23 (1972):
270-84.

12.3.31 1978(u).   "Terence   Hutchison's   Reluctant
Ultra-Empiricism." In his 1978(m), pp. 493-504; Rpt. from
Southern Economic Journal. "Rejoinder to a Reluctant
Ultra-Empiricist." 22, No. 4 (April): 483-93.

12.3.32 1978(v). "Theories of the Firm: Marginalist,
Behavioral, Managerial." In his 1978(m), 391-424.

12.3.33 1978(w). "Three Writers on Social Theory: Madge,
Rose, and Zetterberg." In his 1978(m), pp. 485-88.

12.3.34 1978(x). "The Universal Bogey: Economic Man." In his 1978(m), pp. 283-301.

12.3.35 1978(y). "What Is Meant by Methodology: A Selective Survey of the Literature." In his 1978(m), pp. 5-62.

12.3.36 1978(z). "Why Bother with Methodology?" In his 1978(m), pp. 63-70.

12.3.37 1978(a$_1$). "Why Economists Disagree." In his 1978(m), pp. 375-90.

12.3.38 1967. **Essays in Economic Semantics.** NY: W. Norton.

12.3.39 1953. "Do Economists Know Anything?" **American Scholar** 22, No. 2 (Spring): 167-82.

***

O s k a r   M o r g e n s t e r n:

12.3.40 1976. **Selected Writings of Oskar Morgenstern.** Ed. Andrew Schotter. NY: New York University Press.

12.3.41 1972(a). "Descriptive, Predictive, and Normative Theory." **Kyklos** 225, No. 4: 699-714.

12.3.42 1972(b). "Thirteen Critical Points in Contemporary Economic Theory: An Interpretation." **Journal of Economic Literature** 10, No. 4 (December): 1163-89.

12.3.43 1967. "Game Theory: A New Paradigm of Science." In S. Zwicky and A. G. Wilson, eds. **New Methods of Thought and Procedure.** Berlin/Heidelberg/NY: Springer Verlag, 1967, pp. 203-27.

12.3.44 1963. **On the Accuracy of Economic Observations,** 2nd completely revised edition. NY: Princeton University Press.

12.3.45 1953. "When Is a Problem of Economic Policy Solvable?" In Valentin F. Wagner and Fritz Marbach, eds. **Wirtschaftstheorie und Wirtschaftspolitik. Festschrift für Alfred Amonn zum 70. Geburtstag.** Bern: Francke, 1953, pp. 241-49.

12.3.46 1934. **Die Grenzen der Wirtschaftschaftspolitik.** Vienna: Julius Springer Verlag; Trans. by Vera Smith as **The Limits of Economics.** London: W. Hodge and Co., 1937.

12.3.47 1928. **Wirtschaftsprognose, eine Untersuchung ihrer Voraussetzungen und Möglichkeiten.** Vienna: Julius Springer.

***

12.4.   General Works and Works by Contemporary Austrians

12.4.1   Alter, Max. 1982. "Carl Menger and Homo Oeconomicus: Some Thoughts on Austrian Theory and Methodology." **Journal of Economic Issues** 16, No. 1 (March): 149-60.

12.4.2   Armentano, D.T. 1978. "A Critique of Neoclassical and Austrian Monopoly Theory." In Spadaro, ed., 1978(a), pp. 94-110.

12.4.3   Aufricht, Hans. 1958. "The Methodology of Schumpeter's 'History of Economic Analysis.'" **Zeitschrift für Nationalökonomie** 18 (December): 384-441.

12.4.4   Baranzini, Mauro and Roberto Scazzieri, eds. 1986(a). **Foundations of Economics**. Oxford: Basil Blackwell.

12.4.5   Baranzini, Mauro and Roberto Scazzieri. 1986(b). "Knowledge in Economics: A Framework." In their 1986(a), pp. 2-87.

12.4.6   Barry, Norman P. 1981. "Re-stating the Liberal Order: Hayek's Philosophical Economics." In J.R. Shackleton and Gareth Locksley, eds. **Twelve Contemporary Economists**. London: Macmillan, 1981, pp. 87-107.

12.4.7   Barry, Norman P. 1979. **Hayek's Social and Economic Philosophy**. Atlantic Highlands, N.J.: Humanities Press.

12.4.8   Batemarco, Robert. 1985. "Positive Economics and Praxeology: The Clash of Prediction and Explanation." **Atlantic Economic Journal** 13, No. 2 (July): 31-37.

12.4.9   Bernard, Georges. 1986. "The Wittgenstein Heritage and the Principles of Economics." In Werner Leinfellner, ed. **The Tasks of Contemporary Philosophy**. Vienna: Holder-Pichler, 1986, pp. 121-34.

12.4.10   Bliss, Christopher. 1986. "Progress and Anti-Progress in Economic Science." In Baranzini and Scazzieri, 1986(a), pp. 363-76.

12.4.11   Block, Walter. 1973. "A Comment on 'The Extraordinary Claim of Praxeology' by Professor Gutiérrez." **Theory and Decision** 3: 377-87.

12.4.12   Boehm, Stephan. 1982. "The Ambiguous Notion of Subjectivism: Comment on Lachmann." In Kirzner, ed., 1982(a), pp. 41-52.

12.4.13   Boland, Lawrence A. 1978. "Time in Economics Vs. Economics in Time: The 'Hayek Problem.'" **Canadian Journal of Economics** 11, No. 2 (May): 240-62.

12.4.14   Bostaph, Samuel. 1978. "The Methodological Debate Between Carl Menger and the German Historicists." **Atlantic Economic Journal** 6, No. 3 (September): 3-16.

12.4.15 *Buchanan,   James   M.   1982.   "The   Domain   of Subjective   Economics: Predictive   Science   and   Moral Philosophy." In Kirzner, ed., 1982(a), pp. 7-20.

12.4.16   Caldwell,   Bruce   J.   1986.   "Towards   a   Broader Conception of Criticism." **History of Political Economy** 18, No. 4 (Winter): 675-81.

12.4.17   Caldwell,   Bruce   J.   1984.   "Praxeology   and   Its Critics: An Appraisal." **History of Political Economy** 16, No. 3 (Fall): 363-79.

12.4.18   Chalk, Alfred F. 1958. "Schumpeter's Views on the Relationship of Philosophy of Economics." **Southern Economic Journal** 24, No. 3 (January): 271-81.

12.4.19   Chisholm,   Roderick   M.   1986.   "Bretano   on Preference, Desire and Intrinsic Value." In Grassl and Smith, eds., 1986, pp. 182-95.

12.4.20   Coats, A.W. 1978. "Methodology in Economics: A Subordinate Theme in Machlup's Writings." In Dreyer, 1978, pp. 23-35.

12.4.21   Cubeddu,   Raimondo.   1987.   "Popper   et   l'école autrichienne." 21, No. 10 (October): 41-62.

12.4.22   Dnes,   Anthony   W.   1986.   "Individualism   in Contemporary Political Economy: A Review Article." **Scottish Journal of Political Economy** 33, No. 4 (November): 391-96.

12.4.23   Dolan, Edwin G. 1976(a). "Austrian Economics As Extraordinary Science." In his 1976(b), pp. 3-15.

12.4.24   Dolan, Edwin G., ed. 1976(b). **The Foundations of Modern Austrian Economics**. Kansas City: Sheed and Ward.

12.4.25   Dreyer, Jacob S. 1978. **Breadth and Depth in Economics: Fritz Machlup—the Man and His Ideas**. Lexington, MA: Lexington Books.

12.4.26   Egger, John B. 1978. "The Austrian Method." In Spadaro, ed., 1978(a), pp. 19-39.

12.4.27   Eisner,   Robert.   1978.   "Machlup   on   Academic Freedom." In Dreyer, 1978, pp. 3-12.

12.4.28   Endres, A.M. 1984. "Institutional Elements in Carl Menger's Theory of Demand: A Comment" (Carl Menger and **Homo Oeconomicus**:   Some   Thoughts   on   Austrian   Theory   and Methodology). **Journal   of   Economic   Issues** 18,   No. 3

(September): 897-902.

12.4.29 Fabian, Reinhard and Peter M. Simons. 1986. "The Second Austrian School of Value Theory." In Grassl and Smith, eds., 1986, pp. 37-100.

12.4.30 Falkena, H.B. 1982. "On the Logical Structure of Non-Fallible Economic Theories." **South African Journal of Economics** 50 (March): 225-37.

12.4.31 Frisch, Helmut, ed. 1982. **Schumpeterian Economics**. NY: Praeger.

12.4.32 Garrison, Roger W. 1982. "Austrian Economics As the Middle Ground: Comment on Loasby." In Kirzner, ed., 1982(a), pp. 131-38.

12.4.33 Garrison, Roger W. 1978. "Austrian Macroeconomics: A Diagrammatical Exposition." In Spadaro, ed., 1978(a), pp. 167-204.

12.4.34 Grassl, Wolfgang. 1986. "Markets and Morality: Austrian Perspectives on the Economic Approach to Human Behavior." In Grassl and Smith, eds. 1986, pp. 139-81.

12.4.35 Grassl, Wolfgang and Barry Smith, eds. 1986. **Austrian Economics: Historical and Philosophical Background**. London: Croom Helm.

12.4.36 Haller, Rudolf. 1986. "Emanuel Herrmann: On an Almost Forgotten Chapter of Austrian Intellectual History." In Grassl and Smith, eds., 1986, pp. 196-209.

12.4.37 Harris, Seymour Edwin, ed. 1969. **Schumpeter: Social Scientist**. Freeport, NY: Books for Libraries Press.

12.4.38 Hennings, Klaus H. 1986. "The Exchange Paradigm and the Theory of Production and Distribution." In Baranzini and Scazzieri, 1986, pp. 221-243.

12.4.39 *Hicks, Sir John and W. Weber, eds. 1973. **Carl Menger and the Austrian School of Economics**. Oxford: Oxford University Press.

12.4.40 High, Jack. 1982. "Alertness and Judgement: Comment on Kirzner." In Kirzner, ed., 1982(a), pp. 161-68.

12.4.41 Hirsch, Abraham. 1986. "Caldwell on Praxeology and Its Critics: A Reappraisal." **History of Political Economy** 18, No. 4 (Winter): 661-68.

12.4.42 Hutchison, T.W. 1980. "Review of K. Menger's **Selected Papers in Logic and Foundations, Didactics, Economics**." **Journal of Economic Literature** 18 (September): 1090-91.

12.4.43 Hutchison, T.W. 1979. "Review of Hayek's **New Studies in Philosophy, Politics, Economics and the History of Ideas.**" **Economic Journal** 89 (March): 179-80.

12.4.44 Hutchison, T.W. 1978. "Review of Lachmann's **Capital, Expectations, and the Market Economy,** and other works." **Economic Journal** 88 (December): 840-43.

12.4.45 Hutchison, T.W. 1973. "Some Themes from **Investigations into Method.**" In Hicks and Weber, 1973, pp. 15-37.

12.4.46 Hutchison, T.W. 1970. "Review of Streissler's **Roads to Freedom.**" **Economica** 37: 191-93.

12.4.47 Hutchison, T.W. 1965. "Review of Menger's **Problems of Economics and Sociology.**" **Economic Journal** 75 (March): 171-72.

12.4.48 Hutchison, T. W. 1963. "Review of Machlup's **Essays on Economic Semantics.**" **American Economic Review** 53: 1104-05.

12.4.49 Hutchison, T.W. 1955. "Review of Schumpeter's **History of Economic Analysis.**" **Econometrica** 23: 349-50.

12.4.50 Hutchison, T.W. 1935. "A Note on Tautologies and the Nature of Economic Theory." **Review of Economic Studies** 2 (February): 159-61.

12.4.51 Kirzner, Israel M, ed. 1982(a). **Method, Process, and Austrian Economics: Essays in Honor of Ludwig von Mises.** Lexington, Mass. and Toronto: Heath, Lexington Books.

12.4.52 Kirzner, Israel M. 1982(b). "Uncertainty, Discovery, and Human Action: A Study of the Entrepreneurial Profile in the Misesian System." In Kirzner, ed., 1982(a), pp. 139-59.

12.4.53 Kirzner, Israel M. 1980. "The 'Austrian' Perspective." **The Public Interest** (Special Issue: The Crisis in Economic Theory): 111-122.

12.4.54 Kirzner, Israel M. 1978. "Economics and Error." In Spadaro, ed., 1978(a), pp. 57-76.

12.4.55 Kirzner, Israel M. 1976(a) (1960). **The Economic Point of View: An Essay in the History of Economic Thought,** 2nd ed. Ed. and with an introduction by Laurence S. Moss. Kansas City: Universal Press Syndicate.

12.4.56 Kirzner, Israel M. 1976(b). "Equilibrium Versus Market Process." In Dolan, 1976(b), pp. 115-25.

12.4.57 Kirzner, Israel M. 1976(c). "On the Method of

Austrian Economics." In Dolan, 1976(b), pp. 40-51.

12.4.58 Kirzner, Israel M. 1976(d). "Philosophical and Ethical Implications of Austrian Economics." In Dolan, 1976(b), pp. 75-88.

12.4.59 Kirzner, Israel M. 1976(e). "The Theory of Capital." In Dolan, 1976(b), pp. 139-44.

12.4.60 Kirzner, Israel M. 1965. "What Economists Do." **Southern Economic Journal** 31 (January): 257-61.

12.4.61 Kirzner, Israel M. 1962. "Rational Action and Economic Theory." **Journal of Political Economy** 70, (Austrian): 380-85.

12.4.62 Lachmann, Ludwig M. 1986. "Austrian Economics Under Fire: The Hayek-Sraffa Duel in Retrospect." In Grassl and Smith, pp. 225-42.

12.4.63 Lachmann, Ludwig M. 1982(a). "Ludwig von Mises and the Extension of Subjectivism." In Kirzner, ed., 1982(a), pp. 31-40.

12.4.64 Lachmann, Ludwig M. 1982(b). "The Salvage of Ideas: Problems of the Revival of Austrian Economic Thought." **Zeitschrift für die gesamte Staatswissenschaft** 138, No. 4 (December): 629-45.

12.4.65 Lachmann, Ludwig M. 1978. "An Austrian Stocktaking: Unsettled Questions and Tentative Answers." In Spadaro, ed., 1978(a), pp. 1-18.

12.4.66 Lachmann, Ludwig M. 1977(a). "Austrian Economics in the Present Crisis of Economic Thought." In his 1977(b), pp. 25-44.

12.4.67 Lachmann, Ludwig. 1977(b). **Capital, Expectations, and the Market Process: Essays on the Theory of the Market Economy.** Kansas City: Sheed Andrews and McMeel.

12.4.68 Lachmann, Ludwig. 1976(a). "Austrian Economics in the Age of the Neo-Ricardian Counterrevolution." In Dolan, 1976(b), pp. 215-23.

12.4.69 Lachmann, Ludwig. 1976(b). "From Mises to Shackle: An Essay on Austrian Economics and 'The Kaleidic Society'." **Journal of Economic Literature** 14, No. 1 (March): 54-62.

12.4.70 Lachmann, Ludwig. 1976(c). "On Austrian Capital Theory." In Dolan, 1976(b), pp. 145-51.

12.4.71 Lachmann, Ludwig. 1976(d). "On the Central Concept of Austrian Economics: Market Process." In Dolan, 1976(c), pp. 126-32.

12.4.72 Lachmann, Ludwig. 1976(e). "Toward a Critique of Macroeconomics." In Dolan, 1976(b), pp. 152-59.

12.4.73 Lachmann, Ludwig. 1973. "Sir John Hicks As a Neo-Austrian." **South African Journal of Economics** 41 (September): 195-207; Rpt. in his 1977(b), pp. 251-66.

12.4.74 Lachmann, Ludwig. 1971. "Ludwig von Mises and the Market Process." In F.A. Hayek, ed. **Toward Liberty: Essays in Honor of Ludwig von Mises**. Menlo Park, CA: Institute for Humane Studies, Vol. 2, pp. 38-52; Rpt. in his 1977(b), pp. 181-96.

12.4.75 Lachmann, Ludwig. 1970. **The Legacy of Max Weber. Three Essays**. London: Heinemann.

12.4.76 Lachmann, Ludwig. 1969. "Methodological Individualism and the Market Economy." In Erich Streissler, et al., ed. **Roads to Freedom: Essays in Honour of Friedrich A. von Hayek**. London: Routledge and Kegan Paul, pp. 89-104; Rpt. in his 1977(b), pp. 149-65.

12.4.77 Lachmann, Ludwig. 1967. "Causes and Consequences of the Inflation of Our Time." **South African Journal of Economics** 35 (December); Rpt. in his 1977(b), pp. 289-307.

12.4.78 Lachmann, Ludwig. 1966(a). "Model Constructions and the Market Economy." In his 1977(b), pp. 112-32; Trans. of his "Marktwirtschaft und Modelkonstruktionen." **Ordo** 17 (1966): 261-79.

12.4.79 Lachmann, Ludwig. 1966(b). "The Significance of the Austrian School of Economics in the History of Ideas." In his 1977(b), pp. 45-64; Trans. of his "Die geistesgeschichtliche Bedeutung der österreichischen Schule in der Volkswirtschaftslehre." **Zeitschrift für Nationalökonomie** 26 (February 1966): 152-67.

12.4.80 Lachmann, Ludwig. 1966(c). "Sir John Hicks on Capital and Growth." **South African Journal of Economics** 34 (June); Rpt. in his 1977(b), pp. 235-50.

12.4.81 Lachmann, Ludwig. 1963. "Cultivated Growth and the Market Economy." **South African Journal of Economics** 31 (September); Rpt. in his 1977(b), pp. 323-37.

12.4.82 Lachmann, Ludwig. 1959. "Professor Shackle on the Economic Significance of Time." **Metroeconomica** 11 (April/August): 64-73; Rpt. in his 1977(b), pp. 81-93.

12.4.83 Lachmann, Ludwig. 1958. "Mrs. Robinson on the Accumulation of Capital." **South African Journal of Economics** 26 (June); Rpt. in his 1977(b), pp. 214-34.

12.4.84 Lachmann, Ludwig. 1956. "The Market Economy and the Distribution of Wealth." In Mary Sennholz, ed. **On**

Freedom and Free Enterprise: Essays in Honor of Ludwig von Mises. NY: D. Van Nostrand; Rpt. in his 1977(b), pp. 308-22.

12.4.85 Lachmann, Ludwig. 1954. "Some Notes on Economic Thought, 1933-53." **South African Journal of Economics** 22 (March); Rpt. in his 1977(b), pp. 133-48.

12.4.86 Lachmann, Ludwig. 1951. "The Science of Human Action." **Economica** 18 (November): 412-27; Rpt. in his 1977(b), pp. 94-111.

12.4.87 Lachmann, Ludwig. 1950. "Economics As a Social Science." **South African Journal of Economics** 18, No. 3 (September): 231-41; Rpt. in his 1977(b), pp. 166-80.

12.4.88 Lachmann, Ludwig. 1947. "Complementarity and Substitution in the Theory of Capital." **Economica** N.S. 14 (May): 108-19; Rpt. in his 1977(b), pp. 197-213.

12.4.89 Lachmann, Ludwig. 1943. "The Role of Expectations in Economics As a Social Science." **Economica** 10 (February): 12-23; Rpt. in his 1977(b), pp. 65-80.

12.4.90 Lachmann, Ludwig. 1940. "A Reconsideration of the Austrian Theory of Industrial Fluctuations." **Economica** N.S. 7 (May): 179-96; Rpt. in his 1977(b), pp. 267-88.

12.4.91 Lange, Oskar. 1971 (1966). "Die Bedeutung der Praxeologie für die politische Ökonomie." In Reimut Jochimsen and Helmut Knobel, eds. **Gegenstand und Methoden der Nationalökonomie.** Köln: Kiepenheuer & Witsch, 1971, pp. 166-74.

12.4.92 Langlois, Richard N. 1982. "Austrian Economics As Affirmative Science: Comment on Rizzo." In Kirzner, ed., 1982(a), pp. 75-84.

12.4.93 Lavoie, Donald C. 1982. "The Development of the Misean Theory of Interventionism." In Kirzner, ed., 1982(a), pp. 169-83.

12.4.94 Levy, David M. 1985. "The Impossibility of a Complete Methodological Individualist: Reduction When Knowledge Is Imperfect." **Economics and Philosophy** 1, No. 1 (April): 101-08.

12.4.95 Littlechild, Stephen. 1983. "Subjectivism and Method in Economics." In Jack Wiseman, ed. **Beyond Positive Economics?** London: The British Association for the Advancement of Science, 1983, pp. 38-49.

12.4.96 Littlechild, Stephen. 1982. "Equilibrium and the Market Process." In Kirzner, ed., 1982(a), pp. 85-102.

12.4.97 Littlechild, Stephen. 1978. "The Problem of Social

Cost." In Spadaro, ed., 1978(a), pp. 77-93.

12.4.98 Loasby, Brian J. 1982. "Economics of Dispersed and Incomplete Information." In Kirzner, ed., 1982(a), pp. 111-130.

12.4.99 Malkiel, Burton G. 1978. "Fritz Machlup As a Teacher." In Dreyer, 1978, pp. 13-45.

12.4.100 Marget, A.W. 1929. "Morgenstern on the Methodology of Economic Forecasting." **Journal of Political Economy** 37, No. 3 (June): 312-39.

12.4.101 Menger, Karl. 1979(a). "Remarks on the Law of Diminishing Returns: A Study in Meta-Economics." In his **Selected Papers in Logic and Foundations, Didactics, Economics**. Dordrecht/London: Reidel, 1979, pp. 279-302.

12.4.102 Menger, Karl. 1979(b). "The Role of Uncertainty in Economics." In his **Selected Papers in Logic and Foundations, Didactics, Economics.** Dordrecht/London: Reidel, 1979, pp. 259-78.

12.4.103 Menger, Karl. 1973. "Austrian Marginalism and Mathematical Economics." In J.R. Hicks and W. Weber, eds. 1973, pp. 38-60.

12.4.104 Menges, Guy. 1982. "Methodological Ambivalence: The Case of Max Weber." **Social Research** 49, No. 3 (Autumn): 589-615.

12.4.105 Mini, Piero V. 1968. "Does Economics Exist? A Note on Professor Machlup's Methodology." **Journal of Economics Issues** 2, No. 1 (June): 224-27.

12.4.106 Moss, Laurence S. 1978. "The Emergence of Interest in a Pure Exchange Economy: Notes on a Theorem Attributed to Ludwig von Mises." In Spadaro, ed., 1978(a), pp. 157-66.

12.4.107 Murray, A. H. 1945. "Professor Hayek's Philosophy." **Economica** 12 (August): 149-62.

12.4.108 Nozick, Robert. 1977. "On Austrian Methodology." **Synthese** 36: 353-92.

12.4.109 Nyiri, J.C. 1986. "Intellectual Foundations of Austrian Liberalism." In Grassl and Smith, eds., 1986, pp. 102-38.

12.4.110 O'Driscoll, Gerald P., Jr. 1982. "Monopoly in Theory and Practice." In Kirzner, ed., 1982(a), pp. 189-213.

12.4.111 O'Driscoll, Gerald P. 1978. "Spontaneous Order and the Coordination of Economic Activities." In Spadaro, ed., 1978(a), pp. 111-42.

12.4.112 O'Driscoll, Gerald P., Jr. 1977. **Economics As A Coordination Problem: The Contributions of Friedrich A. Hayek.** Foreword by F.A. Hayek. Kansas City: Sheed Andrews and McMeel.

12.4.113 O'Driscoll, Gerald Patrick and Mario J. Rizzo. 1984. **The Economics of Time and Ignorance.** London: Basil Blackwell.

12.4.114 O'Driscoll, Gerald P. and Sudha R. Shenoy. 1976. "Inflation, Recession, and Stagflation." In Dolan, 1976(b), pp. 185-211.

12.4.115 Paqué, Karl-Heinz. 1985. "How Far Is Vienna from Chicago? An Essay on the Methodology of Two Schools of Dogmatic Liberalism." **Kyklos** 38, No. 3: 412-34.

12.4.116 Pasour, E.C., Jr. 1982. "Monopoly Theory and Practice--Some Subjectivist Implications: Comments on O'Driscoll." In Kirzner, ed., 1982(a), pp. 215-23.

12.4.117 Rizzo, Mario J. 1982. "Mises and Lakatos: A Reformulation of Austrian Methodology." In Kirzner, ed., 1982(a), pp. 53-72.

12.4.118 Rizzo, Mario J., ed. 1979. **Time, Uncertainty and Disequilibrium: Exploration of Austrian Themes.** Lexington, Mass./Toronto: Lexington Books/D.C. Heath.

12.4.119 Rizzo, Mario J. 1978. "Praxeology and Econometrics: A Critique of Positivist Economics." In Spadaro, ed., 1978(a), pp. 40-56.

12.4.120 Rothbard, Murray N. 1982. "Interventionism: Comment on Lavoie." In Kirzner, ed., 1982(a), pp. 185-88.

12.4.121 Rothbard, Murray N. 1979. **Individualism and the Philosophy of the Social Sciences.** Foreword by Friedrich A. Hayek. Cato Paper No. 4. San Francisco: Cato Institute.

12.4.122 Rothbard, Murray N. 1978. "Austrian Definitions of the Supply of Money." In Spadaro, ed., 1978(a), pp. 143-56.

12.4.123 Rothbard, Murray N. 1976(a). "The Austrian Theory of Money." In Dolan, 1976(b), pp. 160-84.

12.4.124 Rothbard, Murray. 1976(b). "New Light on the Prehistory of the Austrian School." In Dolan, 1976(b), pp. 52-74.

12.4.125 Rothbard, Murray. 1976(c). "Praxeology: The Methodology of Austrian Economics." In Dolan, 1976(b), pp. 19-39.

12.4.126 Rothbard, Murray. 1976(d). "Praxeology, Value

Judgements, and Public Policy." In Dolan, 1976(b), pp. 89-111.

12.4.127 Rothbard, Murray. 1957. "In Defense of 'Extreme Apriorism.'" **Southern Economic Journal** 23, No. 3 (January): 314-20.

12.4.128 Rothbard, Murray. 1951. "Praxeology: Reply to Mr. Schuller." **American Economic Review** 41 (December): 943-46.

12.4.129 Rotwein, Eugene. 1986. "Flirting with Apriorism: Caldwell on Mises." **History of Political Economy** 18, No. 4 (Winter): 669-73.

12.4.130 Salerno, Joseph T. 1982. "Ludwig von Mises and the Monetary Approach to the Balance of Payments: Comment on Yeager." In Kirzner, ed., 1982(a), pp. 247-56.

12.4.131 Schneider, Erich. 1975 (1970). **Joseph A. Schumpeter: Life and Work of a Great Social Scientist.** Trans. and introduction by W.E. Kuhn. BBR Monograph No. 1. University of Nebraska Lincoln, Bureau of Business Research.

12.4.132 Schweitzer, Arthur. 1970. "Typological Method in Economics: Max Weber's Contribution." **History of Political Economy** 2, No. 1 (Spring): 66-96.

12.4.133 Shackle, G.L.S. 1983. "Review Article: Decisions, Process and the Market." **Journal of Economic Studies** 10, No. 3: 56-66.

12.4.134 Shearmur, Jeremy. 1986. "The Austrian Connection: Hayek's Liberalism and the Thought of Carl Menger." In Grassl and Smith, 1986, pp. 210-24.

12.4.135 Simpson, David. 1983. "Joseph Schumpeter and the Austrian School of Economics." **Journal of Economic Studies** 10, No. 4: 15-28.

12.4.136 Smith, Barry. 1986. "Austrian Economics and Austrian Philosophy." In Grassl and Smith, eds., 1986, pp. 1-36.

12.4.137 Spadaro, Louis M., ed. 1978(a). **New Directions in Austrian Economics.** Kansas City: Universal Press Syndicate.

12.4.138 Spadaro, Louis M. 1978(b). "Toward a Program of Research and Development for Austrian Economics." In Spadaro, ed., 1978(a), pp. 205-27.

12.4.139 Stonier, Alfred W. 1943. "Note on F.A. Hayek's 'Scientism and the Study of Society,' with a rejoinder by Hayek." **Economica** 10 (May): 188-89.

12.4.140 Streissler, Erich W. 1972. "To What Extent Was the

Austrian School Marginalist?" **History of Political Economy** 4 (Fall): 426-41.

12.4.141 Streissler, Erich W. 1969. "Structural Economic Thought. On the Significance of the Austrian School Today." **Zeitschrift für Nationalökonomie** 29, Nos. 3-4 (December): 237-66.

12.4.142 Streissler, Erich and W. Weber. 1973. "The Menger Tradition." In Hicks and Weber, 1973, pp. 226-32.

12.4.143 Sufrin, Sidney C. 1987. "Schumpeter-Walras and Pragmatism." **Revista Internazionale di Scienze Economiche e Commerciali.** 34, No. 9 (September): 823-28.

12.4.144 Vaughn, Karen I. 1982. "Subjectivism, Predictability, and Creativity: Comment on Buchanan." In Kirzner, ed., 1982(a), pp. 21-29.

12.4.145 White, Lawrence H. 1982. "Mises, Hayek, Hahn, and the Market Process: Comment on Littlechild." In Kirzner, ed., 1982(a), pp. 103-110.

12.4.146 Yeager, Leland B. 1982. "Individual and Overall Viewpoints in Monetary Theory." In Kirzner, ed., 1982(a), pp. 225-46.

(See also the new journal **The Review of Austrian Economics,** ed. by M.N. Rothbard, which promises to bring out articles on methodological topics. Volume 1 appeared in 1987.)

***

13

Knowledge and Economics

Knowledge is a typically, but not exclusively, Austrian theme, as this section so aptly shows. The role of knowledge and learning finds a place in most Austrian works, not only those listed here. See here the works by Baranzini and Scazzieri, Hayek, O'Driscoll and Rizzo, and Machlup. Loasby, Robbins, and Shackle's works are influenced by and compatible with Austrian views. (The latter are not categorized as Austrians in this work, but often are in other works.)

Hutchison's **Knowledge and Ignorance** is a gem. Here Hutchison shows convincingly how socially and politically crucial questions involving the limits of economic knowledge are.

Boulding accurately sums up the paradox of knowledge in economics (1966, p. 8):

> where knowledge is an essential part of
> the system, knowledge about the system
> changes the system itself.

***

13.1 Arouh, Albert. 1987. "The Mumpsimus of Economists and the Role of Time and Uncertainty in the Progress of Economic Knowledge." **Journal of Post Keynesian Economics** 9, No. 3 (Spring): 395-423.

13.2 [*]Arrow, Kenneth. 1974. "Limited Knowledge and Economic Analysis." **American Economic Review** 64, No. 1 (March): 1-10.

13.3 Baranzini, Mauro and Roberto Scazzieri, eds. 1986. "Knowledge in Economics: A Framework." In their **Foundations of Economics.** Oxford: Basil Blackwell, 1986, pp. 2-87.

13.4 Bensusan-Butt, D.M. 1980. **On Economic Knowledge: A Special Miscellany**. Canberra: Australian National University.

13.5 Boland, Lawrence A. 1979. "Knowledge and the Role of Institutions in Economic Theory." **Journal of Economic Issues** 13 (December): 957-72.

13.6 Boland, Lawrence A. 1969. "Economic Understanding and Understanding Economics." **South African Journal of Economics** 37 (June): 144-60.

13.7 Boulding, Kenneth E. 1966. "The Economics of Knowledge and the Knowledge of Economics." **American Economic Association Papers and Proceedings** 56, No. 2 (May): 1-13.

13.8 *Hayek, Friedrich A. von. 1937. "Economics and Knowledge." **Economica** 4, Nos. 13-16 (February): 33-54.

13.9 Higgins, Benjamin. 1951. "What Do Economists Know?" In his **What Do Economists Know? Six Lectures on Economics in the Crisis of Democracy**. Victoria: Melbourne Univeristy Press, 1951, pp. 1-29.

13.10 Hutchison, T.W. 1977. **Knowledge and Ignorance in Economics**. Chicago: University of Chicago Press.

13.11 Lawson, Tony. 1987. "The Relative/Absolute Nature of Knowledge and Economic Analysis." **Economic Journal** 97, No. 388 (December): 951-70.

13.12 Loasby, Brian. 1983. "Knowledge, Learning and Enterprise." In Jack Wiseman, ed. **Beyond Positive Economics?** London: The British Association for the Advancement of Science, 1983, pp. 104-21.

13.13 Loasby, Brian. 1982. "Economics of Dispersed and Incomplete Information." In Israel M. Kirzner, ed. **Method, Process, and Austrian Economics**. Lexington, Mass./Toronto: Lexington/Heath, 1982, pp. 111-30.

13.14 Machlup, Fritz. 1953. "Do Economists Know Anything?" **American Scholar** 22, No. 2 (Spring): 167-82.

13.15 Mosak, Jakob L. 1966. "Discussion: The Production and Use of Economic Knowledge." **American Economic Association Papers and Proceedings** 56 (May): 556-58.

13.16 O'Driscoll, Gerald Partick and Mario J. Rizzo. 1984. **The Economics of Time and Ignorance**. London: Basil Blackwell.

13.17 Papineau, David. 1980. "Review of **Knowledge and Ignorance in Economics** by T.W. Hutchison." **British Journal for the Philosophy of Science** 31: 98-103.

13.18 Perlman,   Mark.   1978(b).   "Review   of   Hutchison's **Knowledge and Ignorance in Economics." Journal of Economic Literature** 16 (June): 582-85.

13.19 Robbins,   Lionel.   1949.   "The   Economist   in   the Twentieth Century." **Economica** N.S. 16 (May): 93-105.

13.20 Shackle, G.L.S. 1983. "The Bounds of Unknowledge." In Jack Wiseman, ed. **Beyond Positive Economics?** London: The British Association for the Advancement of Science, 1983, pp. 28-37.

13.21 Shackle,   G.L.S.   1972.   **Epistemics and Economics: A Critique   of   Economic   Doctrines.** Cambridge: Cambridge University Press.

13.22 Sowell, Thomas. 1980. **Knowledge and Decisions.** NY: Basic Books.

***

14

The Is-Ought Problem
in Economics

This problem has been as much the subject matter of philosophers as of economists. The problem starts with David Hume, who argued that "ought" propositions cannot be deduced from "is" propositions in his **A Treatise of Human Nature**. That is, it is a logical error to assert that ethical propositions can be deduced from reasoned statements. Hence it was assumed that facts and values were held apart by logic.

Almost all of the classical economists held this view, including Senior, J.S. Mill, Cairnes, Bagehot, Sidgwick, J.N. Keynes, J.B. Clark, Pigou, Robbins, etc. Consider, for instance, this passage from Robbin's **The Nature and Significance of Economic Science**, 3rd. edition, 1984, pp. 148-49:

> Between the generalisations of positive and normative studies there is a logical gulf fixed which no ingenuity can disguise and no juxtaposition in space or time can bridge over . . . . Propositions involving the verb "ought" are different in kind from propositions involving the verb "is".

Unfortunately the is-ought dichotomy is not as clean as once believed. In the 1960's the philosopher John Searle attacked the dichotomy. Hudson collects some of the most important papers; a good discussion and summary of the debate is provided by Rohatyn. In economics it was Gunnar Myrdal who exposed the is-ought distinction for being too extreme. In economics this dichotomy is, of course, tied to the positive-normative distinction. Hutchison's wonderful book on the positive-normative distinction and the role of value-judgements in economics is recommended. (Hutchison, by the way, finds the is-ought dichotomy useful.)

The general message for today's economist is, as
Streeten argues in his introduction to Myrdal's **Value in
Social Theory** (p. xiii), that

> to-day we accept perhaps too easily the
> belief that the distinction between **is** and
> **ought** is always obvious, clear-cut, and
> easy to draw.

***

14.1 Albert, Hans. 1956. "Das Werturteilsproblem im Lichte
der logischen Analyse." **Zeitschrift für die gesamte
Staatswissenschaft** 112: 410-39.

14.2 Dwyer, Larry. 1983. "'Value Freedom' and the Scope of
Economic Inquiry, II. The Fact/Value Continuum and the
Basis for Scientific and Humanistic Policy." **American
Journal of Economics and Sociology** 42, No. 3 (July):
353-68.

14.3 Harrison, Jonathan. 1967. "Ethical Naturalism." **The
Encyclopedia of Philosophy**. 1967 ed.

14.4 Hudson, W.D., ed. 1969. **The Is-Ought Question: A
Collection of Papers on the Central Problem in Moral
Philosophy**. London: MacMillan.

14.5 Hutchison, T.W. 1964. **'Positive' Economics and Policy
Objectives**. London: George Allen and Unwin Ltd.

14.6 Morgenstern, Oskar. 1972. "Descriptive, Predictive
and Normative Theory." **Kyklos** 225, No. 4: 699-714.

14.7 *Myrdal, Gunnar. 1958. **Value in Social Theory: A
Selection of Essays on Methodology**. Ed. by Paul Streeten.
London: Routledge and Kegan Paul.

14.8 *Myrdal, Gunnar. 1953. **The Political Element in the
Development of Economic Theory**. Trans. Paul Streeten.
London: Routledge and Kegan Paul.

14.9 Rohatyn, D.A. 1975. **Naturalism and Deontology: An
Essay on the Problems of Ethics**. Mouton: The Hague.

14.10 Salkever, Stephen G. 1980. "'Cool Reflexion' and the
Criticism of Values: Is, Ought, and Objectivity in Hume's
Social Science." **American Political Science Review** 74, No.
1 (March): 70-77.

***

15

Semantics

The classic work in semantics is Machlup's **Essays in Economic Semantics.** This work is dedicated to cleaning up economic terminology; many economic terms have multiple meanings. For instance, he gives more than twenty-five meanings of "structure" in economics. He also treats micro- and macroeconomics, marginal analysis, marginal product, forced and induced saving, cost-push and demand-pull inflation, and more.

The definition of economics has always been a source of disagreement. See Hume, Hawley, and Rivett. Eucken warns that simply talking about definitions of economic terminology is futile and he discusses this earlier infertile phase of economics, a phase which he designates as **Begriffsnationalökonomie.**

Galbraith talks in his light, witty way about how poorly economists write. Salant provides good examples of poor word choice in economics.

Dickson's work is a wonderful little book on semantic questions connected with the application of mathematics in economics. He studies mainly the words variable, function, derivative, quantity, relation, and differential, especially as used by R.G.D. Allen.

***

15.1 Arndt, H.W. 1985. "Political Economy: A Reply." **Economic Record** 61, No. 175 (December): 752.

15.2 Arndt, H.W. 1984. "Political Economy." **Economic Record** 60, No. 170 (September): 266-73.

15.3 Black, F. 1982. "The Trouble with Econometric Models." **Financial Analysts Journal** 38 (March/April): 29-37.

15.4 Carlile, William Warrand. 1909. "The Language of Economics." **Journal of Political Economy** 17 (July): 434-47.

15.5 De Alessi, Louis. 1965. "Economic Theory As a Language." **Quarterly Journal of Economics** 79, No. 3 (August): 472-77.

15.6 Dickson, Harald. 1967. **Variable, Function, Derivative: A Semantic Study in Mathematics and Economics.** Göteborg, Sweden: Scandanavian University Books.

15.7 Eucken, Walter. 1971 (1940). "Kritik der 'Begriffsnationalökonomie'." In Reimut Jochimsen and Helmut Knobel. **Gegenstand und Methoden der Nationalökonomie.** Köln: Kiepenheuer & Witsch, 1971, pp. 161-65.

15.8 Fritz, Richard G. and Judy M. 1985. "Linguistic Structure and Economic Method." **Journal of Economic Issues** 19, No. 1 (March): 75-101.

15.9 Galbraith, John K. 1978. "Writing, Typing, and Economics." **The Atlantic Monthly** 241 (March): 102-05.

15.10 Groenewegen, P. D. 1985. "Professor Arndt on Political Economy: A Comment." **Economic Record** 61, No. 175 (December): 744-51.

15.11 Hausman, Daniel. 1983. "Are There Causal Relations Among Dependent Variables?" **Philosophy of Science** 50, No. 1 (March): 58-81.

15.12 Hawley, Frederick Barnard. 1913. "The Definition of Economics." **American Economic Review** 3 (September): 606-609.

15.13 Hume, L.J. 1956. "The Definition of Economics." **Economic Record** 32: 152-57.

15.14 Knight, Frank. 1961. "Methodology in Economics." **Southern Economic Journal** 27, No. 3 (January): 185-93 and 27, No. 4 (April): 273-83.

15.15 Machlup, Fritz. 1967. **Essays in Economic Semantics.** NY: W. Norton.

15.16 Milgate, Murray. 1979. "On the Origin of the Notion of 'Intertemporal Equilibrium.'" **Economica** 46: 1-10.

15.17 Neale, Walter C. 1982. "Languages and Economics." **Journal of Economic Issues** 16, No. 2 (June): 355-69.

15.18 Patten, Simon N. 1891. "The Need of New Economic Terms." **Quarterly Journal of Economics** 5 (April): 372-74.

15.19 Rivett, Kenneth. 1955. "The Definition of Economics."

Economic Record 31 (November): 215-31.

15.20 Salant, Walter S. 1969. "Writing and Reading in Economics." **Journal of Political Economy** 77, No. 4 (July/August): 545-58.

***

16

The Rhetoricians: McCloskey and Klamer

This is the latest school of economic philosophy to appear. Its beginning can be marked by the appearance of McCloskey's "The Rhetoric of Economics" in the **Journal of Economic Literature** in 1983 and in 1985 by his book of the same title. McCloskey has since been joined by Arjo Klamer in emphasizing the rhetorical aspects of economic argument.

The thrust of McCloskey's argument is that "modernism" (philosophical positivism as embedded in "positive economics," i.e., current economic methodology) provides neither an account of what economists do, nor what they should do. McCloskey and his followers are against the following textbook representations of method: prediction is the main goal; observation is the final arbiter of truth; introspection is useless; quantitative representation is all-important; science and nonscience are clearly demarcated; likewise, there is a dichotomy between scientific justification and discovery and between positive and normative; nonanalytic and nonsynthetic statements are to be rejected. This school criticizes all methodological positions; the best way to understand all argument is through rhetoric (which is, of course, an epistemological view). For instance, the theme of Klamer's interesting work, **The New Classical Macroeconomics**, is that the new classical economics can best be understood as a rhetorical phenomenon.

The works by Skinner and Adam Smith underscore the fact that rhetoric and economics is actually an old theme.

***

16.1 Ancil, Ralph E. 1987. "On the Rhetoric of Economics." **Review of Social Economy** 45, No. 3 (December): 259–75.

16.2 Blandy, R. 1985. "Soft Science." **Economic Record** 61, No. 175 (December): 693–706.

16.3   Butos, William N. 1987. "Rhetoric and Rationality: A Review Essay." **Eastern Economic Journal** 13, No. 3 (July–September): 295–304.

16.4   Caldwell, Bruce and A.W. Coats. 1984. "The Rhetoric of Economists: A Comment on McCloskey." **Journal of Economic Literature** 22 (June): 575–78.

16.5   Coats, A.W. and Steven Pressman. 1987. "The Rhetoric of Economics: Further Comments." **Eastern Economic Journal** 13, No. 3 (July–September): 305–07.

16.6   Hollis, Martin. 1985. "The Emperor's Newest Clothes." **Economics and Philosophy** 1, No. 1 (April): 128–33.

16.7   Howitt, Peter. 1986. "Conversations with Economists: A Review Essay." **Journal of Monetary Economics** 18, No. 1 (July): 103–18.

16.8   Klamer, Arjo. 1985. "Economics As Discourse." Paper presented at a conference in honour of Professor J.J. Klant, Amsterdam, December 1985.

16.9   Klamer, Arjo. 1984(a). "Levels of Discourse in New Classical Economics." **History of Political Economy** 16, No. 2: 263–90.

16.10 Klamer, Arjo. 1984(b). **The New Classical Macroeconomics: Conversations with the New Classical Economists and Their Opponents.** Bristol: Harvester Press.

16.11 Klamer, Arjo. 1983. "Empirical Arguments in New Classical Economics." **Economie appliquée** 36, No. 1: 229–54.

16.12 McCloskey, Donald N. 1987. "The Rhetoric of Economics: Responses to My Critics." **Eastern Economic Journal** 13, No. 3 (July–September): 308–11.

16.13 McCloskey, Donald. 1986. "Economics As an Historical Science." In William Parker. **Economic History and the Modern Economist.** Oxford, Basil Blackwell, 1986, pp. 63–9.

16.14 McCloskey, Donald. 1985(a). "A Conversation with Donald N. McCloskey About Rhetoric." **Eastern Economic Journal** 11, No. 4 (October–December): 293–96.

16.15 McCloskey, Donald. 1985(b). "Review of Boland's **The Foundations of Economic Method.**" **Journal of Economic Literature** 23 (June): 618–19.

16.16 McCloskey, Donald. 1985(c). **The Rhetoric of Economics.** Madison: University of Wisconsin Press.

16.17 McCloskey, Donald. 1985(d). "Sartorial Epistemology in Tatters: A Reply to Martin Hollis." **Economics and**

Philosophy 1, No. 1 (April): 134-37.

16.18 McCloskey, Donald. 1984(a). "The Literary Character of Economics." **Daedalus** 113, No. 3 (Summer): 97-119.

16.19 McCloskey, Donald. 1984(b). "Reply to Caldwell and Coats." **Journal of Economic Literature** 22, No. 2 (June): 279-80.

16.20 McCloskey, Donald. 1983. "The Rhetoric of Economics." **Journal of Economic Literature** 21 (June): 481-517.

16.21 Mirowski, Philip. 1987. "Shall I Compare Thee to a Minkowski Ricardo-Leontief-Metzler Matrix of the Masak-Hicks Type? Or, Rhetoric, Mathematics, and the Nature of Neoclassical Economic Theory." **Economics and Philosophy** 3, No. 1 (April): 67-95.

16.22 Perlman, Mark. 1987. "Concerning Winters of Discontent: Does Methodology Or Rhetoric Contain the Answer to a Possible Malaise?" **International Journal of Social Economics** 14, Nos. 7/8/9: 9-18.

16.23 Skinner, Andrew S. 1983. "Adam Smith: Rhetoric and the Communication of Ideas." In A.W. Coats. **Methodological Controversy in Economics: Historical Essays in Honor of T.W. Hutchison.** Greenwich, CT: Jai Press, pp. 71-88.

16.24 Smith, Adam. 1983 (1748-49). **Lectures on Rhetoric and Belle Lettres.** Ed. J.C. Bryce. Oxford: Clarendon.

***

17

The Role of History and Philosophy in Economics

The massive growth in economic theory and mathematical economics seems to have pushed economic history and the history of economic analysis into the background. In addition, economists have always sought to minimize the role of philosophy in economics: economics emerged from moral philosophy and sought to distance itself to the greatest possible extent from philosophy. For this reason this section must be seen as a subsection of the section on scope and offers the question "What contribution to economics do history and philosophy make?"

There is a large and ever-growing literature on the contribution to and role of history in economics. In this section, for instance, we have Cesarano, Coats (1978), Corry, Cunningham, de Marchi and Lodewijks, Dopfer, Farum, Fetter, Gerschenkron, D. Gordon, Grammp, Horowitz, Hutchison, Loos, Lutz, McCloskey, Neumark, Niehans, North (1965 & 1974), O'Brien, Skinner, Solow, Stigler, Tarascio, Taylor, Usher, Viner, and Winch. Note that in 1969 Stigler wrote an article entitled "Does Economics Have a Useful Past?" and in 1976 Donald McCloskey published an article on "Does the Past Have Useful Economics?" The "new economic history," or quantitative economic history, has generated a literature of its own: see Fogel, McClelland, North (1978), and Woodman. None of the above authors denies that economic history is of importance; the great number of articles testifying to history's importance must then be the proof that the discipline is still ignoring the importance of a full integration and utilization of historical knowledge. This is the message of the Parker volume.

On philosophy and economics, see Becker, Bernadelli, Brooks, Collingwood, S. Gordon, Hausman, Hutchison, Linstromberg, Macfie, and Wold. Although only twenty years ago most economists would not have considered philosophers' ideas about economics to be interesting, the 1980's has been a decade of cooperation. The new journal **Economics**

and Philosophy, "designed to foster collaboration between economists and philosophers," is one outgrowth of this. Hausman's article on "How to Do Philosophy of Economics" sets the tone of cooperation from the side of a philosopher, but one with working knowledge of economics.

***

17.1 *Arrow, Kenneth J. 1985. "Maine and Texas." **American Economic Association Papers and Proceedings** 75, No. 2 (May): 320-23; Rpt. in longer version as "History: the View from Economics" in Parker, 1986(a), pp. 13-20.

17.2 Ashley, W.J. 1907. "A Survey of the Past History and Present Position of Political Economy." Report of the British Association for the Advancement of Science." **Economic Journal** (December); Rpt. in R.L. Smyth, ed. **Essays in Economic Method.** London: Gerald Duckworth and Co., 1962, pp. 223-26.

17.3 Ashley, W.J. 1893. "On the Study of Economic History." **Quarterly Journal of Economics** 7: 115-36.

17.4 Becker, Arthur Peter. 1948. "Some Philosophical Aspects of Economics." **Philosophy of Science** 15, No. 3 (July): 242-46.

17.5 Bernadelli, Harro. 1936. "What Has Philosophy to Contribute to the Social Sciences, and to Economics in Particular?" **Economica** 3 N.S. (November): 443-54.

17.6 Brooks, John Graham. 1893. "Philosophy and Political Economy." **Quarterly Journal of Economics** 8 (October): 93-97.

17.7 Buchanan, D. H. 1947. "The Use of Economic History in the Solution of Current Economic Problems." **Southern Economic Journal** 13 (April): 370-77.

17.8 Cesarano, Filippo. 1983. "On the Role of the History of Economic Analysis." **History of Political Economy** 15, No. 1 (Spring): 63-82.

17.9 Checkland, S.G. 1951. "The Advent of Academic Economics in England." **Manchester School of Economic and Social Studies** 19, No. 1 (January): 43-70.

17.10 Coats, A.W. 1983. "The First Decade of HOPE (1969-79)." **History of Political Economy** 15, No. 3 (Fall): 303-19.

17.11 Coats, A.W. 1980. "The Historical Context of the 'New' Economic History." **Journal of Economic History** 9, No. 1 (Spring): 185-207.

17.12 Coats, A.W. 1978. "Reflections on the Role of the

History of Economics in the Training of Economists." In **Studi in Memoria di Federigo Melis** (author/editor unknown), Vol. 5, Rome: Giannini.

17.13 Coats, A.W. 1972. "Situational Determinism in Economics: The Implications of Latsis' Argument for the Historian of Economics." **British Journal for the Philosophy of Science** 23 (1972): 285-88.

17.14 Coats, A.W. 1971. "The Role of Scholarly Journals in the History of Economics: An Essay." **Journal of Economic Literature** 9: 29-44.

17.15 Coats, A.W. 1968. "The Origins and Early Development of the Royal Economic Society." **Economic Journal** 78, No. 310 (June): 349-71.

17.16 Coats, A.W. 1964. "The American Economic Association, 1904-29." **American Economic Review** 54, No. 4 (June): 261-85.

17.17 Coats, A.W. 1961. "Alfred Marshall and Richard T. Ely." **Economica** 28 N.S. (May): 191-94.

17.18 Coats, A.W. and S.E. Coats. 1973. "The Changing Social Composition of the Royal Economic Society 1890-1960 and the Professionalization of British Economics." **British Journal of Sociology** 24, No. 2 (June): 165-87.

17.19 Collingwood, R.G. 1926. "Economics As a Philosophical Science." **International Journal of Ethics** (later named **Ethics**) 36, No. 2 (January): 162-85.

17.20 Corry, Bernard A. 1975. "Should Economists Abandon HOPE?" **History of Political Economy** 7, No. 2: 252-60.

17.21 Craver, Earlene and Axel Leijonhufvud. 1987. "Economics in America: the Continental Influence." **History of Political Economy** 19, No. 2: 173-82.

17.22 Cunningham, W. 1892. "The Perversion of Economic History" (with Alfred Marshall's reply). **Economic Journal** 2 (September): 491-519.

17.23 David, Paul A. 1985. "Clio and the Economics of QWERTY." **American Economic Papers and Proceedings** 75, No. 2 (May): 332-37; Rpt. in longer version as "Understanding the Economics of QWERTY: The Necessity of History" in Parker, 1986(a), pp. 30-49.

17.24 de Marchi, Neil and John Lodewijks. 1983. "HOPE and the Journal Literature in the History of Economic Thought." **History of Political Economy** 15, No. 3 (Fall): 321-43.

17.25 Dopfer, Kurt. 1986. "The Histonomic Approach to Economics: Beyond Pure Theory and Pure Experience." **Journal** of Economic Issues 20, No. 4 (December): 989-1010.

17.26 Ely, Richard T. 1936. "The Founding and Early History of the American Economic Association." American Economic Association Papers and Proceedings 26 (March): 141-50.

17.27 Farnum, H. W. 1912. "The Economic Utilization of History." American Economic Association Papers and Procedures 2 (March): 5-18.

17.28 Fetter, Frank W. 1965. "The Relation of the History of Economic Thought to Economic History." American Economic Review: Supplement 55, No. 2 (May): 136-42, and discussion, pp. 143-49.

17.29 Fogel, Robert William. 1982. "'Scientific' History and Traditional History." In L. Jonathan Cohen, et al., eds. Logic, Methodology and Philosophy of Science VI. Amsterdam: North-Holland, 1982, pp. 15-61.

17.30 Gerschenkron, Alexander. 1969. "History of Economic Doctrines and Economic History." American Economic Association Paper and Proceedings 59, No. 2 (May): 1-17.

17.31 Goodwin, Craufurd D.W. 1980. "Toward a Theory of the History of Economics." History of Political Economy 12, No. 4 (Winter): 610-19.

17.32 Gordon, Donald F. 1965. "The Role of the History of Economic Thought in the Understanding of Modern Economic Thought." American Economic Review: Supplement 55, No. 2 (May): 119-27.

17.33 Gordon, Scott. 1978. "Should Economists Pay Attention to Philosophers?" Journal of Political Economy 86, No. 4 (August): 717-28.

17.34 Grammp, William D. 1965. "On the History of Thought and Policy." American Economic Association Papers and Proceedings 55, No. 2 (May): 128-35.

17.35 Grubel, Herbert G. and Anthony D. Scott. 1967. "The Characteristics of Foreigners in the U.S. Economics Profession." American Economic Review 57, No. 1 (March): 131-45.

17.36 Guthrie, William. 1987. "The Roles of Intellectual Pedigrees in Economic Science." American Journal of Economics and Sociology 46, No. 1 (January): 49-60.

17.37 Harrison, Royden. 1963. "Two Early Articles by Alfred Marshall." Economic Journal 73 (September): 422-30.

17.38 Hausman, Daniel. 1984. "Philosophy and Economic Methodology." In Peter Asquith and P. Kitcher, eds. PSA 1984, Vol. 2. East Lansing, MI: Philosophy of Science

Association, 1984, pp. 231-49.

17.39 Hausman, Daniel. 1980. "How to Do Philosophy of Economics." In Peter Asquith and Ronald N. Giere, eds. **PSA 1980**, Vol. I. East Lansing, MI: Philosophy of Science Association, 1980, pp. 353-62.

17.40 Heilbroner, Robert. 1979. "Modern Economics As a Chapter in the History of Economic Thought." **History of Political Economy** 11, No. 2 (Summer): 192-98.

17.41 Hill, Lewis. E. 1968. "Spengler on the History of Economics: A Comment." **Journal of Economic Issues** 2, No. 4 (December): 435-36.

17.42 Horowitz, Daniel. 1974. "Historians and Economists: Perspectives on the Development of American Economic Thought." **History of Political Economy** 6, No. 4: 454-62.

17.43 Hutchison, T.W. 1977. "On the History and Philosophy of Science and Economics." In his **Knowledge and Ignorance in Economics**. Chicago: University of Chicago Press, 1977, pp. 34-61.

17.44 Kindleberger, Charles P. 1986. "A Further Comment." In Parker, 1986(a), pp. 83-92.

17.45 Koot, Gerard. 1980. "English Historical Economics and the Emergence of Economic History in England." **History of Political Economy** 12, No. 2: 174-205.

17.46 *Leontief, Wassily. 1963. "When Should History Be Written Backwards?" **Economic History Review** 16, No. 1 (August): 1-8.

17.47 *Leontief, Wassily. 1948. "Note on the Pluralistic Interpretation of History and the Problem of Interdisciplinary Cooperation." **Journal of Philosophy** 45, No. 23 (November): 617-24.

17.48 Linstromberg, R.C. 1969. "The Philosophy of Science and Alternative Approaches to Economic Thought." **Journal of Economic Issues** 3, No. 2 (June): 177-91.

17.49 Loos, Isaac A. 1918. "Historical Approach to Economics." **American Economic Review** 8 (September): 549-63.

17.50 Lutz, F.A. 1944. "History and Theory in Economics." **Economica** N.S. 11 (November): 210-14.

17.51 Macfie, A.L. 1963. "Economics--Science, Ideology, Philosophy?" **Scottish Journal of Political Economy** 10: 212-25.

17.52 Macfie, A.L. 1956. "Economic Choice As a Philosophic Theory." **Scottish Journal of Political Economy** 3 (June):

146-58.

17.53 McClelland, Peter D. 1975. **Causal Explanation and Model Building in History, Economics and the New Economic History.** Ithaca, NY: Cornell University Press.

17.54 McCloskey, Donald N. 1986. "Economics As an Historical Science." In Parker, 1986(a), pp. 63-69.

17.55 McCloskey, Donald N. 1976. "Does the Past Have Useful Economics?" **Journal of Economic Literature** 14, No. 2 (June): 434-61.

17.56 Nabors, Lawrence. 1966. "The Positive and Genetic Approaches." In Sherman Roy Krupp, ed. **The Structure of Economic Science.** Englewood-Cliffs: Prentice-Hall, 1966, pp. 68-82.

17.57 Neumark, Fritz. 1975. "Zyklen in der Geschichte ökonomischer Ideen." **Kyklos** 28, No. 2: 257-85.

17.58 Niehans, Jürg. 1981. "Economics: History, Doctrine, Science, Art." **Kyklos** 34, No. 2: 165-77.

17.59 North, Douglass C. 1978. "The New Economic History After Twenty Years." **American Behavioral Scientist** 21, No. 2 (November-December): 187-200.

17.60 North, Douglas C. 1965. "The State of Economic History." **American Economic Association Papers and Proceedings** 60 (May): 86-91.

17.61 O'Brien, D.P. 1983. "Theories of the History of Science: A Test Case." In A.W. Coats. **Methodological Controversy in Economics: Historical Essays in Honor of T.W. Hutchison.** Greenwich, CT: Jai Press, pp. 89-124.

17.62 Parker, William N., ed. 1986(a). **Economic History and the Modern Economist.** Oxford: Basil Blackwell.

17.63 Parker, William N. 1986(b). "An Historical Introduction" and "Afterword." In Parker, 1986(a), pp. 1-10 and 93-99.

17.64 Postan, M. M. 1971. **Facts and Relevance: Essays on Historical Method.** NY/London: Cambridge University Press.

17.65 Pribam, Karl. 1953. "Development of Economic Thought: Patterns of Economic Reasoning." **American Economic Association Papers and Proceedings** 43: 243-58.

17.66 Rostow, W.W. 1986. "Professor Arrow on Economic Analysis and Economic History." In Parker, 1986(a), pp. 70-76.

17.67 Samuels, Warren. 1974. "The History of Economic

Thought As Intellectual History." **History of Political Economy** 6, No. 3 (Fall): 305-23.

17.68 Skinner, Andrew S. 1985. "Smith and Shackle: History and Epistemics." **Journal of Economic Studies** 12, No. 1/2: 13-30.

17.69 Skinner, Andrew S. 1965. "Economics and History--The Scottish Enlightment." **Scottish Journal of Political Economy** 12 (February): 1-22.

17.70 *Solow, R.M. 1985. "Economic History and Economics." **American Economic Association Papers and Proceedings** 75 (May): 328-31; Rpt. in longer version as "Economics: Is Something Missing?" in Parker, 1986(a), pp. 21-29.

17.71 Spellman, William and Bruce Gabriel. 1978. "Graduate Students in Economics 1940-74." **American Economic Review** 68 (March): 182-87.

17.72 *Stigler, George J. 1969. "Does Economics Have a Useful Past?" **History of Political Economy** 1, No. 2 (Fall): 217-30.

17.73 Tarascio, Vincent J. 1975. "Intellectual History and the Social Sciences: The Problem of Methodological Pluralism." **Social Science Quarterly** 56, No. 1 (June): 37-54.

17.74 Tarascio, Vincent J. 1971. "Some Recent Developments in the History of Economic Thought in the United States." **History of Political Economy** 3, No. 2 (Fall): 419-97.

17.75 Taylor, O.H. 1957. "Frank Knight's Perspective 'On the History and Method of Economics.'" **Review of Economics and Statistics** 39 (August): 342-45.

17.76 Temin, Peter and Geoffrey Peters. 1985. "Is History Stranger Than Theory? The Origin of Telephone Separations." **American Economic Papers and Proceedings** 75, No. 2 (May): 324-27; Rpt. with same title but authored only by Temin and in longer form in Parker, 1986(a), pp. 50-59.

17.77 Tuma, Elias. 1971. **Economic History and the Social Sciences: Problems of Methodology.** London/Berkeley: University of California Press.

17.78 Usher, Abbott Payson. 1949. "The Significance of Modern Empiricism for History and Economics." **Journal of Economic History** 9, No. 2 (November): 137-55.

17.79 Viner, Jacob. 1963. "The Economist in History." **American Economic Association Papers and Proceedings** 53, No. 2 (May): 1-22, with "discussion" (G.J. Stigler), pp. 23-25.

17.80 Winch, D.N. 1962. "What Price the History of Economic Thought?" **Scottish Journal of Political Economy** 9, No. 3 (November): 193-204.

17.81 Wisman, Jon D. 1980. "The Sociology of Knowledge As a Tool for Research into the History of Economic Thought." **American Journal of Economics and Sociology** 39, No. 1 (January): 83-94.

17.82 Wold, Herman O. 1969. "Mergers of Economics and Philosophy of Science." **Synthese** 20, No. 4 (December): 427-82.

17.83 Woodman, Harold D. 1972. "Economic History and Economic Theory: The New Economic History in America." **Journal of Interdisciplinary History** 3: 323-50.

17.84 Wright, Gavin. 1986. "History and the Future of Economics." In Parker, 1986(a), pp. 77-82.

***

18

Ethics, Values, and Morality

Myrdal has spent a lifetime writing on values and the role they play in the social sciences. His **Objectivity in Social Science** (1969) is a classic. His view is that economics cannot be a nonnormative discipline.

Most orthodox economists consider themselves to be ethically neutral (i.e., value-free or the German expression for this, **wertfrei**) scientists and ethical neutrality to be desirable. J.N. Keynes, for example, wrote in his **Scope and Method of Political Economy** (p. 40):

> The proposition that it is possible to study economic uniformities without passing ethical judgements or formulating economic precepts seems in fact so little to need proof, when the point at issue is clearly grasped, that it is difficult to say anything in support of it that shall go beyond mere truism.

Apparently Keynes believes that economics consists entirely of descriptive statements and thus cannot have ethical implications. This position then rests on Hume's is-ought dichotomy. This view, of course, has been challenged by Myrdal and by institutional economists in general. Whether one views economics as essentially nonnormative or not seems to turn on one's view of the strictness of the positive-normative dichotomy. See Hutchison, and section 14 above on the is-ought dichotomy.

In his "Science and Ideology" Schumpeter argues that some parts of economics can be value-free. Weber's classic work on objectivity is consistent with Schumpeter's thesis. Klappholz's essay and Sen's book are highly recommended because they are good discussions on why values and ethics can be important for science.

***

18.1   Achatz, Thomas and Franz Haslinger. 1980. "Economics Vs. Moral Philosophy: Comment." **Theory and Decision** 12 (September): 279-88.

18.2   Archibald, G.C. 1959. "Welfare Economics, Ethics and Essentialism." **Economica** 26 (November): 316-27.

18.3   Ayres,   Charles   E.   1935.   "Moral   Confusion   in Economics." **Ethics** 45 (January): 170-99.

18.4   Baier,   Kurt.   1977.   "Rationality   and   Morality." **Erkenntnis** 11: 197-223.

18.5   Barbach,   Ronald   H.   1954.   "Economics   and   Moral Judgements." **Australasian Journal of Philosophy** 32 (May): 30-47.

18.6   Becker,   Arthur   Peter.   1948.   "Some   Philosophical Aspects of Economics." **Philosophy of Science** 15, No. 3 (July): 242-36.

18.7   Boulding, Kenneth E. 1978. "Do the Values of Science Lead to a Science of Value?" **Social Science Quarterly** 11 (March): 548-50.

18.8   Boulding, Kenneth E. 1969. "Economics As a Moral Science." **American Economic Review** 59, No. 1 (March): 1-12.

18.9   Brennan, Timothy. 1979. "Explanation and Value in Economics." **Journal of Economic Issues** 13, No. 4 (December): 911-32.

18.10 *Buchanan, James M. 1978. "Markets, States, and the Extent of Morals." **American Economic Association Papers and Proceedings** 68, No. 2 (May): 364-68.

18.11 Coats,   A.W.   1960.   "The   Politics   of   Political Economists." **Quarterly Journal of Economics** 74, No. (November): 666-669.

18.12 Dwyer, Larry. 1982(a). "The Alleged Value Neutrality of Economics: An Alternative View." **Journal of Economic Issues** 16 (March): 75-106.

18.13 Dwyer,   Larry.   1982(b).   "'Value   Freedom'   and   the Scope of Economic Inquiry: 1. Positivism's Standard View and   the   Political   Economists."   **American   Journal   of Economics and Sociology** 41, No. 2 (April): 159-68.

18.14 Gerschenkron,   Alexander.   1961.   "Reflections   on Ideology As a Methodological and Historical Problem." In Hugo Hegeland, ed. **Money, Growth and Methodology and Other Essays in Economics.** Sweden: Lund, 1961, pp. 179-94.

18.15 Gordon, Scott. 1977. "Social Science and Value Judgements." **Canadian Journal of Economics** 10, No. 4 (November): 529–46.

18.16 Goschen, G. J. 1893. "Ethics and Economics." **Economic Journal** 3 (September): 377–87.

18.17 Guthrie, William G. 1982. "The Methodological and the Ethical Context of Positive Economics: A Comment on McKenzie." **Journal of Economic Issues** 16 (December): 1109–1116.

18.18 Harsanyi, John C. 1977. "Morality and the Theory of Rational Behavior." **Social Research** 44, No. 4 (Winter): 623–56.

18.19 Heilbroner, Robert. 1973. "Economics As a 'Value-Free' Science." **Social Science** 40: 129–43; Rpt. in William L. Marr and Baldev Raj, eds. **How Economists Explain: A Reader in Methodology**. Lanham, MD: University Press of America, 1983, pp. 27–44.

18.20 Higgins, Benjamin. 1949. "Economics and Ethics." **Australasian Journal of Philosophy** 27 (August): 113–33.

18.21 Homans, G.C. 1978. "Values in Social Science: Rejoinder." **Social Science Quarterly** 58, No. 4 (March): 551–52.

18.22 Hook, Sidney, ed. 1967. **Human Values and Economic Policy**. NY: New York University Press.

18.23 Hutchison, T.W. 1964. **'Positive' Economics and Policy Objectives**. London: George Allen and Unwin Ltd.

18.24 Klappholz, Kurt. 1964. "Value Judgements and Economics." **British Journal for the Philosophy of Science** 15, No. 58 (August): 97–114.

18.25 Knight, Frank H. 1923. "The Ethics of Competition." **Quarterly Journal of Economics** 37 (August): 597–624.

18.26 Knight, Frank. 1922(a). "Ethics and the Economic Interpretation." **Quarterly Journal of Economics** 36 (May): 454–81.

18.27 Knight, Frank. 1922(b). "Round Table Conference on the Relation Between Economics and Ethics." **American Economic Association Papers and Proceedings** 12 (March): 192–201.

18.28 Kurz, Mordecai. 1978. "Altruism As an Outcome of Social Interaction." **American Economic Association Papers and Proceedings** 68, No. 2 (May): 216–22.

18.29 Levy, David. 1982. "Rational Choice and Morality: Economics and Classical Philosophy." **History of Political Economy** 14, No. 1 (Spring): 1-36.

18.30 Lindenberg, Siegwart. 1983. "Utility and Morality." **Kyklos** 36, No. 3: 450-68.

18.31 Martin, David D. 1956. "Value Judgements in Economics: A Comment." **Southern Economic Journal** 23, No. 2 (October): 183-87.

18.32 McConnell, Campbell R. 1957. "Value Judgements in Economics: A Rejoinder." **Southern Economic Journal** 23, No. 3 (January): 325-27.

18.33 Meek, Ronald L. 1964. "Value-Judgements in Economics." **British Journal for the Philosophy of Science** 15, No. 5 (August): 89-96.

18.34 Meyer, Willi. 1975. "Values, Facts, and Science: On the Problem of Objectivity in Economics." **Zeitschrift für die gesamte Staatswissenschaft** 131, No. 3 (July): 514-39.

18.35 Mitchell, Wesley C. 1944. "Facts and Values in Economics." **Journal of Philosophy** 41 (April): 212-19.

18.36 *Myrdal, Gunnar. 1972/1973. "The Place of Values in Social Policy." Ch. 3 of his **Against the Stream: Critical Essays on Economics**. NY: Pantheon, 1972/1973, pp. 33-51.

18.37 *Myrdal, Gunnar. 1969. **Objectivity in Social Research**. NY: Pantheon.

18.38 *Myrdal, Gunnar. 1961. "'Value-Loaded' Concepts." In Hugo Hegeland, ed. **Money, Growth and Methodology and Other Essays in Economics**. Sweden: Lund, 1961, pp. 273-88.

18.39 *Myrdal, Gunnar. 1958. **Value in Social Theory: A Selection of Essays on Methodology**. Ed. by Paul Streeten. London: Routledge and Kegan Paul.

18.40 *Myrdal, Gunnar. 1953. **The Political Element in the Development of Economic Theory**. Trans. Paul Streeten. London: Routledge and Kegan.

18.41 Ng, Yew-Kwang. 1972. "Value Judgements and Economists' Role in Policy Recommendation." **Economic Journal** 82, No. 327 (September): 1014-18.

18.42 Pasinetti, Luigi L. 1986. "Theory of Value--A Source of Alternative Paradigms in Economic Analysis." In Mauro Baranzini and Roberto Scazzieri, eds. **Foundations of Economics**. Oxford: Basil Blackwell, 1986, pp. 409-31.

18.43 Paul, Ellen Frankel. 1979. **Moral Revolution and Economic Science: The Demise of Laissez-Faire in**

Nineteenth-Century British Economy. Westport, CN: Greenwood Press.

18.44 Rothbard, Murray N. 1960. "The Politics of Political Economists: Comment." **Quarterly Journal of Economics** 74, No. 4 (November): 659-65.

18.45 Rothenberg, Jerome. 1966. "Values and Value Theory in Economics." In Sherman Roy Krupp, ed. **The Structure of Economic Science**. Englewood Cliffs: Prentice-Hall, 1966, pp. 221-42.

18.46 Schotta, Charles, Jr. 1966. "Values in Economic Analysis: A Methodological Issue." **Kyklos** 19, No. 2: 289-98.

18.47 Schumpeter, Joseph A. 1954. **History of Economic Analysis**. NY: Oxford University Press; Part I: "Scope and Method," pp. 3-47 and his "Science and Ideology." **American Economic Review** 39, No. 2 (March): 345-59.

18.48 Sen, Amartya. 1987. **On Ethics and Economics**. Oxford: Basil Blackwell.

18.49 Shackle, G.L.S. 1962. "Values and Intentions." **Kyklos** 15, No. 2: 828-32.

18.50 *Solow, Robert M. 1971. "Science and Ideology in Economics." **The Public Interest** 23 (Spring): 94-107.

18.51 *Stigler, George. 1960. "Reply" (to Coats and Rothbard's comments on his "The Politics of Political Economics," 1959). **Quarterly Journal of Economics** 74, No. 4 (November): 670-71.

18.52 *Stigler, George. 1959. "The Politics of Political Economists." **Quarterly Journal of Economics** 73, No. 4 (November): 522-32.

18.53 Strasnick, Steven. 1981. "Neo-Utilitarian Ethics and the Ordinal Representation Assumption." In Joseph C. Pitt, ed. **Philosophy in Economics**. Dordrecht: D. Reidel, 1981, pp. 63-92.

18.54 Tarascio, Vincent J. 1971. "Value Judgements in Economic Science." **Journal of Economic Issues** 5, No. 1 (March): 98-102.

18.55 Tool, Mark R. 1980. "The Social Value Theory of Orthodoxy: A Review and Critique." **Journal of Economic Issues** 14, No. 2 (June): 309-26.

18.56 Weber, Max. 1949 (1904). "'Objectivity' in Social Science and Social Policy." In his **The Methodology of the Social Sciences**. Trans. and ed. by Edward A. Shils and Henry A. Finch. Glencoe, Ill.: The Free Press, 1949;

Originally   appeared   as   "Die   Objektivität
sozialwissenschaftlicher und sozialpolitischer Erkenntnis."
Archiv für Sozialwissenschaft und Sozialpolitik 19 (1904):
24-87.

18.57 Weber, Wilhelm and Ernst Toptisch. 1952. "Das
Wertfreiheitsproblem seit Max Weber." **Zeitschrift für
Nationalökonomie** 13: 158-201; Rpt. in Reimut Jochimsen and
Helmut Knobel, eds. **Gegenstand und Methoden der
Nationalökonomie.** Köln: Kiepenheuer & Witsch, 1971, pp.
132-45.

18.58 Weisskopf. Walter A. 1951. "Hidden Value Conflicts in
Economic Thought." **Ethics** 61 (April): 195-204.

***

19

The Analogy to Biology and Evolutionary Economics

The analogy to biology has always competed with the analogy to physics in economics. Alfred Marshall wrote in his **Principles of Economics** (9th variorum ed., p. 772):

> But economics has no near kinship with any physical science. It is a branch of biology broadly interpreted.

This view has survived until today, and has even been taken over by some biologists, e.g., Wilson, who believes economics is a subdivisision of a larger field called "sociobiology."

Hirshleifer's "Economics from a Biological Viewpoint" is a good (52-page) summary of the contributions from biology made by biologists and economists. Alchian's work has incorporated biological analogies into the theory of the firm. In addition, Nelson and Winter have developed an evolutionary theory of the firm. Veblen's work on evolutionary economics is a classic. Losee is a philosopher of science; his work is concerned with the limitations of evolutionist philosophy.

Mechanistic and organistic analogies in economics are discussed by Johansen, Koslowski, and Thoben.

***

19.1 Alchian, Armen A. 1953. "Biological Analogies in the Theory of the Firm: Comment." **American Economic Review** 43, No. 4 (September): 600-603.

19.2 Chase, Richard. 1980. "Structural-Functional Dynamics in the Analysis of Socio-economic Systems: Adaptation of Structural Change Processes to Biological Systems of Human Interaction." **American Journal of Economics and Sociology** 39, No. 1 (January): 49-64.

19.3 Foa, Bruno. 1982. "Marshall Revisited in the Age of DNA." **Journal of Post Keynesian Economics** 5, No. 1 (Fall): 3-16.

19.4 Frazer, William J., Jr. 1978. "Evolutionary Economics, Rational Expectations, and Monetary Policy." **Journal of Economic Issues** 12, No. 2 (June): 343-72.

19.5 Gowdy, John M. 1985. "Evolutionary Theory and Economic Theory: Some Methodological Issues." **Review of Social Economy** 43, No. 3 (December): 316-24.

19.6 Gowdy, John M. 1983. "Biological Analogies in Economics: A Comment (Marshall Revisited in the Age of DNA)." **Journal of Post Keynesian Economics** 5, No. 4 (Summer): 676-78.

19.7 Hirshleifer, J. 1977. "Economics from a Biological Viewpoint." **Journal of Law and Economics** 20, No. 1 (April): 1-52.

19.8 Homan, Paul T. 1928. "Issues in Economic Theory: An Attempt to Clarify." **Quarterly Journal of Economics** 42 (May): 333-65.

19.9 Johansen, Leif. 1983. "Mechanistic and Organistic Analogies in Economics: The Place of Game Theory." **Kyklos** 36, No. 2: 304-07.

19.10 Jones, Lomar B. 1986. "The Institutionalists and **On the Origin of Species**: A Case of Mistaken Identity." **Southern Economic Journal** 52, No. 4 (April): 1043-55.

19.11 Junker, Louis J. 1981. "Instrumentalism, the Principle of Continuity and the Life Process." **American Journal of Economics and Sociology** 40, No. 4: 381-400.

19.12 Karsten, Siegfried G. 1983. "Dialectics, Functionalism, and Structuralism in Economic Thought." **American Journal of Economics and Sociology** 42, No. 2 (April): 179-92.

19.13 Kornai, Janos. 1983. "The Health of Nations: Reflections on the Analogy Between the Medical Science and Economics." **Kyklos** 36, No. 2: 191-212.

19.14 Koslowski, Peter. 1983. "Mechanistische und organistische Analogien in der Wirtschaftswissenschaft --eine verfehlte Alternative." **Kyklos** 36, No. 2: 308-12.

19.15 Losee, John. 1977. "Limitations of an Evolutionist Philosophy of Science." **Studies in History and Philosophy of Science** 8: 349-52.

19.16 Marshall, Alfred. 1961 (1920). "The Scope and Method

of Economics." Appendix C of his **Principles of Economics,** ninth (variorum edition). London: Macmillan and Co. for the Royal Economic Society.

19.17 Nelson, Richard R. and Sidney G. Winter. 1982. **An Evolutionary Theory of Economic Change.** Cambridge, MA: The Belknap Press of Harvard University Press.

19.18 Nelson, Richard R. and Sidney G. Winter. 1974. "Neoclassical vs. Evolutionary Theory of Economic Growth: Critique and Prospectus." **Economic Journal** 84 (December): 886-905.

19.19 *Samuelson, Paul A. 1978. "Maximizing and Biology." **Economic Inquiry** 16, No. 2 (April): 171-83.

19.20 Thoben, H. 1982. "Mechanistic and Organistic Analogies in Economics Reconsidered." **Kyklos** 35, No. 2: 292-306.

19.21 Veblen, Thorstein. 1948. "Why Is Economics Not an Evolutionary Science?" In Max Lerner, ed. **The Portable Veblen.** NY: Viking Press, 1948, pp. 215-40.

19.22 Wilson, Edward O. 1977. "Biology and the Social Sciences." **Daedalus** (Fall): 127-40.

*****

20

Consensus and Dissension in Economics

Benjamin Higgins (1951) begins his essay "Economists Never Agree" with the following story.

> Everyone has encountered, in one version or another, the remark which I heard attributed to Winston Churchill: "Whenever I ask England's six leading economists a question, I get seven answers--two from Mr. Keynes."

It is true that economists are known for never agreeing. This lack of agreement goes back to economics' very beginnings: James Mill's (1836) piece is a paradigm example.

Higgins argues that there are really three kinds of disagreement among economists: disagreement on matters outside of economics (e.g., in ethics or politics), disagreement on method, and disagreement on the borders of knowledge. Duhs believes the dissension is due to varying views about the nature of man and different political philosophies and ideologies. (See also Cole, et al. for a similar view.) Chase believes the disagreements are irreconcilable because of the nature of economics: its historical character, the fact that economic policy influences economic agents, the relativity of "economic truth" which varies from school to school. Frey, et al. attempt to quantify consensus and dissension among economists: they survey a population of over 900 U.S. French, German, Austrian, and Swiss economists and find that there is agreement that the price mechanism is a desirable social choice mechanism. Dissension exists on normative or currently controversial issues (e.g., supply economics). There is more agreement on micro than macro issues. Kearl, et al. also analyse disagreement among economists and come to similar conclusions. They deny that "wide disagreement" exists. Certainly it is true that

macroeconomic   topics   are   more   controversial   than
microeconomic at the moment, due to the "dissolution of the
Keynesian   consensus"   (Dean,   1980).   Here   this   section
overlaps into "crises" (§ 6) and "theory" (§ 8). Machlup's
"Why   Economists   Disagree"   is,   as   always,   written   in
crystal-clear form. He argues that there are four causes
of disagreement: (1) different word meanings, (2) different
logical reasoning, (3) different factual assumptions (for
which there is usually little or no historical evidence),
and (4) different value judgements.

***

20.1   Chase,   Richard   X.   1977.   "Why   Economists   Disagree."
American Journal of Economics and Sociology 36, No. 4
(October): 429-32.

20.2   Cole, Ken, John Cameron, and Chris Edwards. 1983. **Why
Economists Disagree.** London/NY: Longman.

20.3   Dean,   James   W.   1980.   "The   Dissolution   of   the
Keynesian Consensus." **The Public Interest** (Special Issue:
The Crisis in Economic Theory): 19-34; Rpt. in Daniel Bell
and Irving Kristol, eds. **The Crisis in Economic Theory.** NY:
Basic, 1981, pp. 19-34.

20.4   Duhs,   L.A.   1982.   "Why   Economists   Disagree: The
Philosophy   of   Irreconcilability."   **Journal   of   Economic
Issues** 16, No. 1 (March): 221-36.

20.5   Frey,   Bruno   S.,   et   al.   1984.   "Consensus   and
Dissension   Among   Economists: An   Empirical   Inquiry."
American Economic Review 74, No. 5 (December): 986-94.

20.6   Higgens, Benjamin. 1951. "Economists Never Agree." In
his **What Do Economists Know?** Victoria/London: Melbourne
and Cambridge University Presses, 1951, pp. 30-60.

20.7   Kearl,   J.R.,   et   al.   1979.   "A   Confusion   of
Economists?" **American Economic Association Papers and
Proceedings** 69, No. 2 (May): 28-37.

20.8   Lugg,   Andrew.   1978.   "Disagreement   in   Science."
Zeitschrift für allgemeine Wissenschaftstheorie 9, No. 2:
276-92.

20.9   Machlup,   Fritz.   1978.   "Why   Economists   Disagree."   In
his **Methodology of Economics and Other Social Sciences.** NY:
Academic Press, pp. 375-90.

20.10 Mill, James. 1966 (1836). "Whether Political Economy
Is Useful." In Donald Winch, ed. **James Mill: Selected
Economic Writings.** Chicago: University of Chicago Press,
1966, pp. 371-82.

***

21

The Cambridge Controversy

In the fifties Joan Robinson and other Cambridge (England) economists launched an attack on the orthodox (i.e., neoclassical) marginal productivity theory of distribution, especially Hick's two-input-one-input model of factor pricing. Blaug describes and evaluates "Switching, Reswitching, and All That" in his **Methodology of Economics Or How Economists Explain** (1980). Harcourt's work is an excellent survey and appraisal of this rather complex subject.

More recently Cohen (1984) concludes that the resolution of the Cambridge controversy of the 1960's was disappointing because a full theoretical assessment of the controversy has been ignored. Bernstein (1985) argues that Cohen's dependence on "the growth of knowledge method" is flawed. He emphasizes that understanding, not prediction, is important. Cohen (1985) replies that Bernstein misunderstood him.

Dow (1980) analyses the Cambridge controversy by way of analogy to Kuhn's philosophy of science in a similar exchange in the **Journal of Post Keynesian Economics**. She concludes that formalism in economics must not be allowed to reign supreme. (In her discussion, she assumes that the application of Kuhn's philosophy to economics is useful.) Salanti argues that the Cambridge school failed even though it pointed out a flaw in neoclassical theory. Dow replies that Salanti argues from a positivist position.

***

21.1 Bernstein, Michael A. 1985. "The Methodological Resolution of the Cambridge Controversies: A Comment." **Journal of Post Keynesian Economics** 7, No. 4 (Summer): 607-11.

21.2 Blaug, Mark. 1980. **The Methodology of Economics Or How**

Economists Explain. Cambridge: Cambridge University Press, Ch. 10, "Switching, Reswitching, and All That," pp. 202-08.

21.3 Cohen, Avi J. 1985. "Issues in the Cambridge Controversies." **Journal of Post Keynesian Economics** 7, No. 4 (Summer): 612-15.

21.4 Cohen, Avi J. 1984. "The Methodological Resolution of the Cambridge Controversies." **Journal of Post Keynesian Economics** 6, No. 4 (Summer): 614-29.

21.5 Dow, Sheila. 1982. "Neoclassical Tautologies and the Cambridge Controversies: Reply to Salanti." **Journal of Post Keynesian Economics** 5, No. 1 (Fall): 132-34.

21.6 Dow, Sheila. 1980. "Methodological Morality in the Cambridge Controversies." **Journal of Post Keynesian Economics** 2, No. 3 (Spring): 368-80.

21.7 Harcourt, G.C. 1976. "The Cambridge Controversies: Old Ways and New Horizons--Or Dead End?" **Oxford Economic Papers** 28, No. 1 (March): 25-65.

21.8 Salanti, Andrea. 1982. "Neoclassical Tautologies and the Cambridge Controversies: Comment on Dow." **Journal of Post Keynesian Economics** 5, No. 1 (Fall): 128-31.

***

22

Institutionalism

Charles Ayres once said of his fellow institutionalists:

> even today there is no clearly defined
> body of principles on which institu-
> tionalists are generally agreed and by
> which they are known. But if there is
> anything all institutionalists have in
> common it is dissatisfaction with
> 'orthodox' price theory (quoted in Dugger,
> 1977, p. 449).

Identifying the institutionalists and their particular theories or body of ideas is indeed not so simple. Sometimes it is difficult to discern differences between political economists, institutionalists, historical economists in the tradition of the German historical school, and Post Keynesians.

The three founders of American institutionalism were Thorstein Veblen (1857-1929), John R. Commons (1862-1945), and Wesley Mitchell (1874-1948). Not only a dissatisfaction with the price mechanism is common ground for most contemporary institutionalists. Most are also against formalism and abstraction. They usually advocate history and insist on economics' normative character. In addition, they often believe the scope of economics should be broadened. For instance, Veblen emphasizes the role of tradition and custom (i.e., of "institutions") in economics, Commons the role of law, and Mitchell the need for more empirical work. Contemporary institutionalists such as Galbraith, Gramm, and Samuels would insist on the inclusion of power as a necessary element for understanding the modern economy. Hutchison mentions that some of the contemporary property rights theorists are considered to be "neoinstitutionalists" because of their emphasis on law and economics.

The voice of the institutionalists is the **Journal of Economic Issues**. The articles which appear below are by institutionalists and on institutionalism (some written by non-institutionalists).

***

22.1 Atkins, Willard, et al. 1936. "Institutional Economics: Discussion." **American Economic Association Papers and Proceedings** 26 (March): 250-54.

22.2 Ayres, C.E. 1971. "On the Possibility of a Political Economics: Comment." **Journal of Economic Issues** 5, No. 3 (September): 96.

22.3 Ayres, C.E. 1967. "Ideological Responsibility." **Journal of Economic Issues** 1, Nos. 1-2 (June): 3-11.

22.4 Ayres, C.E. 1918. "The Function and Problems of Economic Theory." **Journal of Political Economy** 26 (January): 69-90.

22.5 Bolin, Meb. 1983. "The Independent, Simultaneous Development of Instrumental Thoughts in Various Disciplines." **Journal of Economic Issues** 17, No. 2 (June): 345-52.

22.6 Bronfenbrenner, Martin. 1985. "Early American Leaders--Institutional and Critical Traditions." **American Economic Review Special Issue** 75, No. 6 (December): 13-27.

22.7 *Buchanan, James M. and Warren J. Samuels. 1975. "On Some Fundamental Issues in Political Economy: An Exchange of Correspondence." **Journal of Economic Issues** 9, No. 1 (March): 15-38.

22.8 Burns, E.M. 1931. "Does Institutionalism Complement Or Compete with 'Orthodox Economics'?" **American Economic Review** 21 (March): 80-87, and correction 21 (June): 287.

22.9 Clark, J.M. 1925. "Problems of Economic Theory: Discussion." **American Economic Association Papers and Proceedings** 15 (March): 56-58.

22.10 Clark, J.M. 1921. "Soundings in Non-Euclidean Economics." **American Economic Association Papers and Proceedings** 11 (March): 132-43.

22.11 Clark, J.M. 1919. "Economic Theory in an Era of Social Readjustment." **American Economic Association Papers and Proceedings** 9 (March): 280-90.

22.12 Clark, J.M. 1918. "Economists and Modern Psychology, Parts I & II." **Journal of Political Economy** 26 (January): 1-30 and 26 (February): 136-66.

22.13 Commons, John R. 1936. "Institutional Economics." **American Economic Association Papers and Proceedings** 26 (March): 237-49.

22.14 Culbertson, John M. 1984. "The New Potential of Evolutionary Institutional Economics." **Journal of Economic Issues** (June): 611-18.

22.15 Dagum, Camilo. 1979. "Methods and Data in Economic Inquiry: Comment." **Journal of Economic Issues** 13, No. 2 (June): 387-90.

22.16 Dalton, George. 1968. "Economics, Economic Development, and Economic Anthropology." **Journal of Economic Issues** 2, No. 2 (June): 173-86.

22.17 Dugger, William M. 1984. "Veblen and Kropotkin on Human Evolution." **Journal of Economic Issues** 18, No. 4 (December): 971-85.

22.18 Dugger, William M. 1977. "Institutional and Neoclassical Economics Compared." **Social Science Quarterly** 58, No. 3: 449-61.

22.19 Dugger, William M. 1976. "Ideological and Scientific Functions of the Neoclassical Theory of the Firm." **Journal of Economic Issues** 10, No. 2 (June): 314-23.

22.20 Dyer, Alan W. 1986. "Veblen on Scientific Creativity: The Influence of Charles S. Pierce." **Journal of Economic Issues** 20, No. 1 (March): 21-41.

22.21 Field, Alexander James. 1979. "On the Explanation of Rules Using Rational Choice Models." **Journal of Economic Issues** 13, No. 1 (March): 49-72.

22.22 Fischer, Charles C. 1986. "Institutionalism Versus Orthodoxy: The Articulation of Methodological Alternatives." **American Journal of Economics and Sociology** 45, No. 3 (July): 359-72.

22.23 Fischer, Charles C. 1981. "A Comment on 'The Method Is the Ideology.'" **Journal of Economic Issues** 15, No. 1 (March): 193-96.

22.24 Gäfgen, G. 1974. "On the Methodology and Political Economy of Galbraithian Economics." **Kyklos** 27: 705-31.

22.25 Galbraith, John K. 1978. "On Post Keynesian Economics." **Journal of Post Keynesian Economics** 1, No. 1 (Fall): 8-11.

22.26 Galbraith, John K. 1973. "Power and the Useful Economist." **American Economic Review** 63, No. 1 (March): 1-11.

22.27 Gordon, Robert Aaron. 1976. "Rigor and Relevance in a Changing Institutional Setting." **American Economic Review** 66, No. 1 (March): 1-14.

22.28 Gramm, Warren S. 1973. "Natural Selection in Economic Thought: Ideology, Power, and the Keynesian Counterrevolution." **Journal of Economic Issues** 7, No. 1 (March): 1-27.

22.29 Gruchy, Allan G. 1984. "Neo-Institutionalism, Neo-Marxism, and Neo-Keynesianism: An Evaluation." **Journal of Economic Issues** 18, No. 2 (June): 547-56.

22.30 Gruchy, Allan G. and Fritz Machlup. 1952. "Issues in Methodology: Discussion." **American Economic Association Papers and Proceedings** 42, No. 2 (May): 67-73.

22.31 Hamilton, W.H. 1919. "The Institutional Approach to Economic Theory." **American Economic Association Paper and Proceedings** 9 (March): 309-18.

22.32 Heilbroner, Robert. 1970(a). "On the Limited 'Relevance' of Economics." **The Public Interest** 21 (Fall): 80-93.

22.33 Heilbroner, Robert. 1970(b). "On the Possibility of a Political Economics." **Journal of Economic Issues** 4, No. 4 (December): 1-22.

22.34 Higgens, Benjamin. 1947. "The Economic Man and Economic Science" (Review of John S. Gamb's **Beyond Supply and Demand: A Reappraisal of Institutional Economics** (1946)). **Canadian Journal of Economics and Political Science** 13 (November): 587-99.

22.35 Hill, Lewis E. and Donald W. Owen. 1984. "The Instrumental Philosophy of Economic History and the Institutionalist Theory of Normative Value." **Journal of Economic Issues** 18, No. 2 (June): 581-87.

22.36 Hirsch, Abraham. 1976. "The **a posteriori** Method and the Creation of New Theory: W.C. Mitchell As a Case Study." **History of Political Economy** 8, No. 2 (Summer): 195-206.

22.37 Homan, Paul T. 1932. "An Appraisal of Institutional Economics." **American Economic Review** 22 (March): 10-17.

22.38 Homan, Paul T., et al. 1931. "Economic Theory: Institutionalism: What It Is and What It Hopes to Become." **American Economic Association Papers and Proceedings** 21 (March): 134-41.

22.39 Hutchison, T. W. 1984. "Institutional Economics Old and New." **Zeitschrift für Staatswissenschaft** 140, No. 1 (March): 20-29.

22.40 Kapp, K. William. 1976. "The Nature and Significance of Institutional Economics." **Kyklos** 29, No. 2: 209–32.

22.41 Karsten, Siegfried G. 1973. "Dialectics and the Evolution of Economic Thought." **History of Political Economy** 5, No. 2 (Fall): 399–419.

22.42 Keller, Robert R., John R. McKean and Rodney D. Peterson. 1982. "Preference and Value Formation: A Convergence of Enlightened Orthodox and Institutional Analysis?" **Journal of Economic Issues** 16, No. 4 (December): 941–54.

22.43 Kickhofer, W.H. 1932. "Institutional Economics. Round Table Conference." **American Economic Review Papers and Proceedings** 22 (March): 105–16.

22.44 Klein, Philip A. 1974. "Economics: Allocation Or Valuation?" **Journal of Economic Issues** 8, No. 4 (December): 785–811.

22.45 Knight, Frank H. 1952. "Institutionalism and Empiricism in Economics." **American Economic Association Papers and Proceedings** 42, No. 2 (May): 45–55.

22.46 Kowalik, Tadeusz. 1978. "The Institutional Framework of Dobb's Economics." **Cambridge Journal of Economics** 2, No. 2 (June): 141–51.

22.47 Methodology in Economics Symposium Issues: Part I & II. 1979/1980. **Journal of Economic Issues** 14, No. 4 (December 1979) and 14, No. 1 (March 1980).

22.48 McKenzie, Richard B. 1981. "The Necessary Normative Context of Positive Economics." **Journal of Economic Issues** 15 (September): 703–19.

22.49 McKenzie, Richard B. 1978. "On the Methodological Boundaries of Economic Analysis." **Journal of Economic Issues** 12, No. 3 (September): 627–45.

22.50 Mitchell, Wesley C. 1924. "Commons on the Legal Foundations of Capitalism." **American Economic Review** 14 (June): 240–53.

22.51 Mitchell, Wesley C. 1914. "Human Behavior and Economics: A Survey of Recent Literature." **Quarterly Journal of Economics** (November): 1–47.

22.52 *Myrdal, Gunnar. 1978. "Institutional Economics." **Journal of Economic Issues** 12, No. 4 (December): 771–83.

22.53 *Myrdal, Gunnar. 1933. "Das Zweck-Mittel-Denken in der Nationalökonomie." **Zeitschrift für Nationalökonomie** 4: 305–29.

22.54 Nichols,   Alan.   1969.   "On   Savings   and
Neo-Institutionalism." **Journal of Economic Issues** 3, No. 3
(September): 63-66.

22.55 Perelman,   Michael.   1976.   "Energy,   Entropy   and
Economic Value." **Australian Economic Papers** 15, No. 26
(June): 1-10.

22.56 Petr,   Jerry   L.   1984.   "Fundamentals   of   an
Institutionalist Perspective on Economic Policy." **Journal
of Economic Issues** 8, No. 1 (March): 1-17.

22.57 Pinney,   Harvey.   1940.   "The   Institutional   Man."
Journal of Political Economy 48 (August): 543-62.

22.58 Rashid, Salim. 1981(a). "Methods in Economic Science:
Comment." **Journal of Economic Issues** 15, No. 1 (March):
183-88.

22.59 Rashid,   Salim.   1981(b).   "Political   Economy   and
Geology   in   the   Nineteenth   Century: Similarities   and
Contrasts." **History of Political Economy** 13, No. 4
(Winter): 726-44.

22.60 Rotwein, Eugene. 1979. "The Methodological Basis of
Institutional Economics: Comment." **Journal of Economic
Issues** 13, No. 4: 1029-33.

22.61 Roy, Paul-Martel. 1985. "L'approch structuraliste
-institutionnaliste nord-américaine: une forme de réalisme
en économie." **Economies et sociétés** 20, No. 4 (April):
57-75.

22.62 Samuels, Warren J. 1987. "An Essay on the Nature and
Significance of the Normative Nature of Economics." **Journal
of Post Keynesian Economics** 10, No. 3 (Spring): 347-54.

22.63 Samuels, Warren J. 1984. "Galbraith on Economics As a
System of Professional Belief." **Journal of Post Keynesian
Economics** 7, No. 1 (Fall): 61-76.

22.64 Samuels,   Warren   J.   1981.   "A   Necessary   Normative
Content of Positive Economics?" **Journal of Economic Issues**
15, No. 3 (September): 721-27.

22.65 Samuels, Warren J., ed. 1980. **The Methodology of
Economic Thought: Critical Papers from the Journal of
Economic Issues**. New Brunswick, N.J.: Transaction Books.

22.66 Samuels,   Warren   J.   1969.   "On   the   Future   of
Institutional Economics." **Journal of Economic Issues** 3, No.
3 (September): 67-72.

22.67 Shafer,   Joseph   E.   1933.   "The   Institutionalist
Economics   of   Professor   Commons: A   Rejoinder." **American**

Economic Review 23 (March): 87-91.

22.68 Shafer, Joseph E. 1932. "Institutional Economics of Professor Commons (followed by Common's comment)." **American Economic Review** 22 (June): 261-68.

22.69 Sherman, Howard J. 1984. "Contemporary Radical Economics." **Journal of Economic Education** 15, No. 4 (Fall): 265-74.

22.70 Silverstein, Nathan L. 1932. "An Appraisal of Institutional Economics: Comment." **American Economic Review** 22 (June): 268-69.

22.71 Simich, J. L. and R. Tilman. 1980. "Critical Theory and Institutional Economics: Frankfurt's Encounter with Veblen." **Journal of Economic Issues** 14, No. 3 (September): 631-48.

22.72 Stanfield, J. Ron. 1983. "Institutional Analysis: Toward Progress in Economic Science." In Alfred S. Eichner, ed. **Why Economics Is Not Yet a Science**. London: Macmillan/Sharpe, 1983, pp. 187-204.

22.73 Stanfield, J. Ron. 1979. "Phenomena and Epiphenomena in Economics." **Journal of Economic Issues** 13, No. 4 (December): 885-98.

22.74 Sturgeon, James I. 1984. "Induction and Instrumentalism in Institutional Thought." **Journal of Economic Issues** 18, No. 2 (June): 599-609.

22.75 Tilman, Rich. 1983. "Social Value Theory, Corporate Power, and Political Elites: Appraisals of Lindblom's **Politics and Markets**." **Journal of Economic Issues** 17, No. 1: 115-31.

22.76 Tool, Marc R. 1981. "Observations on the Fischer Comment (The Method Is the Ideology)." **Journal of Economic Issues** 15, No. 1 (March): 197-99.

22.77 Veblen, Thorstein. 1925. "Economic Theory in the Calculable Future." **American Economic Association Papers and Proceedings** 15 (March): 48-55.

22.78 Wegehenkel, Lothar. 1984. "Institutional Economics Old and New: Comment." **Zeitschrift für die gesamte Staatswissenschaft** 140, No. 1 (March): 30-33.

22.79 Weisskopf, Walter. 1981. "Reply to Professor Fischer" (The Method Is the Ideology). **Journal of Economic Issues** 15, No. 1 (March): 196-97.

22.80 Weisskopf, Walter. 1979. "The Methodology Is the Ideology: From a Newtonian to a Heisenbergian Paradigm in Economics." **Journal of Economic Issues** 13 (December):

869-84.

22.81 Weisskopf, Walter. 1977. "Normative and Ideological Elements in Social and Economic Thought." **Journal of Economic Issues** 11 (March): 103-17.

22.82 Weisskopf, Walter. 1973. "The Image of Man in Economics." **Social Research** (Autumn): 547-63.

22.83 White, Morton G. 1947. "The Revolt Against Formalism in American Social Thought of the Twentieth Century." **Journal of the History of Ideas** 8, No. 2 (April): 131-52.

22.84 Wible, James R. 1985. "Institutional Economics, Positive Economics, Pragmatism, and Recent Philosophy of Science: Reply to Liebhafsky and Liebhafsky." **Journal of Economic Issues** 19, No. 4 (December): 984-95.

22.85 Wilber, Charles K. and R. S. Harrison. 1979. "The Methodological Basis of Institutional Economics: A Reply." **Journal of Economic Issues** 13, No. 4 (December): 1033-37.

22.86 Winrich, J. Steven. 1984. "Self-reference and the Incomplete Structure of Neoclassical Economics." **Journal of Economic Issues** 18, No. 4 (December): 987-1005.

22.87 Wolfe, A.B. 1939. "Thoughts on Perusal of Wesley Mitchell's Collected Essays." **Journal of Political Economy** 47 (February): 1-29.

***

23

Marxism

Most of the entries here are on Marxism rather than by Marxists. Frey's "Renaissance of Political Economy" (in German) serves as a good survey of the extreme wing of modern economics: the unorthodox and the radicals. Not only the Marxists belong to these groups. The Cambridge (England) school with its capital controversy actually belongs to this category because the Cambridge theorists often (wrongly) assume that a failure in neoclassical economics means that Marxism is the only alternative (Frey, 1974, p. 378). Like the institutionalists, modern Marxists are not always very easy to categorize. Bronfenbrenner (p. 26) lists as the leading dissidents influenced by Marx since 1945: Paul Baran, Samuel Bowles, Herbert Gintis, David Gordon, John Gurley, David Harris, E.K. Hunt, David Laibman, Leo Rogin, Edward Nell, James O'Connor, John Roemer, Anwar Shaikh, Howard Sherman, Paul Sweezy, and Thomas Weisskopf.

Kuhn's work has been used by Marxists to show that neoclassical economics is flawed. That was the task of the special issue of the **Review of Radical Political Economics** (the mouthpiece of Marxist economists), "Radical Paradigms in Economics." (See Peabody and Zweig.) Ward's **What's Wrong with Economics?** uses Kuhn's framework of normal science and revolutions to explain growth of economic thought; this work has been praised by the mainstream.

The opposite side of the coin is presented by Blaug's works, which use Lakatos' philosophy of science to show that Marxism is a degenerating research programme which should be abandoned.

On orthodox Marxism (i.e., on Marx's works) see Bartley, Hunt, Hutchison's chapter one: "Friedrich Engels and Marxian Political Economy," and Weaver and Wisman. The labor theory of value has been analysed by Cohen, Sen, Sensat, and Leontief. Leontief's "The Significance of

154   Economic Methodology

Marxian Economics for Present-Day Economic Theory" is, although written in 1938, highly recommended. He (p. 8) believes Marx's "strength lies in realistic, empirical knowledge of the capitalist system."

***

23.1 Bartley, William W., III. 1987. "Alienation Alienated: The Economics of Knowledge Versus the Psychology and Sociology of Knowledge." In Gerard Radnitzky and Bartley, eds. **Evolutionary Epistemology, Rationality, and the Sociology of Knowledge.** La Salle/London: Open Court, 1987, pp. 423-51.

23.2 Blaug, Mark. 1983. "A Methodological Appraisal of Radical Economics." In A.W. Coats. **Methodological Controversy in Economics: Historical Essays in Honor of T.W. Hutchison.** Greenwich, CT: Jai Press, 1983, pp. 211-46.

23.3 Blaug, Mark. 1980. **A Methodological Appraisal of Marxian Economics.** Amsterdam: North-Holland.

23.4 Bronfenbrenner, Martin. 1985. "Early American Leaders--Institutional and Critical Traditions." **American Economic Review Special Issue** 75, No. 6 (December): 13-27.

23.5 Cohen, G.A. 1979. "The Labor Theory of Value and the Concept of Exploitation." **Philosophy and Public Affairs** 8, No. 4 (Summer): 338-60.

23.6 Dreyer, Jacob S. 1974. "The Evolution of Marxist Attitudes Toward Marxist Techniques." **History of Political Economy** 6, No. 1: 48-75.

23.7 Frey, Bruno S. 1974. "Die Renaissance der politischen Ökonomie." **Schweizerische Zeitschrift für Volkswirtschaft und Statistik** 110, No. 3 (September): 357-407.

23.8 Gruchy, Allan G. 1984. "Neo-Institutionalism, Neo-Marxism, and Neo-Keynesianism: An Evaluation." **Journal of Economic Issues** 18, No. 2 (June): 547-56.

23.9 Gruchy, Allan G. 1969. "Neoinstitutionalism and the Economics of Dissent." **Journal of Economic Issues** 3, No. 1 (March): 1-17.

23.10 Gurley, John. 1971. "The State of Political Economics." **American Economic Association Papers and Proceedings** 61, No. 2 (May): 53-68.

23.11 Hunt, E. K. 1984. "The Relation Between Theory and History in the Writings of Karl Marx." **Atlantic Economic Journal** 12, No. 4 (December): 1-8.

23.12 Hutchison, T.W. 1981. **The Politics and Philosophy of Economics: Marxians, Keynesians and Austrians.** NY: New York

University Press.

23.13 *Leontief, Wassily W. 1938. "The Significance of Marxian Economics for Present-Day Economic Theory." **American Economic Association Papers and Proceedings** 28 (March): 1-9.

23.14 Peabody, Gerald E. 1971. "Scientific Paradigms and Economics: An Introduction." **Review of Radical Political Economics** 3, No. 2 (July): 1-16.

23.15 "Radical Paradigms in Economics." 1971. **Review of Radical Political Economics** (Special Issue on Radical Paradigms in Economics) 3, No. 2 (July).

23.16 Ranson, Baldwin. 1980. "Rival Economic Epistemologies: The Logic of Marx, Marshall, and Keynes." **Journal of Economic Issues** 14 (March): 77-98.

23.17 Robinson, Joan. 1981. "Marxism: Religion and Science." In her **What Are the Questions? and Other Essays.** Armonk, NY: Sharpe, 1981, pp. 155-64.

23.18 Ruccio, David F. and Lawrence H. Simon. 1986. "Methodological Aspects of a Marxian Approach to Development: An Analysis of the Modes of Production School." **World Development** 14, No. 2 (February: Special Issue): 211-222.

23.19 Russell, James W. 1985. "Method, Analysis, and Politics in Max Weber: Disentangling Marxian Affinities and Differences." **History of Political Economy** 17, No. 4 (Winter): 575-90.

23.20 Sen, Amartya. 1978. "On the Labor Theory of Value: Some Methodological Issues." **Cambridge Journal of Economic** 2, No. 1 (March): 175-90.

23.21 Sensat, Julius O. 1983. "Sraffa and Ricardo on Value and Distribution." **Philosophical Forum** 14, Nos. 3-4 (Spring-Summer): 334-68.

23.22 Sherman, Howard J. 1984. "Contemporary Radical Economics." **Journal of Economic Education** 15, No. 4 (Fall): 265-74.

23.23 Sherman, Howard J. 1979. "'Technology **vis-a-vis** Institutions': A Marxist Commentary." **Journal of Economic Issues** 13, No. 1 (March): 175-91.

23.24 Ward, Benjamin. 1972. **What's Wrong with Economics?** London: Macmillan.

23.25 Weaver, James H. and Jon D. Wisman. 1978. "Smith, Marx, and Malthus--Ghosts Who Haunt Our Future." **The Futurist** 12, No. 2 (April): 93-104.

23.26 Wolff, Richard D. 1975. "Communication: On Marxism and Marginalism." **History of Political Economy** 7, No. 2 (Summer): 270-72.

23.27 Worland, Stephen T. 1972. "Radical Political Economy As a Scientific Revolution." **Southern Economic Journal** 39, No. 2 (October): 274-84.

23.28 Zweig, Michael. 1971. "Bourgeois and Radical Paradigms in Economics." **Review of Radical Political Economics** 3, No. 2 (July): 43-58.

***

24

The German Historical School and the *Methodenstreit*

This section is dedicated to the influence of the German historical school and the **Methodenstreit** (and thus the Austrian school) on economics, and especially on American economics. The members of the German historical school were in part Friedrich List, Wilhelm Roscher, Karl Knies, Karl Bücher, and Gustav von Schmoller.

It was very much the fashion to go to Germany and study in the late 1800's when American economics as a discipline was forming. The influence of Germany on American economics is described by Barber, Baumol, Dunbar, Epstein, Herbst, Laughlin, Nasse, Oncken, Parrish, Rowe, Seager, and Wickett. Baumol's discussion of the evolution of method in economics since the beginnings of the American Economic Association and his contrasts of contemporary methods with early methods makes for interesting reading. Historicism as a phenomenon not necessarily associated with economics is described by Brinkmann, Eisermann, Hoxie, Iggers, Lee, Mandelbaum, Nipperdey, Rashid, Redlich, Rogin, and Rothacker. Popper coined the word historicism and launched the most powerful attack against it ever. His usage of 'historicism' is, however, unusual and not accepted as normal usage of the word. Popper, Suchting, Urbach, and Wilkins analyse Popper's **Poverty of Historicism**. White's article is an analysis of the anti-formalistic movement within historicism. The methodological aspect manifested in this section is the battle between historical and theoretical methods in economics and other disciplines.

***

24.1 Albert, Hans. 1962. "Der moderne Methodenstreit und die Grenzen des Methodenpluralismus." **Jahrbuch für Sozialwissenschaften**. 13: 143-69; Rpt. in Reimut Jochimsen and Helmut Knobel, eds. **Gegenstand und Methoden der Nationalökonomie**. Köln: Kiepenheuer & Witsch, 1971, pp.

255-82.

24.2 Barber, William J. 1987. "Should the American Economic Association Have Toasted Simon Newcomb at Its 100th Birthday Party?" **Journal of Economic Perspectives** 1, No. 1 (Summer): 179-83.

24.3 Baumol, William J. 1985. "On the Method in U.S. Economics a Century Earlier." **American Economic Review Special Issue** 75, No. 6 (December): 1-12.

24.4 Brinkmann, Carl. 1956. "Historische Schule." **Handwörterbuch der Sozialwissenschaften.** Vol. 5, 1956 ed.

24.5 Dunbar, Charles. 1891. "The Academic Study of Political Economy." **Quarterly Journal of Economics** (July): 397-416.

24.6 Eisermann, Gottfried. 1956. **Die Grundlagen des Historismus in der deutschen Nationalökonomie.** Stuttgart: Ferdinand Enke Verlag.

24.7 Epstein, M. 1917. "The Teaching of Economics in Germany After the War." **Economic Journal** 27 (September): 432-35.

24.8 Herbst, Jurgen. 1965. **The German Historical School in American Scholarship.** Ithaca, NY: Cornell University Press.

24.9 Hoxie, R.F. 1906. "Historical Method Vs. Historical Narrative." **Journal of Political Economy** 14 (November): 568-72.

24.10 Hutchison, T.W. 1967. "Review of Popper's **Das Elend des Historizismus.**" **Zeitschrift für Nationalökonomie** 27: 503-04.

24.11 Iggers, Georg. 1973. "Historicism." **Dictionary of the History of Ideas.** 1973 ed.

24.12 Iggers, Georg. 1968. **The German Conception of History.** Middleton, CN: Wesleyan University Press.

24.13 Laughlin, J. Laurence. 1892. "The Study of Political Economy in the United States." **Journal of Political Economy** 1 (December): 1-19 and Appendix I: 143-51.

24.14 Lee, Dwight E. and Robert N. Beck. 1953-54. "The Meaning of 'Historicism'." **American Historical Review** 59: 568-77.

24.15 Mandelbaum, Maurice. 1967. "Historicism." **Encyclopedia of Philosophy.** 1967 ed.

24.16 Menger, Carl. 1968-1970. **Gesammelte Werke.** Ed. and with an introduction by F.A. Hayek, 2nd. ed., 4 Vols.

Tübingen: J. C.B. Mohr.

Vol. II: **Untersuchungen über die Methode der Sozialwissenschaften und der politischen Ökonomie insbesondere.** 1969 (1883); Trans. by Francis J. Nock as **Investigations into the Method of the Social Sciences with Special Reference to Economics.** 1985 (rpt. of 1963). With a new introduction by Lawrence H. White. Ed. by Louis Schneider. NY/London: New York University Press. (Originally published in English as **Problems in Economics and Sociology,** 1963)

Vol. III: **Kleinere Schriften zur Methode und Geschichte der Volkswirtschaftslehre.** 1970 (1884-1915).

24.17 Nasse, Erwin. 1887. "Correspondence: The Economic Movement in Germany." **Quarterly Journal of Economics** 1: 498-506.

24.18 Nipperdey, Thomas. 1985. **Deutsche Geschichte 1800-1866.** 3rd rev. ed. München: C.H. Beck.

24.19 Oncken, August. 1899. "New Tendencies in German Economics." **Economic Journal** 9 (September): 462-69.

24.20 Parrish, John B. 1967. "Rise of Economics As an Academic Discipline: The Formative Years to 1900." **Southern Economic Journal** 34, No. 1 (July): 1-16.

24.21 Passmore, John. 1974. "The Poverty of Historicism Revisited." **History and Theory,** Beiheft 14: **Essays on Historicism** 14, No. 4: 30-47.

24.22 Popper, Sir Karl. 1972 (1963). **Conjectures and Refutations,** 4th ed. London: Routledge and Kegan Paul, chap. 16.

24.23 Popper, Sir Karl. 1966 (1962). **The Open Society,** 5th rev. ed. 2 vols. Princeton: Princeton University Press.

24.24 Popper, Sir Karl. 1960 (1957). **The Poverty of Historicism,** 2nd ed. London: Routledge and Kegan Paul; Originally published in 3 parts in **Economica** N.S.:

Part I: May 1944 (11): 86-103
Part II: August 1944 (11): 119-37
Part III: May 1945 (12): 69-89.

24.25 Rashid, Salim. 1979. "Richard Jones and Baconian Historicism at Cambridge." **Journal of Economic Issues** 13, No. 1 (March): 159-73.

24.26 Redlich, Fritz. 1970. "Arthur Spiethoff on Economic Styles." **Journal of Economic History** 30, No. 3 (September): 640-52.

24.27 Rogin, Leo. 1933. "Werner Sombart and the 'Natural Science Method' in Economics." **Journal of Political Economy** 41 (April): 222-36.

24.28 Rothaker, Erich. 1960. "Das Wort 'Historicismus.'" **Zeitschrift für deutsche Wortforschung** 16: 3-6.

24.29 Rowe, Leo S. 1890. "Instruction in Public Law and Political Economy in German Universities." **Annals of the American Academy of Political and Social Science** (July): 78-102.

24.30 Seager, Henry M. 1893. "Economics at Berlin and Vienna." **Journal of Political Economy** 1 (March): 236-62.

24.31 Suchting, W.A. 1972. "Marx, Popper, and 'Historicism'." **Inquiry** 15: 235-66.

24.32 Urbach, Peter. 1978. "Is Any of Popper's Arguments Against Historicism Valid?" **British Journal for the Philosophy of Science** 29: 117-30.

24.33 White, Morton G. 1947. "The Revolt Against Formalism in American Social Thought of the Twentieth Century." **Journal of the History of Ideas** 8, No. 2 (April): 131-52.

24.34 Wickett, S. M. 1898. "Political Economy at German Universities." **Economic Journal** 8 (March): 146-50.

24.35 Wilkins, Burleigh Taylor. 1978. **Has History Any Meaning? A Critique of Popper's Philosophy of History.** Hassocks: Harvester Press.

(For further references see **History of Theory**'s "Bibliography of Works in the Philosophy of History," **Beiheft** 1, 3, 10, 12, 13, 18, and 23.)

***

25

Miscellaneous Works on Economic Methodology

In this section, the books have been annotated and hence the only additional point to make on the books is that numerous works are classics or near classics. The fact that they appeared before 1960 does not make them obsolete.

In § 25.2 all of the articles which did not find entry into any other section in part I or II of the bibliography have been collected. That the works fall under "miscellaneous" does not indicate their unimportance. Quite to the contrary, one can find here works from Boland, Buchanan, Caldwell, T.W. Hutchison, Coats, Hahn, Hall, Hicks, J.M. Keynes, Koopmans, Leijonhufvud, Leontief, Malinvaud, Marshall, Pareto, and Joan Robinson. The works are simply intractable from the standpoint of the organization here. Quite a few works deal with the question: Is economics a science? The answer to this question often defies easy classification.

In this section one also finds the near Austrians and the economists whose work is compatible with Austrian economics. See, for example, Shackle and the works on Shackle by Akerman, Coddington (1975), Earl and Kay; Robbins and works on Robbins by Aslanbeigui, Parsons, Peston, Piron, Scoon, and Souter; Frank Knight; Littlechild; and Loasby.

The two classical economists whose works have received considerable attention for methodological reasons are Adam Smith and J.S. Mill. Bitterman, Boulding (1971(a)), Hutchison (1976), Recktenwald, and Thompson discuss Smith's philosophy of science. Adam Smith's 1967 (ca. 1750) is the place where he develops his philosophy of science. De Marchi (1986), Ekelund and Olsen, Leary, Losee, and Whitaker treat Mill's philosophy.

***

25.1 Books Published Before 1960:

25.1.1 Cairnes, J.E. 1965 (1888). **The Character and
Logical Method of Political Economy**, 2nd ed. London:
Macmillan and Co.

> This work examines the methods of political economy.
> In this edition Cairnes considers Jevon's view that
> mathematics should be used in economics and rejects
> it. This work is divided into 7 "lectures":
> introduction; on the mental and physical premises of
> political economy; and of the logical character of
> the doctrines thence deduced; on the logical method
> of political economy; on the logical method of
> political economy continued; on the solution of an
> economic problem, and of the degree of perfection of
> which it is susceptible; of the place and purpose of
> definition in political economy; of the Malthusian
> doctrine of population; of the theory of rent.

25.1.2 Eisermann, Gottfried. 1956. **Die Grundlagen des
Historismus in der deutschen Nationalökonomie.** Stuttgart:
Ferdinand Enke Verlag.

> Eisermann discusses the German historical school:
> its political, economic, social, and intellectual
> roots; Müller and List; Roscher, Hildebrand, and
> Knies (i.e., the old historical school). (In German)

25.1.3 Eucken, Walter. 1965 (1940). **Die Grundlagen der
Nationalökonomie**, 8th ed. Berlin: Springer.

> Although in the introduction to this work Eucken
> states that the book is not of a methodological
> nature (p. ix), the work does treat traditional
> methodological problems. The work centers on
> developing a realistic economics. (In German)

25.1.4 Florence, Philip Sargant. 1927. **Economics and Human
Behavior: A Rejoinder to Social Psychologists.** London:
Kegan Paul, Trench, Trubner & Co. Ltd.

> This little book is about relations between rival
> theories of human behavior. The author defends
> economic theory against social psychologists'
> criticisms. Florence summarizes the arguments of the
> social psychologists against economics and attempts
> to refute these arguments. He believes, however, that
> the Benthamite hedonist foundations of economics are
> too dogmatic; economic theories should be worded
> independently of utilitarian views.

25.1.5 Fraser, Lindley M. 1937. **Economic Thought and
Language: A Critique of Some Fundamental Economic Concepts.**
London: A & C Black.

Fraser sets out to assist students of economics in thinking clearly and logically about economics. The terminology economists use is inaccurate and confusing. Many of economists' disagreements are of a terminological nature. The work hopes to clear up language problems. The definitions of economics, economic laws, value, utility, cost, theories of value, commodity, market, money, supply and demand, production and consumption, factor of production, land and labour, capital, enterprise, income, saving and investment, and theories of distribution are discussed.

25.1.6   *Hayek, F.A. 1976 (Rpt. of 1949). **Individualism and Economic Order**. London and Henley: Routledge and Kegan Paul.

This is a collection of previously published articles on aspects of economics. Included are his essays on "Economics and Knowledge," "The Facts of the Social Sciences," "The Use of Knowledge in Society," and other essays.

25.1.7 Higgins, Benjamin. 1951. **What Do Economists Know? Six Lectures on Economics in the Crisis of Democracy**. Victoria/London & NY: Melbourne University Press/Cambridge University Press.

As the title indicates, this work consists of six essays. The first of these asks "What Do Economists Know?" The remaining essays deal with dissension among economists, economic policy, social conflict and economics, and "ethics, politics, and the crisis of democracy."

25.1.8 Kaufmann, Felix. 1958 (1944). **Methodology of the Social Sciences**. NY: Humanities Press.

This work is in many ways a classic. Although the title refers to the social sciences, Kaufmann uses economics as an example, and deals with methodological problems faced by economists. Kaufmann emigrated from Vienna to the U.S. and was a member of the Vienna Circle. (The Viennese influence can be seen in this work.) Part I is devoted to general methodology and part II to methodological issues in social social (i.e., relationship to natural science, behaviorism, physical and social laws, objectivity, value, etc.).

25.1.9   *Koopmans, Tjalling C. 1957. **Three Essays on the State of Economic Science**. NY: McGraw-Hill.

These three essays emphasize formal model construction in theory and in empirical research. The

3 essays are on allocation of resources and the price
system, the construction of economic knowledge, and
the interaction of tools and problems in economics.
This work is a classic.

25.1.10 Knight, Frank. 1956. **On the History and Method of
Economics**. Chicago: University of Chicago Press.

This is a collection of Knight's works on history
and method of economics. Part III deals with
methodological themes: on social science, causation,
truth in economics, statics and dynamics, the
business cycle, and on science.

25.1.11 Menger, Carl. 1968–1970. **Gesammelte Werke**. Ed. and
with an introduction by F.A. Hayek, 2nd ed., 4 Vols.
Tübingen: J.C.B. Mohr.

Vol. II: **Untersuchungen über die Methode der
Sozialwissenschaften und der politischen Ökonomie
insbesondere**. 1969 (1883); Trans. by Francis J. Nock
as **Investigations into the Method of the Social
Sciences with Special Reference to Economics**. 1985.
(rpt. of 1963). With a new introduction by Lawrence
H. White. Ed. by Louis Schneider. NY/London: New York
University Press. (Originally published in English as
Problems of Economics and Sociology, 1963)

Menger's second work, this book is devoted to
investigating the methodological mistakes of the
German historical school, economics as theoretic
science, self-interest, atomism, the historical
aspects of economics, the organic analogy,
contrasts and similarities between the social and
natural sciences. This work is a classic.

Vol. III: **Kleinere Schriften zur Methode und
Geschichte der Volkswirtschaftslehre**. 1970
(1884–1915).

This is a collection of works written between 1884
and 1915. The most famous is his "Die Irrtümer des
Historismus in der Nationalökonomie," which is a
polemic against the German historical school. (In
German)

25.1.12 Mill, John Stuart. 1974 (1874). **Essays on Some
Unsettled Questions of Political Economy**, 2nd ed. Clifton,
NY: Augustus M. Kelley; Essay V: "On the Definition of
Political Economy; and on the Method of Investigation
proper to it" (1836).

This essay is one of the earliest discussions of
methodology of economics and it remains one of the
best. Mill believes the premises of economics are
empirically well-supported and its conclusions follow

deductively from its premises. But it is nonetheless a science of "tendencies" and is thus "hypothetical." This is a classic.

25.1.13 Mill, John Stuart. 1965 (1843). **A System of Logic Ratiocinative and Inductive Being a Connected View of the Principles of Evidence and the Methods of Scientific Investigation.** Vol. VII of the **Collected Works of John Stuart Mill.** Ed. by J.M. Robson and R.F. McRae. Toronto/London: University of Toronto Press/Routledge and Kegan Paul.

This is Mill's principal philosophical work. Deduction, induction, the neutral nature of logic, fallacies, and the logic of the moral sciences are discussed. Chapters VI to X of Book VI, "On the Logic of the Moral Sciences," discuss methodology of the social sciences. This is a classic.

25.1.14 Morgenstern, Oskar. 1934. **Die Grenzen der Wirtschaftspolitik.** Vienna: Julius Springer Verlag. Trans. by Vera Smith as **The Limits of Economics.** London: W. Hodge and Co., 1937.

This work focuses on the problems of applying economic theory, especially the problem presented by political factors.

25.1.15 Morgenstern, Oskar. 1928. **Wirtschaftsprognose, eine Untersuchung ihrer Voraussetzungen und Möglichkeiten.** Vienna: Julius Springer.

Morgenstern discusses prediction. He treats business cycle theory and prediction, the effects and uses of prediction, possibilities for prediction. Morgenstern's view that economic prediction is impossible touched off a great controversy in the literature. (In German)

25.1.16 Mukerjee, Radhakamal. 1925. **Borderlands of Economics.** London: George Allen and Unwin.

This work is a series of lectures which explore the borders of economics. The author hopes to open up new vistas for further research.

25.1.17 *Myrdal, Gunnar. 1958. **Value in Social Theory: A Selection of Essays on Methodology.** Ed. by Paul Streeten. London: Routledge and Kegan Paul.

In this work Myrdal discusses value premises in science, the relation between social theory and social policy, the black problem, valuations and beliefs, valuations and facts, and ends and means in political economy.

25.1.18 *Myrdal, Gunnar. 1953. **The Political Element in the Development of Economic Theory**. Trans. Paul Streeten. London: Routledge and Kegan. (Originally in Swedish, ca. 1929).

> The purpose of this book is to give the reader an historical and critical account of the role politics plays in economic theory. He discusses the ideological background, the classical theory of value, economic liberalism, neoclassical value theory, 'social housekeeping' and social value, public finance theory, and the role of economics in politics. There is an appendix by Paul Streeten which puts the controversies in modern perspective.

25.1.19 Neurath, Otto. 1970 (1944). **Foundations of the Social Sciences**. Vol. II, No. 1 of the **Foundations of the Unity of Science**. Chicago: University of Chicago Press.

> Written from a member of the Vienna Circle, this work is a reminder of how young the social sciences are. Neurath, an economist, treats fundamental methodological problems of economics: the aggregation problem, causality, ceteris paribus, corroboration of hypotheses, unpredictability, empiricism, social engineering, argument in social science, decision, and human action.

25.1.20 Papandreou, Andreas George. 1958. **Economics As a Science**. Chicago: Lippincott.

> Papandreou, Greece's Harvard-educated head of state, examines the character of economics as a science, explores its foundations from a logical point of view, and spells out its limitations. Comparative statics is the focus of his study. He considers deductive systems, the concept of calculus, set theory, functions, structure, generic structures, models versus theories, and empirical relevance.

25.1.21 Schoeffler, Sidney. 1955. **The Failures of Economics: A Diagnostic Study**. Cambridge, Mass.: Harvard University Press.

> The first four sections of this work discuss methodology and methodological problems of economics. The last sections of the work are devoted to case studies. An interesting aspect of this work is that Schoeffler discusses the work of some of economics' most prominent members straightforwardly. The case studies deal with micro- and macroeconomic topics, with econometric modelling and prediction.

25.1.22 Schöpf, Anton. 1966. **Das Prognoseproblem in der Nationalökonomie. Versuch einer Gesamtbetrachtung**. Vol. 2 of **Beiträge zur ganzheitlichen Wirtschafts- und**

Gesellschaftslehre. Berlin: Duncker & Humblot.

> This wonderful little book, unfortunately not translated from German, introduces the reader to the history of prediction in science and then concentrates on the problem of prediction in economics. Discussed are theories, methods, and limits of prediction and the basis of prediction for policy. Schöpf really covers the literature and provides the reader with a lengthy bibliography on the subject.

25.1.23 Schumpeter, Joseph A. 1954. **History of Economic Analysis.** NY: Oxford University Press.

> Part I of Schumpeter's **magnum opus** (pp. 3–50) is one source of his mature methodology. He discusses the history of economics, economics' scientific status, techniques of analysis, developments in neighboring disciplines, and the sociology of economics. It is here that he discusses "vision" as the source of scientific discovery in economics.

25.1.24 Schumpeter, Joseph. 1970 rpt. of 1908. **Das Wesen und der Hauptinhalt der theoretischen Nationalökonomie.** Berlin: Duncker und Humblot.

> He compares economics with other sciences and discusses economics' direction. Then he analyzes the foundations of economics, exchange, methodological individualism, value, static equilibrium, distribution theory, "exact" economics (laws), the biological analogy, sister disciplines, the limits of economics, reforms in economics. (In German)

25.1.25 Senior, Nassau W. 1965 rpt. of 1836. **An Outline of the Science of Political Economy.** NY: Augustus M. Kelley.

> Senior attempts to narrow "political economy" to the "Science which treats of the Nature, the Production, and the Distribution of Wealth." He attempts to separate political economy from other disciplines and to adopt a particular vocabulary suitable to an autonomous discipline.

25.1.26 Shackle, G.L.S. 1968 (rpt. of 1955). **Uncertainty in Economics and Other Reflections.** Cambridge: Cambridge University Press.

> This is a collection of essays on the nature and effects of uncertain expectation. Part I focuses on expectation and uncertainty, part II on interest rates, part III on investment and employment, and part IV on the philosophy of economics.

25.1.27 von Mises, Ludwig. 1949. **Human Action. A Treatise on Economics.** New Haven, CN: Yale University Press.

This work places economic problems within the broader framework of action. Part I deals with human action, part II with action within the framework of society, part III with economic calculation, part IV with catallactics, part V with social cooperation without a market, part VI with the hampered market economy, and part VII with the place of economics in society.

25.1.28 von Wieser, Friedrich Freiherr von. 1884. **Über den Ursprung und die Hauptgesetze des wirtschaftschaftlichen Werthes.** Wien: Alfred Hölder, Abschnitt 1, "Die wissenschaftliche Bedeutung der Sprachbegriffe," pp. 1–10.

The primary goal of this work is to explore value theory (by further developing Carl Menger's theory of value). The first chapter, however, is devoted to the methodology of economics. Von Wieser urges economists to follow the natural sciences more closely.

25.1.29 Weisskopf, Walter. 1955. **The Psychology of Economics.** London: Routledge and Kegan Paul.

This is a study of the psychology and philosophy of economic thought. Weisskopf does not try to debunk economics as unscientific, but instead tries to show that economics has an ethical and fiduciary foundation. He discusses classical value theory and Smith, Ricardo, Marx, and Marshall. The last section deals with the disintegration of economic rationalism.

***

25.2 Articles:

25.2.1 Ackermann, Robert. 1983. "Methodology and Economics." **Philosophical Forum** 14, Nos. 3–4 (Spring–Summer): 389–402.

25.2.2 Akerman, Johan. 1958. "Professor Shackle on Economic Methodology." **Kyklos** 11, No. 3: 341–58.

25.2.3 Albert, Hans. 1973. "Der Gesetzesbegriff im ökonomischen Denken." **Verein für Socialpolitik: Macht und ökonomishes Gesetz.** Berlin: Duncker & Humblot, 1973, pp. 129–61.

25.2.4 *Allais, Maurice. 1968. "L'Economique en tant que science." **Revue d'économie politique** 78, N° 1 (January–February): 5–30; Rpt. as No. 26 of the **Etudes et travaux de l'institute universitaire des hautes études internationales.** Genéve, 1968.

25.2.5   Altar,   M.   and   R.   Stroe.   1982.   "The   National
Wealth--A   Cybernetic   System."   **Economic   Computation   and
Economic   Cybernetic   Studies   and   Research** 16, No. 4: 35-52.

25.2.6   Archibald,   G.C.   1979.   "Method   and   Appraisal   in
Economics."   **Philosophy   of   the   Social   Sciences** 9, No. 3
(September): 304-15.

25.2.7   Archibald,   G.C.,   et   al.   1963.   "Problems   of
Methodology: Discussion."   **American   Economic   Association
Papers   and   Proceedings** 53 (May): 227-36.

25.2.8   *Arrow,   Kenneth   J.   1978.   "The   Future   and   the
Present   in   Economic   Life."   **Economic   Inquiry** 16, No. 2
(April): 157-69.

25.2.9   Ashley,   W.J.   1907.   "The   Present   Position   of
Political   Economy."   **Economic   Journal** 17 (December): 467-89.

25.2.10   Aslanbeigui,   Nahid.   1987.   "Some   Inconsistencies   in
Lionel   Robbin's   Methodology."   **Review   of   Social   Economy** 45,
No. 3 (December): 325-35.

25.2.11   Bartoli,   Pr   H.   1986.   "Au-dela   des   confusions:
propositions   heretiques."   **Economies   et   sociétés** 20, No. 4:
3-56.

25.2.12   Bastable,   C.F.   1894.   "A   Comparison   Between   the
Position   of   Economic   Science   in   1860   and   1894."   Report   of
the   British   Association   for   the   Advancement   of   Science.
Journal   of   the   Royal   Statistical   Society (December); Rpt. in
R.L.   Smyth,   ed.   **Essays   in   Economic   Method.** London: Gerald
Duckworth and Co., 1962, pp. 126-43.

25.2.13   Becker,   William   E.   1987.   "'Measurement'   Or   Finding
Things   Out   in   Economics: A   Comment."   **Journal   of   Economic
Education** 18, No. 2 (Spring): 208-12.

25.2.14   Ben-David,   Joseph.   1975.   "Innovations   and   Their
Recognition   in   Social   Science."   **History   of   Political   Economy**
7, No. 4 (Winter): 434-55.

25.2.15   Bergmann,   Barbara   R.   1987.   "'Measurement'   Or
Finding   Things   Out   in   Economics."   **Journal   of   Economic
Education** 18, No. 2 (Spring): 191-201.

25.2.16   Beveridge,   Sir   William.   1921.   "Economics   As   a
Liberal   Education."   **Economica** 1 (January): 2-19.

25.2.17   Bittermann,   Henry   J.   1940.   "Adam   Smith's   Empiricism
and   the   Law   of   Nature.   Parts   I   and   II."   **Journal   of   Political
Economy** 48 (August): 487-520 and 48 (October): 703-34.

25.2.18   Black,   Duncan.   1950.   "The   Unity   of   Political   and
Economic   Science."   **Economic   Journal** 60 (September): 506-14.

25.2.19 Black, R.D. Collison. 1983. "The Present Position and Prospects of Political Economy." In A.W. Coats. **Methodological Controversy in Economics: Historical Essays in Honor of T.W. Hutchison.** Greenwich, CT: Jai Press, 1983, pp. 55-70.

25.2.20 Bliss, Christopher. 1986. "Progress and Anti-Progress in Economic Science." In Mauro Baranzini and Roberto Scazzieri, eds. **Foundations of Economics.** Oxford: Basil Blackwell, 1986, pp. 363-76.

25.2.21 Boddy, Francis M. 1951. "Straight Thinking Versus Inductive Research in the Solution of Economic Problems." **American Economic Association Papers and Proceedings** 41, No. 2 (May): 119-23.

25.2.22 Boland, Lawrence A. 1985. "Reflections on Blaug's **Methodology of Economics:** Suggestions for a Revised Edition." **Eastern Economic Journal** 11, No. 4 (October-December): 450-54.

25.2.23 Boland, Lawrence A. 1983. "On the Best Strategy for Doing Philosophy of Economics." **British Journal for the Philosophy of Science** 34 (December): 387-93.

25.2.24 Boland, Lawrence A. 1982. "Difficulties with the Element of Time and the 'Principles' of Economics Or Some Lies My Teachers Told Me." **Eastern Economic Journal** 8, No. 1 (January): 47-58.

25.2.25 Boland, Lawrence A. 1981. "Satisficing in Methodology: A Reply to Fels." **Journal of Economic Literature** 19, No. 1 (March): 84-86.

25.2.26 Boland, Lawrence A. 1971. "Discussion: Methodology As an Exercise in Economic Analysis." **Philosophy of Science** 38 (March): 105-117.

25.2.27 Boland, Lawrence. 1970. "Axiomatic Analysis and Economic Understanding." **Australian Economic Papers** 9, No. 14 (June): 62-75.

25.2.28 Bonar, James. 1898. "Old Lights and New in Economic Study." **Economic Journal** 8 (December): 433-53.

25.2.29 Bordo, Michael David. 1975. "John E. Cairnes on the Effects of the Australian Gold Discoveries, 1851-73: An Early Application of the Methodology of Positive Economics." **History of Political Economy** 7, No. 3 (Fall): 337-59.

25.2.30 Bordo, Michael David and Daniel Landau. 1986. "Advocacy and Neo-Classical Economics." **Eastern Economic Journal** 12, No. 2 (April-June): 4-102.

25.2.31 Boucke, O. Fred. 1922. "A Unique Situation in Economic Theory." **American Economic Review** 12 (December):

598-605.

25.2.32 Boulding, Kenneth E. 1971(a). "After Samuelson, Who Needs Adam Smith?" **History of Political Economy** 3, No. 2 (Fall): 225-37.

25.2.33 Boulding, Kenneth E. 1971(b). "The Misallocation of Intellectual Resources in Economics." In Irving Louis Horowitz, ed. **The Use and Abuse of Social Science.** New Brunswick, N.J.: Transaction, 1971, pp. 34-51.

25.2.34 Boulding, Kenneth E. 1967. "The Legitimacy of Economics." **Western Economic Journal** 5 (September): 299-307.

25.2.35 Boulding, Kenneth E. 1966. "The Verifiability of Economic Images." In Sherman Roy Krupp. **The Structure of Economic Science.** Englewood Cliffs: Prentice-Hall, 1966, pp. 129-41.

25.2.36 Boulding, Kenneth E. 1956. "Economics and the Behavioral Sciences: A Desert Frontier?" **Diogenes** 15 (Fall): 1-14.

25.2.37 Brandt, Richard B. 1966. "The Concept of Welfare." In Sherman Roy Krupp, ed. **The Structure of Economic Science.** Englewood Cliffs: Prentice-Hall, 1966, pp. 257-76.

25.2.38 Brennan, Timothy J. 1980. "Toward a Humanistic Reconstruction of Economic Science: Comment." **Journal of Economic Issues** 14, No. 4 (December): 1019-25.

25.2.39 Bronfenbrenner, Martin. 1966(a). "A Middlebrow Introduction to Economic Methodology." In Sherman Roy Krupp, ed. **The Structure of Economic Science.** Englewood Cliffs: Prentice-Hall, 1966, pp. 5-24.

25.2.40 Bronfenbrenner, Martin. 1966(b). "Trends, Cycles, and Fads in Economic Writing." **American Economic Association Papers and Proceedings** 56, No. 2 (May): 538-52.

25.2.41 *Buchanan, James M. 1971. "Is Economics the Science of Choice?" In Erich Streissler, ed. 1970/1969. **Roads to Freedom.** London: Routledge and Kegan Paul, 1971, pp. 47-64.

25.2.42 *Buchanan, James M. 1966. "Economics and Its Scientific Neighbors." In Sherman Roy Krupp, ed. **The Structure of Economic Science.** Englewood Cliffs: Prentice-Hall, 1966, pp. 165-83.

25.2.43 *Buchanan, James M. 1964. "What Should Economists Do?" **Southern Economic Journal** 30, No. 3 (January): 213-22.

25.2.44 Bye, Raymond T. 1957. "Lament for Economics." **Review of Economics and Statistics** 39 (May): 210.

25.2.45 Caldwell, Bruce J. 1985. "Some Reflections on

Beyond Positivism." **Journal of Economic Issues** 19, No. 1 (March): 187-94.

25.2.46   Caldwell, Bruce J. 1980. "Positivist Philosophy of Science and the Methodology of Economics." **Journal of Economics** 14, No. 1 (March): 53-76.

25.2.47   Caldwell, Bruce J. 1979. "Two Suggestions for the Improvement of Methodological Work in Economics." **American Economist** 23 (Fall): 56-61.

25.2.48   Campbell, William F. 1983. "Pericles and the Sophistication of Economics." **History of Political Economy** 15, No. 1 (Spring): 122-35.

25.2.49   Canaan, Edwin. 1902. "The Practical Utility of Economic Science." **Economic Journal** 12 (December): 459-471.

25.2.50   Canterbery, E. Ray and Robert J. Burkhardt. 1983. "What Do We Mean by Asking Whether Economics Is a Science?" In Alfred S. Eichner, ed. **Why Economics Is Not a Science**. London: Macmillan, 1983, pp. 15-40.

25.2.51   Carver, T.N. 1911. "The Meaning of Social Science." **Journal of Political Economy** 19 (February): 128-31.

25.2.52   Cheung, Steven N.S. 1973. "The Fable of the Bees: An Economic Investigation." **Journal of Law and Economics** 16, No. 1 (April): 11-33.

25.2.53   Churchman, C.W. 1966. "On the Intercomparison of Utilities." In Sherman Roy Krupp, ed. **The Structure of Economic Science**. Englewood Cliffs: Prentice-Hall, 1966, pp. 243-56.

25.2.54   Coats, A.W. 1983(a). "Half a Century of Methodological Controversy in Economics: As Reflected in the Writings of T.W. Hutchison." In his **Methodological Controversy in Economics: Historical Essays in Honor of T.W. Hutchison**. Greenwich, CT: Jai Press.

25.2.55   Coats, A.W. 1983(b). "The Revival of Subjectivism in Economics." In Jack Wiseman, ed. **Beyond Positive Economics?** London: The British Association for the Advancement of Science, 1983, pp. 87-103.

25.2.56   Coats, A.W. 1982. "The Methodology of Economics: Some Recent Contributions." **Kyklos** 35: 310-21.

25.2.57   Coats, A.W. 1980. "The Culture and the Economists: Some Reflections on Anglo-American Differences." **History of Political Economy** 12, No. 4 (Winter): 588-609.

25.2.58   Coats, A.W. 1967. "Sociological Aspects of British Economic Thought." **Journal of Political Economy** 75, No. 5 (October): 706-29.

25.2.59 Coats, A.W. 1963. "The Origins of the 'Chicago School(s).'" **Journal of Political Economy** 71 (October): 487-93.

25.2.60 Coats, A.W. 1960. "The First Two Decades of the American Economic Association." **American Economic Review** 50, No. 4 (September): 555-74.

25.2.61 Coddington, Alan. 1983. "Economists and Policy." In William Marr and Baldev Raj, eds. **How Economists Explain: A Reader in Methodology.** Lanham, MD: University Press of America, 1983, pp. 229-38.

25.2.62 Coddington, Alan. 1975. "Creaking Semaphore and Beyond: A Consideration of Shackle's **'Epistemics and Economics'.**" **British Journal for the Philosophy of Science** 26: 151-63.

25.2.63 Colander, David and Arjo Klamer. 1987. "The Making of an Economist." **Journal of Economic Perspectives** 1, No. 2 (Fall): 95-111.

25.2.64 Coleman, James S. 1984. "Introducing Social Structure into Economic Analysis." **American Economic Association Papers and Proceedings** 74, No. 2 (May): 84-88.

25.2.65 Collard, D.A. 1964. "Swans, Falling Bodies, and Five-Legged Dogs." **Quarterly Journal of Economics** 78 (November): 645-46.

25.2.66 Copeland, Morris A. 1931. "Economic Theory and the Natural Science Point of View." **American Economic Review** 21 (March): 67-79.

25.2.67 Cropsey, Joseph. 1956. "What Is Welfare Economics?" **Ethics** 65 (January): 209-13.

25.2.68 Cross, Rod. 1984. "Methodology in Economics" (review article). **Scottish Journal of Political Economy** 31, No. 1 (February): 100-10.

25.2.69 Crossland, Philip P. and Iran Weinel. 1983. "Modern Empiricism and Quantum Leap Theorizing in Economics: A Comment." **Journal of Economic Issues** 17, No. 4 (December): 1129-38.

25.2.70 Cumming, Robert D. 1981. "Giving Back Words: Things, Money, Persons." **Social Research** 48, No. 2 (Summer): 227-59.

25.2.71 Cummings, John. 1909. "The Conversion of the Economist." **Journal of Political Economy** 17 (April): 206-19.

25.2.72 Cunningham, W. 1892. "The Relativity of Economic Doctrine." **Economic Journal** 2 (March): 1-16.

25.2.73 Cunningham, W. 1889. "The Comtist Criticism of Economic Science." Report of the British Association for the Advancement of Science. In R.L. Smyth, ed. **Essays in Economic Method**. London: Gerald Duckworth and Co., 1962, pp. 98-111.

25.2.74 Davenport, H.J., et al. 1916. "Tendencies in Economic Theory: Discussion." **American Economic Association Papers and Proceedings** 6 (March): 162-69.

25.2.75 Davidson, Paul. 1980. "Post Keynesian Economics." **The Public Interest** (Special Issue: The Crisis in Economic Theory): 151-73.

25.2.76 Davis, J.B. 1987. "Three Principles of Post Keynesian Methodology." **Journal of Post Keynesian Economics** 9, No. 4 (Summer): 552-64.

25.2.77 De Marchi, Neil. 1986. "Discussion: Mill's Unrevised Philosophy of Economics: A Comment on Hausman." **Philosophy of Science** 53 (March): 89-100.

25.2.78 De Marchi, Neil. 1983. "The Case for James Mill." In A.W. Coats. **Methodological Controversy in Economics: Historical Essays in Honor of T.W. Hutchison**. Greenwich, CT: Jai Press, 1983, pp. 155-84.

25.2.79 De Marchi, Neil. 1976. "Anomaly and the Development of Economics: the Case of the Leontief Paradox." In Spiro T. Latsis, ed. **Method and Appraisal in Economics**. Cambridge: Cambridge University Press, 1976, pp. 109-27.

25.2.80 De Marchi, Neil. 1973. "The Noxious Influence: A Correction of Jevon's Charge." **Journal of Law and Economics** 16, No. 1 (April): 179-90.

25.2.81 Dennis, Ken. 1987. "Boland on Boland: A Further Rebuttal." **Journal of Economic Issues** 21, No. 1 (March): 388-93.

25.2.82 Dennis, Ken. 1982. "Economic Theory and the Problem of Translation, Part I." **Journal of Economic Issues** 16, No. 3 (September): 691-712.

25.2.83 Dorfman, Robert. 1958. "Economic Science" (Review of Koopman's **Three Essays on the State of Economic Science**). **Kyklos** 11, No. 4: 534-38.

25.2.84 Dow, Sheila C. 1983. "Schools of Thought in Macroeconomics: The Method Is the Message." **Australian Economic Papers** 22, No. 40 (June): 30-47.

25.2.85 Dow, Sheila C. 1982-83. "Substantive Mountains and Methodological Molehills: A Rejoinder." **Journal of Post Keynesian Economics** 5 (Winter): 304-08.

25.2.86 Dow, Sheila C. 1981. "Weintraub and Wiles: The Methodological Basis of Policy Conflict." **Journal of Post Keynesian Economics** 3, No. 3 (Spring): 325-39.

25.2.87 Dow, Sheila C. and Peter E. Earl. 1984. "Methodology and Orthodox Monetary Policy." **Economie appliquée** 37, No. 1: 143-63.

25.2.88 Downey, E.H. 1910. "The Futility of Marginal Utility." **Journal of Political Economy** 18 (April): 253-68.

25.2.89 Drucker, Peter F. 1980. "Toward the Next Economics." **The Public Interest** (Special Issue: The Crisis in Economic Theory): 4-18.

25.2.90 Dugger, William M. 1983. "Two Twists in Economic Methodology: Positivism and Subjectivism." **American Journal of Economics and Sociology** 42, No. 1 (January): 75-91.

25.2.91 Dwyer, Larry. 1987. "Some Implications of a Pragmatist Conception of the Aims of Economic Enquiry." **International Journal of Social Economics** 14, No. 6: 22-35.

25.2.92 Dykema, Eugene R. 1986. "No View Without a Viewpoint: Gunnar Myrdal." **World Development** 14, No. 2 (February: Special Issue): 147-63.

25.2.93 Eagly, Robert V. 1974. "Contemporary Profile of Conventional Economists." **History of Political Economy** 6, No. 1: 76-91.

25.2.94 Earl, Peter E. 1983(a). A Behavioral Theory of Economists' Behavior." In Alfred S. Eichner, ed. **Why Economic Is Not Yet a Science**. London: Macmillan/Sharpe, 1983, pp. 90-125.

25.2.95 Earl, Peter E. 1983(b). "The Consumer in His/Her Social Setting: A Subjectivist View." In Jack Wiseman, ed. **Beyond Positive Economics?** London: The British Association for the Advancement of Science, 1983, pp. 176-91.

25.2.96 Earl, Peter E. and Neil M. Kay. 1985. "How Economists Can Accept Shackle's Critique on Economic Doctrines Without Arguing Themselves Out of Their Jobs." **Journal of Economic Studies** 12, No. 1/2: 34-48.

25.2.97 Eichner, Alfred S. 1986. "Can Economics Become a Science?" **Challenge** 29, No. 5 (November/December): 4-12.

25.2.98 Eichner, Alfred S. 1983. "Why Economics Is Not Yet a Science." **Journal of Economic Issues** 17, No. 2 (June): 507-20; and in his **Why Economics Is Not Yet a Science**. London: Macmillan/Sharpe, 1983, pp. 205-41.

25.2.99 Ekelund, Robert B., Jr. and Emile S. Olsen. 1973.

"Comte, Mill, Cairnes: The Positivist-Empiricist Interlude in Late Classical Economics." **Journal of Economic Issues** 7, No. 3 (September): 383-416.

25.2.100 Ely, Richard T. 1910. "Suggestions to Teachers of General Economics." **Journal of Political Economy** 18 (June): 437-40.

25.2.101 Engelhardt, Werner Wilhelm. 1983. "Zum Situations- und Problembezug von Entscheidungsmodellen bei Johann Heinrich von Thünen." **Zeitschrift für Wirtschafts- und Sozialwissenschaften** 103, No. 6: 561-88.

25.2.102 Eusepi, Giuseppe. 1987. "General Implications of Subjectivism and Dynamics in Buchanan's Works." **Economia Internazionale** 40, No. 1 (February): 55-66.

25.2.103 Fabian, Robert G. 1967. "An Empirical Principle for Deductive Theory in Economics." **Southern Economic Journal** 34 (July): 53-66.

25.2.104 Fach, Wolfgang. 1973. "Über einige Schwierigkeiten der neuen politischen Ökonomie: das Beispiel der Koalitionstheorie." **Zeitschrift für die gesamte Staatswissenschaft** 129, No. 2 (May): 347-74.

25.2.105 Fels, Rendigs. 1981. "Boland Ignores Simon: A Comment." **Journal of Economic Literature** 19 (March): 83-84.

25.2.106 Ferber, Robert and Werner Z. Hirsch. 1978. "Some Experimentation and Economic Policy: A Survey." **Journal of Economic Literature** 16, No. 4 (December): 1379-1414.

25.2.107 Fetter, Frank A. 1920. "Price Economics Versus Welfare Economics: Contemporary Opinion." **American Economic Review** 10 (December): 719-37.

25.2.108 Fisher, Irving, et al. 1921. "Traditional Economic Theory: Discussion." **American Economic Association Papers and Proceedings** 11 (March): 143-47.

25.2.109 Foley, Duncan. 1975. "Problems Vs. Conflicts: Economic Theory and Ideology." **American Economic Association Papers and Proceedings** 65, No. 2 (May): 231-36.

25.2.110 Fournaker, Lawrence E. 1958. "The Cambridge Didactic Style." **Journal of Political Economy** 66 (February): 65-73.

25.2.111 Frank, Lawrence K. 1924. "The Emancipation of Economics." **American Economic Review** 14 (March): 17-38.

25.2.112 Georgescu-Roegen, Nicholas. 1981. "Methods in Economic Science: A Rejoinder." **Journal of Economic Issue** 15, No. 1: 188-93.

25.2.113 Georgescu-Roegen, Nicholas. 1979. "Methods in Economic Science." **Journal of Economic Issues** 13 (June): 317-28.

25.2.114 Gill, Flora. 1981. "Some Methodological Implications of the Marginal Revolution." **Australian Economic Papers** 20, No. 36 (June): 72-82.

25.2.115 Gilmore, Eugene Allen. 1917. "The Relation of Law and Economics" (with discussion by J.P. Hall and H. Oliphant). **Journal of Political Economy** 25 (January): 69-83.

25.2.116 Gnanadoss, B. 1985. "The Concept of Field in Economic Analysis." **Indian Economic Journal** 32, No. 4 (April-June): 75-79.

25.2.117 Gordon, Donald F. 1955. "Operational Propositions in Economic Theory." **Journal of Political Economy** 63 (April): 150-62.

25.2.118 Gorman, W.M. 1984. "Towards a Better Methodology?" In Peter Wiles and Guy Routh, eds. **Economics in Disarray.** Oxford: Basil Blackwell, 1984, pp. 260-88, and reply by Wiles, pp. 289-92.

25.2.119 Gramm, Warren S. 1975. "Chicago Economics: From Individualism True to Individualism False." **Journal of Economic Issues** 9, No. 4 (December): 753-75.

25.2.120 Grammp, William D. 1983. "An Episode in the History of Thought and Policy." In A.W. Coats. **Methodological Controversy in Economics: Historical Essays in Honor of T.W. Hutchison.** Greenwich, CT: Jai Press, 1983, pp. 137-54.

25.2.121 Green, Edward J. 1980. "On the Role of Fundamental Theory in Positive Economics." In Joseph C. Pitt, ed. **Philosophy in Economics.** Dordrecht: D. Reidel, 1981, pp. 5-15.

25.2.122 Gruchy, Allan G. and Fritz Machlup. 1952. "Issues in Methodology: Discussion." **American Economic Association Papers and Proceedings** 42, No. 2 (May): 67-73.

25.2.123 Grunberg, Emile. 1978. "'Complexity' and 'Open Systems' in Economic Discourse." **Journal of Economic Issues** 12, No. 3 (September): 541-60.

25.2.124 Hahn, Frank. 1982. "On Some Difficulties of the Utilitarian Economist." In Amartya Sen and Bernard Williams, eds. **Utilitarianism and Beyond.** Cambridge/Paris: Cambridge University Press/Editions de la maison des sciences de l'homme, 1982, pp. 187-98.

25.2.125 Haldane, R.B. 1905. "Modern Logicians and Economic Methods." **Economic Journal** 15 (December): 494-504.

25.2.126 Hall, Sir Robert. 1959. "Reflections on the Practical Application of Economics." **Economic Journal** 69 (December): 639-52.

25.2.127 Hamilton, David. 1984. "Economics: Science Or Legend?" **Journal of Economic Issues** 18 (June): 565-72.

25.2.128 Hamilton, Walton H. 1915. "Economic Theory and 'Social Reform'." **Journal of Political Economy** 23 (June): 562-84.

25.2.129 Hands, Douglas W. 1984(a). "The Role of Crucial Counter-Examples in the Growth of Economic Knowledge: Two Case Studies in the Recent History of Economic Thought." **History of Political Economy** 16, No. 1 (Spring): 59-67.

25.2.130 Hands, Douglas W. 1984(b). "What Economics Is Not: An Economist's Response to Rosenberg." **Philosophy of Science** 51, No. 3 (September): 495-503.

25.2.131 Harvey-Phillips, M.B. 1983. "T.R. Malthus on the 'Metaphysics of Political Economy': Ricardo's Critical Ally." In A.W. Coats. **Methodological Controversy in Economics: Historical Essays in Honor of T.W. Hutchison.** Greenwich, CT: Jai Press, 1983, pp. 185-210.

25.2.132 Hausman, Daniel M. 1985. "Classical Wage Theory and the Causal Complications of Explaining Distribution." In Joseph C. Pitt, ed. **Change and Progress in Modern Science.** Vol. 27 of **The University of Western Ontario Series in Philosophy of Science.** Dordrecht: Reidel, 1985, pp. 171-97.

25.2.133 Hausman, Daniel M. 1981. "John Stuart Mill's Philosophy of Economics." **Philosophy of Science** 48, No. 3 (September): 363-85.

25.2.134 Hawley, Frederick B. 1902. "A Positive Theory of Economics." **Quarterly Journal of Economics** 16: 233-64.

25.2.135 Hawtrey, R.G. 1946. "The Need for Faith." **Economic Journal** 56 (September): 351-65.

25.2.136 Hayden, F. Gregory. 1982(a). "Organzing Policy Research Through the Social Fabric Matrix: A Boolian Digraph Approach." **Journal of Economic Issues** 16, No. 4 (December): 1013-26.

25.2.137 Hayden, F. Gregory. 1982(b). "Social Fabric Matrix: From Perspective to Analytical Tool." **Journal of Economic Issues** 16, No. 3 (September): 637-62.

25.2.138 Henley, Andrew. 1987. "Economic Orthodoxy and the Free Market System: A Christian Critique." **International Journal of Social Economics** 14, No. 10: 56-66.

25.2.139 Hennings, Klaus H. 1986. "The Exchange Paradigm and the Theory of Production and Distribution." In Mauro Baranzini and Roberto Scazzieri, eds. **Foundations of Economics**. Oxford: Basil Blackwell, 1986, pp. 221-43.

25.2.140 Henry, John F. 1986. "On Economic Theory and the Question of Solvability." **Journal of Post Keynesian Economics** 8, No. 3 (Spring): 371-86.

25.2.141 Hey, John D. 1983. "Towards the Double Negative Economics." In Jack Wiseman, ed. **Beyond Positive Economics?** London: The British Association for the Advancement of Science, 1983, pp. 160-75.

25.2.142 Hicks, Sir John. 1986. "Is Economics a Science?" In Mauro Baranzini and Roberto Scazzieri, eds. **Foundations of Economics**. Oxford: Basil Blackwell.

25.2.143 *Hicks, Sir John. 1983. "A Discipline Not a Science." In his **Classics and Moderns**. Vol. III of his **Collected Essays on Economic Theory**. Oxford: Basil Blackwell, 1983, pp. 365-75.

25.2.144 *Hicks, Sir John. 1979. "The Formation of an Economist." **Banca Nazionale del Lavoro Quarterly Review** 32, 130: 195-204; Rpt. in his **Classics and Moderns**, Vol III. Oxford: Basil Blackwell, 1983, pp. 355-64.

25.2.145 Hildreth, Clifford. 1951. "Economic Theory, Statistics, and Economic Practice: Discussion." **American Economic Papers and Proceedings** 41, No. 2 (May): 124-26.

25.2.146 Hill, Lewis E. 1979. "The Metaphysical Preconceptions of the Economic Science." **Review of Social Economy** 37 (October): 189-97.

25.2.147 Hill, Lewis E. 1970. "Beyond Positive Economics." **American Journal of Economics and Sociology** 29, No. 3 (July): 329-34.

25.2.148 Hirsch, Abraham. 1985. "Review of Bruce Caldwell's **Beyond Positivism: Economic Methodology in the Twentieth Century**." **Journal of Economic Issues** 19, No. 1 (March): 175-85.

25.2.149 Hirsch, Abraham. 1978. "J.E. Cairnes' Methodology in Theory and Practice: A Note." **History of Political Economy** 10, No. 2: 322-28.

25.2.150 Hirsch, Abraham. 1976. "Ideological and Scientific Functions of the Neoclassical Theory of the Firm: Comment." **Journal of Economic Issues** 10, No. 2 (June): 324-27.

25.2.151 Hirsch, Abraham and Neil de Marchi. 1986. "Making a Case When Theory Is Unfalsifiable: Friedman's Monetary History." **Economics and Philosophy** 2, No. 1 (April): 1-21.

25.2.152 Hirsch, Abraham and Eva. 1975. "The Heterodox Methodology of Two Chicago Economists." **Journal of Economic Studies** 9 (December): 645-64.

25.2.153 Hirschmann, Albert O. 1985. "Against Parsimony: Three Easy Ways of Complicating Some Categories of Economic Discourse." **Economics and Philosophy** 1, No. 1 (April): 7-21; Rev. version of his 1984 work with the same title in **American Economic Association Papers and Proceedings** 74, No. 2 (May): 89-96.

25.2.154 Hollander, Jacob H. 1916. "Economic Theorizing and Scientific Progress." **American Economic Association Papers and Proceedings** 6 (March): 124-39.

25.2.155 Hollander, Samuel. 1983. "William Whewell and John Stuart Mill on the Methodology of Political Economy." **Studies in History and Philosophy of Science** 14, No. 2 (June): 127-68.

25.2.156 Hollander, Samuel. 1977. "Adam Smith and the Self-Interest Axiom." **Journal of Law and Economics** 20, No. 1 (April): 133-52.

25.2.157 Hood, William C. 1948. "Some Aspects of the Treatment of Time in Economic Theory." **Canadian Journal of Economics and Political Science** 14: 453-68.

25.2.158 Hooker, C.A. 1979. "Discussion Review: Hollis and Nell's **Rational Economic Man: A Philosophical Critique of Neo-Classical Economics.**" **Philosophy of Science** 46: 470-90.

25.2.159 Hoxie, Robert F. 1901. "On the Empirical Method of Economic Instruction." **Journal of Political Economy** 9 (September): 481-526.

25.2.160 Hoy, David Couzens. 1980. "Philosophy: An Assessment: Hermeneutics." **Social Research** 47, No. 4 (Winter): 649-71.

25.2.161 Hutchison, T.W. 1983. "From 'Dismal Science' to 'Positive Economics'--A Century-and-a-Half of Progress?" In Jack Wiseman, ed. **Beyond Positive Economics?** London: The British Association for the Advancement of Science, 1983, pp. 192-211.

25.2.162 Hutchison, T.W. 1979. "Die Natur- und die Sozialwissenschaften und die Entwicklung und Unterentwicklung der Ökonomik: Methodologische Vorschriften für weniger entwickelte Wissenschaften." In Hans Albert and Kurt H. Stapf, eds. **Theorie und Erfahrung.** Stuttgart: Klett, 1979, pp. 245-68.

25.2.163 Hutchison, T.W. 1976. "Adam Smith and the Wealth of Nations." **Journal of Law and Economics** 19, No. 3 (October): 507-28.

25.2.164 Hutchison, T.W. 1970. "Economic Thought and Policy: Generalizations and Ambiguities." In H. van der Wee, V.A. Vinogradov, and G.G. Kotovsky, eds. **International Congress on Economic History** (5th, 1970). The Hague: Mouton, 197-, pp. 119-33.

25.2.165 Hutchison, T.W. 1941. **"The Significance and Basic Postulates of Economic Theory**: A Reply to Professor Knight." **Journal of Political Economy** 49, No. 5 (October): 732-50.

25.2.166 Hutchison, T.W. 1937. "Theoretische Ökonomie als Sprachsystem." **Zeitschrift für Nationalökonomie** 8, No. 1: 78-90.

25.2.167 Ingram, J.K. 1878. "The Present Position and Prospects of Political Economy." Report of the British Association for the Advancement of Science; Rpt. in R.L. Smyth, ed. **Essays in Economic Method.** London: Gerald Duckworth and Co., pp. 41-72.

25.2.168 Jalladeau, Joel. 1975. "The Methodological Conversion of John Bates Clark." **History of Political Economy** 7, No. 2 (Summer): 209-26.

25.2.169 Jameson, Kenneth P. 1986. "Latin American Structuralism: A Methodological Perspective." **World Development** 14, No. 2 (February: Special Issue): 223-32.

25.2.170 Jefferson, Michael. 1983. "Economic Uncertainty and Business Decision-Making." In Jack Wiseman, ed. **Beyond Positive Economics?** London: The British Association for the Advancement of Science, 1983, pp. 122-59.

25.2.171 Jevons, W.S. 1870. "Economic Policy." Report of the British Association for the Advancement of Science. **Journal of the Royal Statistical Society** 33; Rpt. in R.L. Smyth, ed. **Essays in Economic Method.** London: Gerald Duckworth, 1962, pp. 25-40.

25.2.172 Johnson, Harry G. 1977. "The American Tradition in Economics." **Nebraska Journal of Economics** 16, No. 3 (Summer): 17-26.

25.2.173 Johnson, Harry G. 1973. "National Styles in Economic Research: The United States, the United Kingdom, Canada, and Various European Countries." **Daedalus** 102, No. 2 (Spring): 65-74.

25.2.174 Johnson, Harry G. 1968(a). "A Catarrh of Economists." **Encounter** 30 (May): 50-54.

25.2.175 Johnson, Harry G. 1968(b). "The Economic Approach to Social Questions." **Economica** 35, No. 137 (February): 1-21.

25.2.176 Johnson, L.E. 1983. "Economic Paradigms: A Missing Dimension." **Journal of Economic Issues** 17, No. 4 (December): 1097-1111.

25.2.177 Jones, Evan. 1977. "Positive Economics Or What?" **Economic Record** 3 (September): 350-63.

25.2.178 Juster, F. Thomas. 1974. "The Use of Surveys for Policy Research." **American Economic Review** 64, No. 2 (May): 355-64.

25.2.179 Kapp, E. William. 1970. "Environmental Disruption and Social Costs: A Challenge to Economics." **Kyklos** 23, No. 4: 833-48.

25.2.180 Katona, George. 1978. "Psychology and Economics: Discussion." **American Economic Association Papers and Proceedings** 68, No. 2 (May): 75-76.

25.2.181 Katouzian, Homa. 1983. "Towards the Progress of Economic Knowledge." Jack Wiseman, ed. **Beyond Positive Economics?** London: The British Association for the Advancement of Science, 1983, pp. 50-64.

25.2.182 Katouzian, Homa. 1974. "Scientific Method and Positive Economics." **Scottish Journal of Economics** 21, No. 3 (November): 279-86.

25.2.183 Kearl, J.R., et al. 1979. "What Economists Think." **American Economic Association Papers and Proceedings** 69, No. 2 (May): 28-37.

25.2.184 Keynes, John Maynard. 1972 (ca. 1930). "Economic Possibilities for Our Grandchildren." In his **Essays in Persuasion**. Vol. IX of **The Collected Writings of John Maynard Keynes**. London: Macmillan, 1972, pp. 321-32.

25.2.185 Klant, J.J. 1985. "The Slippery Transition." In Tony Lawson and Hashem Pesaran, eds. **Keynes' Economics**. Croom Helm, 1985, pp. 80-98.

25.2.186 Klant, J.J. 1982. "The Natural Order." Expanded and revised version of "Idealisatie: Idee en ideaal." In **Economie en ideaal**. Ed. by Gaay Fortman. Samson: Alphen aan de Rijn, 1982, pp. 1-47.

25.2.187 Klappholz, Kurt and Joseph Agassi. 1959. "Methodological Prescriptions in Economics." **Economica** 26, No. 101 (February): 60-74.

25.2.188 Klein, Daniel B. 1985. "Deductive Economic Methodology in the French Enlightenment: Condillac and Destutt de Tracy." **History of Political Economy** 17, No. 1 (Spring): 51-71.

25.2.189 Knight, Frank. 1956. **On the History and Method of**

Economics. Chicago: University of Chicago Press.

25.2.190 Knight, Frank. 1947. "Salvation by Science: the Gospel According to Professor Lundberg." **Journal of Political Economy** 55 (December): 537-52.

25.2.191 Knight, Frank. 1946. "Immutable Law in Economics: Its Reality and Limitations." **American Economic Papers and Proceedings** 36, No. 2 (May): 93-111.

25.2.192 Knight, Frank. 1941. "A Rejoinder." **Journal of Political Economy** 49 (October): 750-53.

25.2.193 Knight, Frank. 1940. "'What Is Truth' in Economics?" **Journal of Political Economy** 48, No. 1 (February): 1-32.

25.2.194 Knight, Frank. 1925. "Economic Psychology and the Value Problem." **Quarterly Journal of Economic** 39: 372-409.

25.2.195 Knight, Frank. 1924. "The Limitations of Scientific Method." In his **The Ethics of Competition and Other Essays.** Freeport, NY: Books for Libraries Press, 1969 (rpt. of 1935), pp. 04-47; Rpt. from Rexford G. Tugwell, ed. **The Trend of Economics.** F.S. Crofts and Co., 1924, pp. 229-67.

25.2.196 Koch, H. 1971. "Die theoretische Ökonomik als individual-analytische Handlungstheorie." **Zeitschrift für die gesamte Staatswissenschaft** 127, No. 4 (October): 585-743.

25.2.197 Koch, James V. 1972. "On 'A Critique of Positive Economics': Comment." **American Journal of Economics and Sociology** 31, No. 3 (July): 327-32.

25.2.198 *Koopmans, Tjalling C. 1979. "Economics Among the Sciences." **American Economic Review** 69, No. 1 (March): 1-13.

25.2.199 *Koopmans, Tjalling C. 1974. "Measurement Without Theory." **Review of Economic Statistics** 29 (August): 161-72.

25.2.200 Krupp, Sherman Roy. 1966. "Types of Controversy in Economics." In his **The Structure of Economic Science.** Englewood Cliffs: Prentice-Hall, 1966, pp. 39-52.

25.2.201 Krupp, Sherman Roy. 1963. "Analytical Economics and the Logic of External Effects." **American Economic Association Papers and Proceedings** 53, No. 2 (May): 220-26, with discussion, pp. 227-36.

25.2.202 Kunreuther, Howard and Paul Slovic. 1978. "Economics, Psychology, and Protective Behavior." **American Economic Association Papers and Proceedings** 68, No. 2

(May): 64-69.

25.2.203 Kuttner, Robert. 1985. "The Poverty of Economics."
The Atlantic Monthly 255, No. 2 (February): 74-84.

25.2.204 Latsis, Spiro. 1976. "The Limitations of
Single-Exit Models: Reply to Machlup." **British Journal for
the Philosophy of Science** 27: 51-60.

25.2.205 Latsis, Spiro. 1972. "Situational Determinism in
Economics." **British Journal for the Philosophy of Science**
23: 207-45.

25.2.206 Lawson, Tony. 1985. "Uncertainty and Economic
Analysis." **Economic Journal** 95, No. 380 (December): 909-27.

25.2.207 Leary, David. 1982. "The Fate and Influence of
John Stuart Mill's Proposed Science of Ethology." **Journal
of the History of Ideas** 43, No. 1 (January-March): 153-62.

25.2.208 Lee, Frederic. 1984. "Whatever Happened to the
Full-Cost Principle (USA)?" In Peter Wiles and Guy Routh,
eds. **Economics in Disarry.** Oxford: Basil Blackwell, 1984,
pp. 233-39.

25.2.209 Leijonhufvud, Axel. 1973. "Life Among the Econ."
Western Economic Journal 11 (September): 327-37.

25.2.210 *Leontief, Wassily W. 1958. "The State of Economic
Science" (Review of **Three Essays on the State of Economic
Science**). **Review of Economics and Statistics** 40, No. 2
(May): 103-106.

25.2.211 Lenk, Hans. 1975. "Wirklichkeitsnähe,
Erklärungskraft und theoretische Fundierung von
Wirtschaftstheorien." In his **Pragmatische Philosophie.**
Hamburg: Hoffmann und Campe, 1975, pp. 211-46.

25.2.212 Lerner, Abba P. 1978. "The Scramble for Keynes'
Mantle." **Journal of Post Keynesian Economics** 1, No. 1
(Fall): 115-23.

25.2.213 Lessa, Carlos. 1979. "Economic Policy: Science Or
Ideology?" **Cepal Review** 8 (August): 119-44.

25.2.214 Littlechild, Stephen. 1983. "Subjectivism and
Method in Economics." In Jack Wiseman, ed. **Beyond Positive
Economics?** London: The British Association for the
Advancement of Science, 1983, pp. 38-49.

25.2.215 Loasby, Brian J. 1985. "Profit, Expectations and
Coherence in Economic Systems." **Journal of Economic Studies**
12, No. 1/2: 21-33.

25.2.216 Loasby, Brian J. 1984. "On Scientific Method."
Journal of Post Keynesian Economics 6, No. 3 (Spring):

394-410.

25.2.217 Losee, John. 1983. "Whewell and Mill on the Relation Between Philosophy of Science and History of Science." **Studies in History and Philosophy of Science** 14, No. 2 (June): 113-26.

25.2.218 Lutz, Mark A. and Kenneth Lux. 1986. "Neo-Humanistic Economics: A Comment." **Review of Social Economy** 44, No. 2 (October): 183-87.

25.2.219 Lyon, Leverett S. 1920. "A Functional Approach to Social-Economic Data." **Journal of Political Economy** 28 (July): 529-64.

25.2.220 MacDougall, Donald. 1974. "In Praise of Economics." **Economic Journal** 84, No. 336 (December): 773-86.

25.2.221 Machlup, Fritz. 1952. "Issues in Methodology: Introductory Remarks." **American Economic Association Papers and Proceedings** 42, No. 2 (May): 36.

25.2.222 MacLennon, Barbara. 1972. "Jevon's Philosophy of Science." **Manchester School of Economics and Social Sciences** 60, No. 1: 53-71.

25.2.223 Malinvaud, E. 1972. "The Scientific Papers of Tjalling C. Koopmans: A Review Article." **Journal of Economic Literature** 10, No. 3 (September): 798-802.

25.2.224 Marschak, Jacob. 1943. "A Discussion of Methods in Economics." **Journal of Political Economy** 49 (June): 441-48.

25.2.225 Marsden, David. 1984. "Homo Economicus and the Labour Market." In Peter Wiles and Guy Routh, eds. **Economics In Disarray**. Oxford: Basil Blackwell, 1984, pp. 121-53, with comment by Lévy-Garboua, pp. 154-58.

25.2.226 Marshall, Alfred. 1897. "The Old Generation of Economists and the New." **Quarterly Journal of Economists** (January): 113-35.

25.2.227 Martin, Anne. 1964. "Empirical and **a Priori** in Economics." **British Journal for the Philosophy of Science** 15, No. 58 (August): 123-36.

25.2.228 McClennan, E.F. 1981. "Constitutional Choice: Rawls Vs. Harsanyi." In Joseph C. Pitt, ed. **Philosophy in Economics**. Dordrecht: Reidel, 1981, pp. 175-203.

25.2.229 McKenzie, Richard B. 1977. "Where Is the Economics in Economic Education?" **Journal of Economic Education** 9, No. 1 (Fall): 5-13.

25.2.230 Menges, Günter. 1982. "Wege in die Realität."

Zeitschrift für die gesamte Staatswissenschaft 138, No. 4 (December): 646-63.

25.2.231 Miller, William L. 1971. "Richard Jones: A Case Study in Methodology." **History of Political Economy** 3, No. 1 (Spring): 198-207.

25.2.232 Mills, Frederick C. 1941. "Economics in a Time of Change." **American Economic Review** 31, No. 1 (March): 1-14.

25.2.233 Mirowski, Philip. 1987. "Book Review: **The Logic of Discovery.**" **Journal of Economic History** 42, No. 1 (March): 295-96.

25.2.234 Mirowski, Philip. 1986(a). "Institutions As a Solution Concept in a Game Theory Context." In his **The Reconstruction of Economic Theory.** Boston: Kluwer-Nijhoff, 1986, pp. 241-63.

25.2.235 Mirowski, Philip. 1986(b). "Introduction: Paradigms, Hard Cores, and Fugleman in Modern Economic Theory." In his **The Reconstruction of Economic Theory.** Boston: Kluwer-Nijhoff, 1986, pp. 1-11.

25.2.236 Mishan, E.J. 1982. "The New Controversy About the Rationale of Economic Evaluation." **Journal of Economic Issues** 16, No. 1 (March): 29-47.

25.2.237 Moses, Bernard. 1902. "Certain Tendencies in Political Economy." **Quarterly Journal of Economics** 11: 233-64.

25.2.238 Mueller, Dennis. 1984. "Further Reflections on the Invisible Hand Theorem." In Peter Wiles and Guy Routh, eds. **Economics in Disarry.** Oxford: Basil Blackwell, 1984, pp. 159-83.

25.2.239 Neild, Robert. 1984. "The Wider World and Economic Methodology." In Peter Wiles and Guy Routh, eds. **Economics in Disarray.** Oxford: Basil Blackwell, 1984, pp. 37-46, with comments by Hart, pp. 47-50.

25.2.240 Neill, Thomas P. 1949. "The Physiocrats' Concept of Economics." **Quarterly Journal of Economics** 63 (November): 532-53.

25.2.241 Nell, Edward J. 1977. "'No Statement Is Immune to Revision.'" **Social Research** 44, No. 4 (Winter): 801-23.

25.2.242 Newcomb, Simon. 1893. "The Problem of Economic Education." **Quarterly Journal of Economics** 7 (July): 375-99.

25.2.243 Nicholas, J.S. 1906. "The Use and Abuse of Authority in Economics." **Economic Journal** 13 (December): 554-66.

25.2.244 Nicholson, J. Shield. 1893. "The Reaction in Favour of the Classical Political Economy." **Journal of Political Economy** 2 (December): 119-32; Rpt. in R.L. Smyth, ed. **Essays in Economic Method**. London: Gerald Duckworth and Co., 1962, pp. 112-25.

25.2.245 Northrop, F.S.C. 1941. "The Impossibility of a Theoretical Science of Economic Dynamics." **Quarterly Journal of Economics** 56 (November): 1-17.

25.2.246 Noyes, C. Reinold. 1950. "Isolation in Economic Method: A Comment." **Quarterly Journal of Economics** 64 (August): 483-87.

25.2.247 Odagiri, Hiroyuki. 1984. "The Firm As a Collection of Human Resources." In Peter Wiles and Guy Routh, eds. **Economics in Disarray**. Oxford: Basil Blackwell, 1984, pp. 190-206, with comment by Hart, pp. 207-10.

25.2.248 Opp, Karl-Dieter. 1969. "Das Experiment in den Sozialwissenschaften." **Zeitschrift für die gesamte Staatswissenschaft** 125, No. 1: 106-22.

25.2.249 Oswald, Donald J. 1987. "Metaphysical Beliefs and the Foundations of Modern Economics." **Review of Social Economy** 45, No. 3 (December): 276-97.

25.2.250 Pantaleoni, M. 1898. "An Attempt to Analyse the Concepts of 'Strong and Weak' in Their Economic Connection." **Economic Journal** 8 (June): 183-205.

25.2.251 Papandreou, A.G. 1950. "Economics and the Social Sciences." **Economic Journal** 60: 715-23.

25.2.252 Papineau, D. 1976. "Ideal Types and Empirical Theories." **British Journal for the Philosophy of Science** 27: 137-46.

25.2.253 Pareto, Vilfredo. 1897. "The New Theories of Economics." **Journal of Political Economy** 5 (September): 485-502.

25.2.254 Parsons, Talcott. 1934. "Some Reflections on 'The Nature and Significance of Economics'." **Quarterly Journal of Economics** 48: 511-45.

25.2.255 Perlman, Mark. 1978. "Reflections on Methodology and Persuasion." In Jacob S. Dreyer, ed. **Breadth and Depth in Economics: Fritz Machlup—the Man and His Ideas**. Lexington, MA: Lexington Books, 1978, pp. 37-45.

25.2.256 Peston, Maurice. 1981. "Lionel Robbins: Methodology, Policy and Modern Theory." In J.R. Shackleton and Gareth Locksley, eds. **Twelve Contemporary Economists**. London: Macmillan, 1981, pp. 183-98.

25.2.257 Peterson, Wallace. 1982. "Growth, Profits, and Property: A Review Article." **Journal of Post Keynesian Economics** 4, No. 3 (Spring): 425-34.

25.2.258 Pfouts, Ralph W. 1973. "Some Proposals for a New Methodology in Economics." **Atlantic Economic Journal** 1, No. 1 (November): 13-22.

25.2.259 Pfouts, Ralph W. 1967. "Artistic Goals, Scientific Method and Economics." **Southern Economic Journal** 33, No. 4 (April): 457-67.

25.2.260 Phelps-Brown, Sir E.H. 1980. "The Radical Reflections of an Economist." **Bianca Nazionale del Lavoro Quarterly Review** 132, No. 33: 3-14.

25.2.261 Piron, Robert. 1962. "On 'The Methodology of Positive Economics': Comment." **Quarterly Journal of Economics** 76: 664-66.

25.2.262 Pokorny, Dusan. 1978. "Two Theories of Science." **Canadian Journal of Economics** 11, No. 3 (August): 387-407.

25.2.263 Postan, Michael M. 1968. "A Plague of Economists? On Some Current Myths, Errors, and Fallacies." **Encounter** 30 (January): 42-47.

25.2.264 Price, L.L. 1895. "On the Relation of Economic Science to Practical Affairs." Report of the British Association for the Advancement of Science. **Journal of the Royal Statistical Society** (December); Rpt. in R.L. Smyth, ed. **Essays in Economic Method.** London: Gerald Duckworth and Co., 1962, pp. 144-64.

25.2.265 Price, L.L. 1892. "Notes on a Recent Economic Treatise" (i.e., Marshall's **Principles of Economics**). **Economic Journal** 2 (March): 17-34.

25.2.266 Pullen, John. 1982. "Malthus on the Doctrine of Proportions and the Concept of Optimimum." **Australian Economic Papers** 21, No. 39 (December): 270-85.

25.2.267 Recktenwald, Horst Claus. 1975. "Adam Smith heute und morgen." **Kyklos** 28, No. 1: 5-22.

25.2.268 Reder, Melvin W. 1982. "Chicago Economics: Permanence and Change." **Journal of Economic Literature** 20, No. 1 (March): 1-38.

25.2.269 Reid, Joseph D., Jr. 1987. "The Theory of Sharecropping: Occam's Razor and Economic Analysis." **History of Political Economy** 19, No. 4 (Winter): 551-69.

25.2.270 Remenyi, Joseph V. 1979. "Core Demi-Core

Interaction: Toward a General Theory of Disciplinary and Subdisciplinary Growth." **History of Political Economy** 11, No. 1 (Spring): 30-63.

25.2.271 Richter, Rudolf. 1965. "Methodologie aus der Sicht des Wirtschaftstheoretikers." **Weltwirtschaftliches Archiv** 95: 242-61; Rpt. in Reimut Jochimsen and Helmut Knobel, eds. **Gegenstand und Methoden der Nationalökonomie.** Köln: Kiepenheuer & Witsch, 1971, pp. 188-203.

25.2.272 Rivett, Kenneth. 1977. "Hollis and Nell on Methodology." **Economic Record** 53, Nos. 142 and 143 (June-September): 239-61.

25.2.273 Rivlin, Alice M. 1974. "How Can Experiments Be More Useful?" **American Economic Review** 64, No. 2 (May): 346-54.

25.2.274 Robbins, Lionel. 1981. "Economics and Political Economy." **American Economic Association Papers and Proceedings** 71, No. 2 (May): 1-10.

25.2.275 Robbins, Lionel. 1938. "Live and Dead Issues in the Methodology of Economics." **Economica** N.S. 5 (August): 342-52.

25.2.276 Robbins, Lionel. 1930. "The Present Position of Economic Science." **Economica** 10 (March): 14-24.

25.2.277 Robertson, D.H. 1949. "On Sticking to One's Last." **Economic Journal** 59 (December): 505-09.

25.2.278 Robinson, Joan. 1981(a). "The Disintegration of Economics." In her **What Are the Questions? and Other Essays.** Armonk, NY: M.E. Sharpe, 1981, pp. 96-104.

25.2.279 Robinson,. Joan. 1981(b). "Survey: 1950's." In her **What Are the Questions? And Other Essays.** Armonk, NY: M.E. Sharpe: 1981, pp. 105-11.

25.2.280 Robinson, Joan. 1981(c). "Thinking About Thinking." In her **What Are the Questions? And Other Essays.** Armonk, NY: M.E. Sharpe, 1981, pp. 54-63.

25.2.281 Robinson, Joan. 1981(d). "Time in Economic Theory." **Kyklos** 33, No. 2: 219-29.

25.2.282 Robinson, Joan. 1977. "What Are the Questions?" **Journal of Economic Literature** 15, No. 4 (December): 1318-39.

25.2.283 Robinson, Joan. 1973. "What Has Become of the Keynesian Revolution." In her **After Keynes.** Oxford: Basil Blackwell, 1973, pp. 1-11.

25.2.284 Rosefielde, Steven. 1976. "Economic Theory in the

Excluded Middle Between Positivism and Rationalism." **Atlantic Economic Journal** 4, No. 2 (Spring): 1-9.

25.2.285 Rosenberg, Alexander. 1987. "Weintraub's Aims: A Brief Rejoinder to Comment on Rosenberg's 'Lakatosian Consolations for Economists.'" **Economics and Philosophy** 3 (April): 143-44.

25.2.286 Rosenberg, Alexander. 1986. "Discussion: What Rosenberg's Philosophy of Economics Is Not." **Philosophy of Science** 53 (March): 127-32.

25.2.287 Rosenberg, Alexander. 1983. "The Explanatory Role of Existence Proofs." **Ethics** 97 (October): 177-86.

25.2.288 Rosenberg, Alexander. 1979. "Can Economic Theory Explain Everything?" **Philosophy of the Social Sciences** 9 (December): 509-29.

25.2.289 Rosenberg, Alexander. 1978(a). "Hollis and Nell: Rational Economic Men." **Philosophy of the Social Sciences** 8: 87-98.

25.2.290 Rosenberg, Alexander. 1978(b). "Weintraub's Aims: A Brief Rejoinder." **Economics and Philosophy** 3, No. 1 (April): 143-44.

25.2.291 Rousseas, Stephen. 1981. "Wiles' Wily Weltanschauung." **Journal of Post Keynesian Economics** 3, No. 3 (Spring): 340-51.

25.2.292 Rousseas, Stephen. 1973. "Paradigm Polishing Versus Critical Thought in Economics." **American Economist** 17 (Fall): 72-78.

25.2.293 Routh, Guy. 1984. "What to Teach Undergraduates." In Peter Wiles and Guy Routh, eds. **Economics in Disarray.** Oxford: Basil Blackwell, 1984, pp. 240-48, with comment by Morris Perlman, pp. 249-59.

25.2.294 Salz, Arthur. 1944. "The Present Position of Economics." **American Economic Association Papers and Proceedings** 34 (March): 15-24.

25.2.295 Sargeant, J.R. 1963. "Are American Economists Better?" **Oxford Economic Papers** N.S. 15, No. 1 (March): 1-7.

25.2.296 Scaperlanda, Anthony. 1986. "Neo-Humanistic Economics and Social Economics, Revisited." **Review of Social Economy** 44, No. 2 (October): 188-92.

25.2.297 Scaperlanda, Anthony. 1985. "Is Neo-Humanistic Economics the New Paradigm for Social Economists?" **Review of Social Economy** 43, No. 2 (October): 173-80.

25.2.298 Schabas, Margaret. 1986. "An Assessment of the Scientific Standing of Economics." In Arthur Fire and Peter Machamer, eds. **PSA 1986**, Vol. 1. East Lansing, MI: Philosophy of Science Association, 1986, pp. 289-97.

25.2.299 Schachter, Gustav. 1973. "Some Developments in Economic Science 1965: Methods, Ideas, Approaches." **American Journal of Economics and Sociology** 32, No. 3 (July): 331-35.

25.2.300 Schmidtchen, Dieter. 1977. "Wider den Vorwurf, das neoklassische Wettbewerbskonzept sei tautologisch: eine Antikritik aus wissenschaftlicher und markttheoretischer Sicht." **Jahrbücher für Nationalökonomie und Statistik** 191, Nos. 5-6 (April): 428-54.

25.2.301 Schmitt, Bernard. 1986. "The Process of Formation of Economics in Relation to the Other Sciences." In Mauro Baranzini and Roberto Scazzieri, eds. **Foundations of Economics.** Oxford: Basil Blackwell, 1986, pp. 103-32.

25.2.302 Schuller, George J. 1949. "Isolationism in Economic Method." **Quarterly Journal of Economics** 63, No. 4 (November): 439-75.

25.2.303 Schumacher, E.F. 1973. "Does Economics Help?" In Joan Robinson, ed. **After Keynes.** Oxford: Basil Blackwell, 1973, pp. 26-36.

25.2.304 Scoon, Robert. 1943. "Professor Robbin's Definition of Economics." **Journal of Political Economy** 51: 310-21.

25.2.305 Seligman, Ben B. 1969. "The Impact of Positivism on Economic Thought." **History of Political Economy** 1, No. 2 (Fall): 256-78.

25.2.306 Seligman, Ben B. 1957. "On the Nature of Economic Growth." **Diogenes** 19 (Fall): 42-61.

25.2.307 Shackle, G.L.S. 1986. "Decision." **Journal of Economic Studies** 13, No. 5: 58-62.

25.2.308 Shackle, G.L.S. 1982. "Means and Meaning in Economic Theory." **Scottish Journal of Political Economy** 29, No. 3 (November): 223-34.

25.2.309 Simon, Lawrence H. and David F. Ruccio. 1986. "A Methodological Analysis of Development Theory: Explanation in Andre Gunder Frank." **World Development** 14, No. 2 (February: Special Issue): 195-209.

25.2.310 Smith, Adam. 1967 (ca. 1750). "The History of Astronomy." In Ralph J. Lindgren, ed. **The Early Writings of Adam Smith.** NY: Augustus M. Kelley, 1967, pp. 53-109.

25.2.311 Smith, Vernon L. 1978. "Psychology and Economics: Discussion." **American Economic Association Papers and Proceedings** 68, No. 2 (May): 76-77.

25.2.312 Smith, Vernon L. 1976. "Experimental Economics: Induced Value Theory. **American Economic Association Papers and Proceedings** 66, No. 2 (May): 274-79.

25.2.313 Söderbaum, Peter. 1983. "Ezra Mishan on Economic Evaluation: A Comment." **Journal of Economic Issues** 17, No. 1 (March): 206-13.

25.2.314 Söderbaum, Peter. 1982. "Positional Analysis and Public Decision Making." **Journal of Economic Issues** 16, No. 2 (June): 391-400.

25.2.315 Solo, Robert A. 1975(a). "Neoclassical Economics in Perspective." **Journal of Economic Issues** 9, No. 4 (December): 627-44.

25.2.316 Solo, Robert A. 1975(b). "What Is Structuralism? Piaget's Genetic Epistemology and the Varieties of Structuralist Thought." **Journal of Economic Issues** 9, No. 4 (December): 605-25.

25.2.317 Souter, R.W. 1933. "'The Nature and Significance of Economic Science' in Recent Discussion." **Quarterly Journal of Economics** 47 (May): 377-413.

25.2.318 Spengler, Joseph J. 1968. "Exogenous and Endogenous Influences in the Formation of Post-1870 Economic Thought: A Sociology of Knowledge Approach." In Robert V. Eagly, ed. **Events, Ideology and Economic Theory.** Detroit: Wayne State University Press, 1968, pp. 159-205.

25.2.319 Stanfield, J.R. 1979. "Phenomena and Epiphenomena in Economics." **Journal of Economic Issues** 13, No. 4 (December): 885-98.

25.2.320 Stewart, Walter W., et al. 1919. "Economic Theory: Discussion." **American Economic Association Papers and Proceedings** 9 (March): 319-24.

25.2.321 *Stigler, George J. 1983. "The Process and Progress of Economists." **Journal of Political Economy** 91 (August): 529-45.

25.2.322 *Stigler, George J. 1965(a). "The Economist and the State." **American Economic Review** 55, No. 1 (March): 1-18.

25.2.323 *Stigler, George J. 1965(b). "Textual Exegesis As a Scientific Problem." **Economica** N.S. 32 (November): 447-50.

25.2.324 *Stigler, George J. 1951. "Economic Theory,

Statistics, and Economic Practice: Discussion." **American Economic Association Papers and Proceedings** 41, No. 2 (May): 126-28.

25.2.325 *Stigler, George J. and Claire Friedland. 1975. "The Citation Practices of Doctorates in Economics." **Journal of Political Economy** 83, No. 3 (June): 477-507.

25.2.326 Stonier, Alfred and Karl Bode. 1937. "A New Approach to the Methodology of the Social Sciences." **Economica** (November): 406-24.

25.2.327 Swanbey, James A. and Robert Premus. 1983. "Practice, Logic, and Problem Solving: A Reply to Crossland and Weinel." **Journal of Economic Issues** 17, No. 4 (December): 1138-42.

25.2.328 Swanbey, James A. and Robert Premus. 1982. "Modern Empiricism and Quantum Leap Theorizing in Economics." **Journal of Economic Issues** 16, No. 3 (September): 713-30; Rpt. in Alfred S. Eichner, ed. **Why Economics Is Not Yet a Science**. London: Macmillan / Sharpe, 1983, pp. 41-60.

25.2.329 Tarascio, Vincent J. 1983. "The Problem of Progress in Economic Science." **Atlantic Economic Journal** 11, No. 2 (July): 29-34.

25.2.330 Tarascio, Vincent J. and Bruce Caldwell. 1979. "Theory Choice in Economics: Philosophy and Practice." **Journal of Economic Issues** 13 (December): 983-1006.

25.2.331 Taylor, O.H. 1929. "Economics and the Idea of Natural Laws." **Quarterly Journal of Economics** 44 (November): 1-39.

25.2.332 Thompson, Herbert. 1965. "Adam Smith's Philosophy of Science." **Quarterly Journal of Economics** (February): 212-33.

25.2.333 Thornton, Robert J. and Jon T. Innes. 1988. "The Status of Master's Programs in Economics." **Journal of Economic Perspectives** 2, No. 1 (Winter): 171-78.

25.2.334 Tichy, von Gieserich E. 1978. "Die allgemeine Theorie der Wirtschaftspolitik und die neue politische Ökonomie." **Jahrbücher für Nationalökonomie und Statistik** 193, No. 4 (August): 289-307.

25.2.335 Tugwell, R.G. 1923. "Economic Theory and Practice: Discussion." **American Economic Association Papers and Proceedings** 13 (March). 107-09.

25.2.336 Vickers, Douglas. 1985. "On Relational Structures and Nonequilibrium in Economic Theory." **Eastern Economic Journal** 11, No. 4 (October-December): 384-404.

25.2.337 Vickers, Douglas. 1983. "Formalism, Finance, and Decisions in Real Economic Time." In A.W. Coats. **Methodological Controversy in Economics: Historical Essays in Honor of T.W. Hutchison**. Greenwich, CT: Jai Press, pp. 247-64.

25.2.338 Viner, J. 1917. "Some Problems of Logical Method in Political Economy." **Journal of Political Economy** 25 (March): 236-60.

25.2.339 Vining, Rutledge. 1969. "On Two Foundation Concepts of the Theory of Political Economy." **Journal of Political Economy** 77, No. 2 (March-April): 199-218.

25.2.340 Vredeveld, George M. 1987. "Economics: Musing Or Reality--Some Thoughts on Bergman's Methodology." **Journal of Economic Education** 18, No. 2 (Spring): 203-07.

25.2.341 Ward, Benjamin. 1966. "Institutions and Economic Analysis." In Sherman Roy Krupp, ed. **The Structure of Economic Science**. Englewood Cliffs: Prentice-Hall, 1966, pp. 184-200.

25.2.342 Ward, Benjamin. 1956. "What Is Welfare Economics?" **Ethics** 66 (January): 116-25.

25.2.343 Watkins, J.W.N. 1953. "Walter Eucken: Philosopher-Economist." **Ethics** 63 (January): 131-36.

25.2.344 Weintraub, E. Roy. 1982-83. "Substantive Mountains and Methodological Molehills." **Journal of Post Keynesian Economics** 75, No. 2 (Winter): 295-303.

25.2.345 Whitaker, J.K. 1975. "John Stuart Mill's Methodology." **Journal of Political Economy** 83, No. 5 (October): 1033-50.

25.2.346 Wilber, Charles K. 1986. "Methodological Debate in Economics: Editor's Introduction." **World Economics** 14, No. 2 (February: Special Issue): 143-45.

25.2.347 Wilber, Charles K. and Steve Francis. 1986. "The Methodological Basis of Hirschman's Development Economics: Pattern Model vs. General Laws." **World Development** 14, No. 2 (February: Special Issue): 181-94.

25.2.348 Wilber, Charles K. and Jon Wisman. 1975. "The Chicago School: Positivism Or Ideal Type." **Journal of Economic Issues** 12, No. 1 (March): 61-89.

25.2.349 Wilde, Louis L. 1981. "On the Use of Laboratory Experiments in Economics." In Peter Wiles and Guy Routh, eds. **Economics in Disarray**. Oxford: Basil Blackwell, 1981, pp. 137-25.

25.2.350 Wiles, Peter. 1984(a). "Epilogue: The Role of

Theory." In Peter Wiles and Guy Routh, eds. **Economics in Disarray**. Oxford: Oxford University Press, 1984, pp. 293-325.

25.2.351 Wiles, Peter. 1984(b). "Whatever Happened to the Full-Cost Principle (UK)?" In Peter Wiles and Guy Routh, eds. **Economics in Disarray**. Oxford: Basil Blackwell, 1984, pp. 211-21, with comment (Austin Robinson), pp. 222-32.

25.2.352 Wiles, Peter. 1981(a). "Methodology and Ideology: Reply." **Journal of Post Keynesian Economics** 3, No. 3 (Spring): 352-58.

25.2.353 Wiles, Peter. 1981(b). "Rejoinder" (Ideology, Methodology, and Neoclassical Economics). **Journal of Post Keynesian Economics** 3, No. 3 (Spring): 352-58.

25.2.354 Wiles, Peter. 1979-80. "Ideology, Methodology, and Neoclassical Economics." **Journal of Post Keynesian Economics** 2, No. 2 (Winter): 155-80.

25.2.355 Winch, Donald. 1972. "Marginalism and the Boundaries of Economic Science." **History of Political Economy** 4, No. 2: 325-43.

25.2.356 Wiseman, Jack. 1983. "Beyond Positive Economics--Dream and Reality." In his **Beyond Positive Economics?** Oxford: Basil Blackwell, 1983, pp. 13-27.

25.2.357 Wisman, Jon D. 1986. "The Methodology of W. Arthur Lewis's Development Economics: Economics As Pedagogy." **World Development** 14, No. 2 (February: Special Issue): 165-80.

25.2.358 Wisman, Jon D. 1979. Legitimation, Ideology-Critique, and Economics." **Social Research** 46 (Summer): 291-320.

25.2.359 Wisman, Jon D. 1978. "The Naturalistic Turn of Orthodox Economics: A Study of Methodological Misunderstanding." **Review of Social Economy** 36 (December): 263-84.

25.2.360 Wisman, Jon and James H. Weaver. 1978. "Smith, Marx, and Malthus: Ghosts Who Haunt Our Future." **The Futurist** 12 (April): 92-104.

25.2.361 Wolozin, Harold. 1974. "Lying and Economic Dogma." **Review of Existential Psychology and Psychiatry** 13, No. 2: 196-203.

25.2.362 Woodbury, Stephan A. 1979. "Methodological Controversy in Labor Economics." **Journal of Economic Issues** 13 (December): 933-72.

25.2.363 Young, Allyn A. 1925. "The Trend of Economics, As

Seen by Some American Economists." **Quarterly Journal of Economics** 39 (February): 155-83.

25.2.364 Young, Warren L. 1982. "Time and Concept Formation in Economics: A Suggested Approach." **Journal of Economic Issues** 16, No. 1: 161-80.

25.2.365 Yunker, James A. 1986. "In Defense of Utilitarianism: An Economists's Viewpoint." **Review of Social Economy** 44, No. 1 (April): 57-79.

25.2.366 Zajdlic, W. 1956. "The Limitations of Social Science." **Kyklos** 9, No. 1: 65-73.

25.2.367 Zimmermann, Horst. 1968. "Wirtschaftspolitische Beratung unter Wertabstinenz." **Zeitschrift für Nationalökonomie** 28, No. 3-4 (December): 305-40.

***

PART TWO

THE PHILOSOPHY OF SCIENCE

1

On the Philosophy of Science

1.1 Introductory Texts

1.1.1 Brown, Harold I. 1977. **Perception, Theory and Commitment: The Philosophy of Science.** Chicago/London: University of Chicago Press.

The philosophy of science has been in flux for the past 30 years. The historical, process-oriented view has challenged the long-standing logico-empiricist tradition. In part I Brown reviews the doctrines of logical empiricism. In part II he discusses "the new philosophy of science." Brown examines both the old and new traditions in the philosophy of science and proposes a new epistemology in his conclusion.

1.1.2 Chalmers, A.F. 1982. **What Is This Thing Called Science?,** 2nd ed. St. Lucia: University of Queensland Press.

This is a popular elementary introduction to the philosophy of science. The intellectual debt to Popper is quite clear. Chalmers outlines the shortcomings of the naive, empiricist account of science and modern attempts to improve them, i.e., the theories of Popper, Lakatos, Kuhn, and Feyerabend are described and criticized.

1.1.3 Giere, Ronald N. 1984 (1979). **Understanding Scientific Reasoning,** 2nd ed. NY: Holt, Rinehart, and Winston.

This is a textbook designed to develop skills in understanding and evaluating scientific reports or findings. Part I deals with the basic concepts of scientific reasoning: statements, (inductive and deductive) arguments, justification, and conditional arguments. In Part II Giere treats reasoning about theories (theoretical models, theoretical hypotheses, laws, theories, generalizations, deterministic and stochastic models), justifying scientific theories, geology and the limits to growth, fallacies of theory testing. Part II focuses on causes, correlations, and causal hypotheses: statistics, correlations, causal hypotheses, probability, justifying statistical hypotheses, and justifying causal hypotheses. In Part IV Giere treats values and decisions: the structures of decisions, and decision strategies.

1.1.4 Hacking, Ian, ed. 1981. **Scientific Revolutions.** Oxford: Oxford University Press.

This is a collection of philosophy of science articles dealing with the problems of logical empiricism, mainly from the historically oriented group of philosophers. The focus is on Kuhn's philosophy. Contributors are Kuhn, Shapere, Putnam, Popper, Lakatos, Hacking, Laudan, and Feyerabend.

1.2   The **Scientific American** and **Science** Series:

Scientific American and **Science** occasionally run articles on philosophy of science topics. Gardner and Quine treat philosophical paradoxes. Nagel discusses the ramifications for Gödel's proof. Salmon discusses confirmation of theories, while Shapere treats Kuhn's concept of the paradigm. Blair and Pollack and Tversky and Kahneman work with rational choice in economics.

***

1.2.1 Blair, Douglas H. and Robert A. Pollak. 1983. "Rational Collective Choice." **Scientific American** 249, No. 2 (August): 76–83.

1.2.2 Gardner, Martin. 1976. "Mathematical Games: On the Fabric of Inductive Logic, and Some Probability Paradoxes." **Scientific American** 234, No. 3 (March): 119–24.

1.2.3 Kahneman, Daniel and Amos Tversky. 1982. "The Psychology of Preferences." **Scientific American** 246: 162–73.

1.2.4 Nagel, Ernst and James R. Newman. 1956. "Gödel's Proof." **Scientific American** 196, No. 6 (June): 71–86.

1.2.5 Quine, Willard van Orman. 1962. "Paradox." **Scientific American** 206, No. 4 (April): 84–96.

1.2.6 Salmon, Wesley C. 1973. "Confirmation." **Scientific American** 228, No. 5 (May): 75–83.

1.2.7 Shapere, Dudley. 1971. "The Paradigm Concept." **Science** 172, No. 3984 (14 May): 706–709.

1.2.8 Tarski, Alfred. 1969. "Truth and Proof." **Scientific American** 220, No. 6 (June): 63-77.

1.2.9 Tversky, Amos and Daniel Kahneman. 1981. "The Framing of Decisions and the Psychology of Choice." **Science** 211 (30 January): 453-58.

1.3   Introductory Texts on Philosophy of Science Written
       for Economists by Economists and Philosophers

1.3.1 Blaug, Mark. 1980. **The Methodology of Economics Or How Economists Explain.** Cambridge: Cambridge University Press.

Blaug devotes Part I of his work to a summary of the ideas of the philosophy of science. His "What you always wanted to know about the philosophy of science but were afraid to ask" treats the received view, Popper, Lakatos, Kuhn, and Feyerabend.

1.3.2 Caldwell, Bruce J. 1982. **Beyond Positivism.** London: Allen and Unwin.

Like Blaug's work, part one is devoted to summarizing the philosophy of science of the twentieth century. Logical positivism, logical empiricism, the attack on logical empiricism, and the growth of knowledge tradition are discussed. (Part II treats economics in light of findings in the philosophy of science.)

1.3.3 Hausman, Daniel M., ed. 1984. **The Philosophy of Economics: An Anthology.** Cambridge: Cambridge University Press; "Introduction," pp. 1-50.

Hausman provides a brief overview of the philosophy of science in his introduction, including a short discussion of the methodology of economics.

1.3.4 Klant, J.J. 1984. **The Rules of the Game: The Logical Structure of Economic Theories.** Trans. Ina Swart. Cambridge: Cambridge University Press.

Klant's discussion of economic theories is interspersed with references to the modern philosophy of science.

1.3.5 Machlup, Fritz. 1978. "What Is Meant by Methodology?" In his **Methodology of Economics and Other Social Sciences.** NY: Academic Press, 1978, pp. 5-62.

Machlup attempts to survey the literature in the philosophy of science to give the unacquainted a taste of methodology. There are brief vignettes about the philosophy of Kant, Windelband, Royce, Croce, Weber, Montague, Bridgman, Whitehead, Cohen,

Reichenbach, Kaufmann, Schutz, Carnap, Margenau,
Popper, Feigl, Braithwaite, Nagel, and Hempel.

1.4   Advanced Works

1.4.1 Newton-Smith, W.H. 1981. **The Rationality of Science.**
London: Routledge and Kegan Paul.

Newton-Smith explores the controversy between the old
philosophy of science and the new historical
approaches. He criticizes the rationalist positions of
Popper and Lakatos, as well as the non-rationalism of
Kuhn and Feyerabend. He develops his own account of
science, an approach which he calls "temporate
rationalism."

1.4.2 Suppe, Frederick, ed. 1977. **The Structure of
Scientific Theories,** 2nd ed. Urbana: University of Illinois
Press.

This is a fat volume which was the outgrowth of a
symposium held on the structure of scientific theories
in Illinois. The purpose of the colloquium was to
bring together main proponents and critics of
traditional philosophy of science to explore the
question "What is the structure of scientific
theories?" The received view, its criticisms, and
alternatives to the received view are treated. The
proceedings of the symposium follow, and Suppe
provides an afterword.

(See also original works of individual philosophers below.)

1.5   Historical Background: Logical Positivism and the Vienna Circle

1.5.1 Achinstein, Peter and Stephen F. Barker, eds. 1969.
The Legacy of Logical Positivism. Baltimore, Maryland: John
Hopkins University Press.

This volume is devoted to the appraisal of logical
positivism and its legacy. Contributors are Feigl,
Toulmin, Hanson, Hesse, Shapere, Hempel, Scriven,
Putnam, Barker, and Achinstein.

1.5.2 Ayer, A.J., ed. 1959. **Logical Positivism.** NY: Free
Press.

This classic is a collection of some of the most
important writings of the logical positivists. Ayer
provides an introduction which traces the history of
the movement (pp. 3-28). Included in the volume are
essays from Russell, Schlick, Carnap, Hempel, Hahn,
Neurath, Ayer, Stevenson, Ramsey, Ryle, and Waismann
(not all of whom are positivists). There is a good,
detailed bibliography.

1.5.3 Feigl, Herbert. 1981. **Inquiries and Provocations: Selected Writings 1929-74**. Vol. 14 of **The Vienna Circle Collection**. Ed. by Robert S. Cohen. Dordrecht: D. Reidel.

This is a collection of essays, the first of which deal with "The Origin and Spirit of Logical Positivism" (pp. 21-37), "The Power of Positivistic Thinking" (pp. 38-55), and "The **Wiener Kreis** in America" (pp. 57-94). Feigl was a member of the Vienna Circle.

1.5.4 Joergensen, Joergen. 1970 (1951). **The Development of Logical Empiricism**. Vol. II, No. 9 of **Foundations of the Unity of Science**. Chicago: University of Chicago Press.

This is a classic account of logical positivism from one of the members of the movement.

1.5.5 Juhos, Béla. 1971. "Formen des Positivismus." **Zeitschrift für allgemeine Wissenschaftstheorie** 2: 27-65.

Juhos describes the development of positivism and empiricism, especially the early development of the movement. He also was a member of the Vienna Circle. (In German)

1.5.6 Kraft, Victor. 1974. "Popper and the Vienna Circle." In Paul Arthur Schilpp, ed. **The Philosophy of Karl Popper**, 2 vols. La Salle: Open Court, 1974, Vol. I, pp. 185-204.

In this article Kraft describes Popper's relationship with the members of the Vienna Circle and vice versa. Although Popper did not belong to the Circle, Kraft claims that he "cannot be thought of as outside it" (p. 185). Kraft was also a member of the Vienna Circle.

1.5.7 Passmore, John. 1967. "Logical Positivism." **Encyclopedia of Philosophy**. 1967 ed.

This much-quoted piece is a good short history of the movement and summary of positivist ideas.

1.5.8 Schleichert, Hubert, ed. 1975. **Logischer Empirismus--der Wiener Kreis. Ausgewählte Texte mit einer Einleitung**. München: Wilhelm Fink Verlag.

This is a collection of the original writings of the logical positivists. Contributors are Schlick, Neurath, Hahn, and Carnap. (In German)

***

2

Works by Sir Karl Popper

Sir Karl Popper is the leading figure of the philosophical school of critical rationalism. The school's name, critical rationalism, stems from Popper's belief that the scientific attitude is the critical attitude.

For the younger Popper, the leading problem of the philosophy of science was demarcation of science from metaphysics and pseudo-science. Popper rejects the view that scientific theories can be verified or given probability values (his rejection of induction). Deductive rather than inductive logic is to be used to evaluate scientific theories. Observation statements are deduced from universal propositions with initial and peripheral conditions (i.e., theories). When experience shows that an observation statement is false, the universal hypothesis is false or falsified. This is one form of his theory of falsification. Popper's use of falsification has not always been consistent. The above version is the one best known to economists.

The above-mentioned theory of falsification, and its various other versions, are not tenable for numerous reasons. Science is not made up of a few, single statements, but of a labyrinth of hypotheses, initial conditions, etc. (i.e., the Duhem problem; see § 10). The works in section 3.2. below go into great detail about the problems which Popper's philosophy has encountered.

Popper's books have been annotated. The works appearing here should be of interest to economists and other social scientists, but do not represent a complete collection of his works.

His articles have also been chosen with an eye towards material that has to do specifically with social science. The following themes may be of interest to economists:

demarcation (his 1974a and b, 1963, 1968); democracy
(1987c); evolution (1987b); the logic of social science
(1967, 1974a, 1976a and b, 1972, 1988); rationality (1967,
1974a); on Kuhn (1970, 1975); on why philosophical theories
cannot be refuted (1964).

***

2.1   Books

2.1.1 1984 (1976). **Ausgangspunkte: meine intellektuelle Entwicklung,** 3rd ed. (revised by author) Hamburg: Hoffmann und Campe Verlag; In English as **Unended Quest. An Intellectual Autobiography.** La Salle: Open Court, 1976; originally published as 1974(a) below.

> This is Popper's intellectual autobiography. It is a
> good introduction to his works in general because he
> discusses their development in short form. He also
> discusses other factors influencing his work, e.g.,
> the war.

2.1.2 1983 (1956). **Realism and the Aim of Science.** Vol. 1 of **The Postscript to The Logic of Scientific Discovery.** Ed. by W.W. Bartley, III. London: Hutchinson.

> This is Popper's first volume of his **Postscript to The
> Logic of Discovery.** It was written in the 50's, but
> not published. Popper expands his views here on
> induction, demarcation, and corroboration, and
> presents his propensity theory of probability. He also
> replies to criticisms.

2.1.3 1982(a) (1956). **The Open Universe: An Argument for Indeterminism.** Vol. II of **The Postscript to The Logic of Scientific Discovery.** Ed. by W.W. Bartley. London: Hutchinson.

> The second volume of the **Postscript** was also written
> in the 1950's. It contains a discussion of determinism
> and indeterminism which were originally appendices to
> **The Logic of Scientific Discovery.**

2.1.4 1982(b) (1956). **Quantum Theory and the Schism in Physics.** Vol. III of **The Postscript to The Logic of Scientific Discovery.** Ed. by W.W. Bartley. London: Hutchinson.

> The third volume of his **Postscript,** also 30+ years old
> was also once an appendix to the mother work. In this
> volume Popper challenges fundamental assumptions of
> current research in physics and sketches a new
> cosmology. The basic theme is that 'something can come
> from nothing.'

2.1.5 1979 (1972). **Objective Knowledge: An Evolutionary**

Approach, rev. ed. Oxford: Oxford University Press.

> In this volume Popper breaks with the tradition of
> subjective knowledge. Popper argues that knowledge is
> not a part of ourselves but is exposed to criticism.
> The volume contains 9 essays, some which have been
> published elsewhere.

2.1.6 1972(a) (1963). **Conjectures and Refutations: The
Growth of Scientific Knowledge**, 4th ed. London: Routledge
and Kegan Paul.

> These essays are variations on the theme that we can
> learn from our mistakes. Knowledge grows and progress
> comes about by learning from mistakes. Science
> proceeds by conjectures and refutations. Because our
> knowledge grows, there is no reason to be a sceptic,
> even though we cannot know for certain.

2.1.7 1972(b) (1959). **The Logic of Scientific Discovery**,
6th ed. London: Hutchinson; Trans. of **Logik der Forschung**,
6th rev. ed. Wien: J. Springer, 1976 (1935).

> This is the work which made Popper famous. The central
> problem of epistemology, he claims, is the problem of
> the growth of knowledge. It is here that Popper first
> discusses falsification and the criterion of
> demarcation.

2.1.8 1966 (1962). **The Open Society and Its Enemies**, 5th
rev. ed. 2 vols. Princeton: Princeton University Press.

> These 2 volumes contain some of Popper's social
> philosophy. This was a war work, aimed at defending
> freedom against totalitarianism and historicist
> superstitions. Popper describes the work as the
> philosophy of politics. Central to the work is his
> treatment of Plato, Marx, and Hegel.

2.1.9 1960 (1957). **The Poverty of Historicism**, 2nd ed.
London: Routledge and Kegan Paul; In German as **Das Elend
des Historizismus**, 5th rev. ed. Trans. of the 2nd Engl. ed.
Tübingen, J.C.B. Mohr.

> In his autobiography Popper describes **The Poverty** as
> "one of his stodgiest pieces of writing." It, too, was
> a war effort. Here Popper coins the word
> "historicism," discusses his theory of "situational
> analysis" and the "zero method." He advocates
> generalizing economic theory so as to become
> applicable to other social sciences. The work is an
> attack on Marxism and the view that man can predict
> the course of history.

2.2   Articles

2.2.1   1988. "The Open Society and Its Enemies Revisited." **The Economist** (23 April): 25-28.

2.2.2   1987(a). "The Myth of the Framework." In Joseph C. Pitt and Marcello Pera, eds. **Rational Changes in Science: Essays on Scientific Reasoning.** Vol. 98 of **Boston Studies in the Philosophy of Science.** Dordrecht: Reidel, 1987, pp. 35-62.

2.2.3   1987(b). "Natural Selection and the Emergence of the Mind." In Gerard Radnitzky and William Bartley, eds. **Evolutionary Epistemology, Rationality, and the Sociology of Knowledge.** La Salle/London: Open Court, 1987, pp. 139-53.

2.2.4   1987(c). "Zur Theorie der Demokratie." **Der Spiegel** (3 August): 54-55.

2.2.5   1976(a). "The Logic of the Social Sciences." In Theodor W. Adorno, et al. **The Positivist Dispute in German Sociology.** Trans. of **Der Positivismusstreit in der deutschen Soziologie** by Glyn Adey and David Frisby. NY: Harper and Row, 1976, pp. 87-104.

2.2.6   1976(b). "Reason Or Revolution?" In Theodor W. Adorno, et al. **The Positivist Dispute in German Sociology.** Trans. of **Der Positivismusstreit in der deutschen Soziologie** by Glyn Adey and David Frisby. NY: Harper and Row, 1976, pp. 288-300.

2.2.7   1975. "The Rationality of Scientific Revolutions." In **Problems of Scientific Revolutions.** Ed. by Rom Harré. Oxford: Clarendon Press, 1975, pp. 72-101; Rpt. in Ian Hacking. **Scientific Revolutions.** Oxford: Oxford University Press, 1981, pp. 80-106.

2.2.8   1974(a). "Autobiography of Karl Popper." In Paul Arthur Schilpp, ed. **The Philosophy of Karl Popper**, 2 vols. La Salle: Open Court, 1974, vol. I, pp. 3-181.

2.2.9   1974(b). "Karl Popper: Replies to My Critics." In Arthur Schilpp, ed. **The Philosophy of Karl Popper**, 2 vols. La Salle: Open Court, 1974, vol. II, pp. 963-1197.

2.2.10   1972. "Prediction and Prophecy in the Social Sciences." In his 1972(a), pp. 336-46.

2.2.11   1970. "Normal Science and Its Dangers." In Imre Lakatos and Alan Musgrave, eds. **Criticism and the Growth of Knowledge.** London: Cambridge University Press, 1970, pp. 51-58.

2.2.12   1968. "Remarks on the Problems of Demarcation and

of Rationality." In Imre Lakatos and Alan Musgrave, eds. **Problems in the Philosophy of Science.** Amsterdam: North-Holland, 1968, pp. 88-102.

2.2.13 1967. "La rationalité et la statut du principe de rationalité." In Emil M. Classen, ed. **Les fondements philosophiques des systèmes économiques: textes de Jacques Rueff et essais rédigés en son honneur.** Paris: Payot, 1967, pp. 142-50.

2.2.14 1964. "Über die Unwiderlegbarkeit philosophischer Theorien einschließlich jener, welche falsch sind." In **Club Voltaire I: Jahrbuch für kritische Aufklärung.** München: Szczesny Verlag, 1964, pp. 271-79.

2.2.15 1963. "The Demarcation Between Science and Metaphysics." In Paul Arthur Schilpp, ed. **The Philosophy of Rudolf Carnap.** La Salle: Open Court, 1963, pp. 183-226.

***

3

On Sir Karl Popper

The articles in § 3.1. discuss or use (directly or indirectly) Popper's ideas of falsification, demarcation, laws, or testing with reference to economics. T.W. Hutchison first introduced economists to Popper's theory of falsification in his **The Significance and Basic Postulates of Economic Theory** in 1938. The early issues for falsification in economics were: (1) economists do not formulate falsifiable hypotheses and (2) economists do not try to falsify their hypotheses. Blaug and Hutchison still defend this position. But since the 1980's, most economists realize that Popper's philosophy of science has problems and his falsification theory is of limited usefulness for economists.

Section 3.2. provides works from philosophers on Popper. They cover all aspects of Popper's philosophy.

Karl Popper's work, along with the works of Hayek and others, triggered a famous debate in the 1950's on methodological individualism, which continues to today. In his **Poverty of Historicism** (1960, p. 136) Popper writes that

> the task of social theory is to construct and to analyse our sociological models carefully in descriptive and nominalist terms, that is to say, **in terms of individuals**, of their attitudes, expectations, relations, etc.--a postulate which may be called 'methodological individualism'.

It is unfortunate that Popper did not participate in the debate which started in the fifties. Most of the works are collected in § 3.3. below.

Scott reaches the conclusion that Popper believes that

laws require testability, but explanation must be based on methodological individualism. Gellner (1956 and 1967) and Goldstein (1965) have both noted that Popper's view of methodological individualism implies psychologism (i.e., is reducible to psychology). This is what Popper wanted to avoid. Much of the debate revolves around the question: Are there non-reducible societal facts and laws? Popper believes that groups should be reducible to individuals; institutions, however, are non-reducible wholes.

Section 3.4. collects miscellaneous articles on Popper, written by social scientists, which do not fall into § 3.1. Lieberson's work is a good general treatment of Popper's philosophy. Cubeddu discusses Popper's place among the Austrians. The rest utilize Popper's ideas in other ways.

***

3.1   Falsification, Demarcation, Laws, and Testing in Economics

3.1.1 Archibald, G.C. 1967. "Refutation Or Comparison?" **British Journal for the Philosophy of Science** 17, No. 4 (February): 279-96.

3.1.2 Armstrong, Wallace Edwin. 1960. **Philosophical Reflections of an Economist.** Southampton: Southampton University Press.

3.1.3 Biermann, Herbert. 1975. "Über die wirtschaftpolitische Relevanz des Popperschen Falsifikationskritieriums." **Jahrbuch für Sozialwissenschaft** 26, No. 1: 1-9.

3.1.4 Blaug, Mark. 1985. "Comment on D. Wade Hands, 'Karl Popper and Economic Methodology: A New Look.'" **Economics and Philosophy** 1: 286-88.

3.1.5 Blaug, Mark. 1980. **The Methodology of Economists Or How Economists Explain.** Cambridge: Cambridge University Press.

3.1.6 Boland, Lawrence A. 1985. "Reflections on Blaug's **Methodology of Economics:** Suggestions for a Revised Edition." **Eastern Economic Journal** 11, No. 4 (October-December): 450-54.

3.1.7 Boland, Lawrence A. 1977. "Testability in Economic Science." **South African Journal of Economics** 45 (March): 93-105.

3.1.8 Boland, Lawrence A. 1969. "Economic Understanding and Understanding Economics." 37 (June): 144-60.

3.1.9 Bray, Jeremy. 1978(a). "Reply to J.G. Meeks" (Bray

on Keynes on Scientific Method) **Journal of Economic Studies** 5, No. 2 (November): 151.

3.1.10 Bray, Jeremy. 1978(b). "Reply to John Naughton" (The Logic of Scientific Method in Economics). **Journal of Economic Studies** 5, No. 2 (November): 166.

3.1.11 Bray, Jeremy. 1977. "The Logic of Scientific Method in Economics." **Journal of Economic Studies** 4, No. 1 (May): 1-28.

3.1.12 Brinkmann, Gerhard. 1970. "Zur Wissenschaftstheorie der Ökonometrie." **Kyklos** 23, No. 2: 205-25.

3.1.13 Brochier, Hubert. 1987. "Les théories économiques sont-elles réfutables." **Economies et sociétés** 21, N° 10 (Octobre): 107-18.

3.1.14 Caldwell, Bruce J. 1984. "Some Problems with Falsification in Economics." **Philosophy of the Social Sciences** 14: 489-95.

3.1.15 Clark, A.F. 1977. "Testability in Economic Sciences: A Comment." **South African Journal of Science** 45: 106-07.

3.1.16 Clauss, Franz Joachim. 1977. "'Null-Wahrscheinlichkeit des allgemeinen Gesetzes'--ein Irrtum Poppers? Kritische Anmerkungen zur falsifikationslogische Wissenschaftslehre." **Ifo-Studien** 23, Nos. 1/2: 177-241.

3.1.17 Dennis, Ken G. 1981. "Provable Theorems and Refutable Hypotheses: The Case of Competitive Theory." **Journal of Economic Issues** 15, No. 1 (March): 95-112.

3.1.18 Falkena, H.B. 1982. "On the Logical Structure of Non-Fallible Economic Theories." **South African Journal of Economics** 50 (March): 225-37.

3.1.19 Good, I.J. 1981. "Some Logic and History of Hypothesis Testing." In Joseph Pitt, ed. **Philosophy in Economics**. Dordrecht: Reidel, 1981, pp. 149-74.

3.1.20 Grunberg, Emile. 1957. "Notes on the Verifiability of Economic Laws." **Philosophy of Science** 24: 337-48.

3.1.21 Hands, Douglas W. 1985. "Karl Popper and Economic Methodology." **Economics and Philosophy** 1: 83-99.

3.1.22 Hands, Douglas W. 1984. "Blaug's Economic Methodology." **Philosophy of the Social Sciences** 14, No. 1: 115-25.

3.1.23 Hutchison, T.W. 1966. "Testing Economic Assumptions: A Comment." **Journal of Political Economy** 74, No. 1 (February): 81-83.

3.1.24 Hutchison, T.W. 1965 (1938). **The Significance and Basic Postulates of Economic Theory.** 74, No. 1 (February): Augustus M. Kelley.

3.1.25 Hutchison, T.W. 1959. "Review of Popper's **The Logic of Scientific Discovery.**" 26 (August): 262-64.

3.1.26 Jetzer, Jean-Pierre. 1987. **Kritscher Rationalismus und Nationalökonomie.** Bern/Frankfurt am Main/NY/Paris: Peter Lang.

3.1.27 Küttner, Michael. 1983. "Kritische Bemerkungen zur Falsifierbarkeit ökonomischer Theorien." In Ekkehard Kappler, ed. **Rekonstruktionen der Betriebswirtschaftslehre als ökonomische Theorie.** Spardorf: Wilfer, 1983, pp. 1-7.

3.1.28 Leeman, Wayne A. 1951. "The Status of Facts in Economic Thought." **Journal of Philosophy** 48 (June): 401-12.

3.1.29 Le Pen, Claude. 1987. "'Falsifiabilité' et théorie économique ou comment rendre une théorie scientifique infalsifiable." **Economies et sociétés** 21, No. 10 (October): 119-28.

3.1.30 Machlup, Fritz. 1978. "The Problem of Verification in Economics." In his **Methodology of Economics and Other Social Sciences.** NY: Academic Press, 1978, pp. 137-58.

3.1.31 Meeks, J.G. 1978. "Bray on Keynes on Scientific Method: A Comment." **Journal of Economic Studies** 5, No. 2 (November): 146-50.

3.1.32 Meidinger, Claude. 1987. "L'empirisme et le statut des hypotheses ad hoc en physique et en économie." **Economies et sociétés** 21, No. 10 (October): 129-52.

3.1.33 Mongin, Philippe. 1986. "Are 'All-and-Some' Statements Falsifiable After All? The Example of Utility Theory." **Economics and Philosophy** 2, No. 2 (October): 185-95.

3.1.34 O'Brien, D.P. 1976. "The Longevity of Adam Smith's Vision: Paradigms, Research Programmes and Falsifiability in the History of Economic Thought." **Scottish Journal of Political Economy** 23, No. 2 (June): 133-51.

3.1.35 Salanti, Andrea. 1987. "Falsificationism and Fallibilism As Epistemic Foundations of Economics: A Critical View." **Kyklos** 40, No. 3: 368-92.

3.1.36 Shearer, J.O. 1939. "(Review of Hutchison's) The Significance and Basic Postulates of Economic Theory." **Economic Record** 15 (June): 136-38.

3.1.37 Shearmur, Jeremy. 1983. "Subjectivism, Falsification, and Positive Economics." In Jack Wiseman, ed. **Beyond**

Positive Economics. London: The British Association for the Advancement of Science, 1983, pp. 65-86.

3.1.38 *Stigler, George J. 1951. "Economic Theory, Statistics, and Economic Practice: Discussion." **American Economic Papers and Proceedings** 41, No. 2 (May): 126-28.

3.1.39 Stonier, Alfred W. 1939. "Review of Hutchison's **The Significance and Basic Postulates of Economic Theory**." **Economic Journal** 49 (March): 114-15.

3.1.40 Swanenberg, August J.M. and Frans A.M. van der Reep. 1982. "Notes on the Testability of Economic Theories: Two Theories About Economic Theory Formation." **Logique et analyse** (March): 57-73.

3.1.41 Whittaker, Edmund. 1940. "Review of Hutchison's **The Significance and Basic Postulates of Economic Theory**." **American Economic Review** 30 (March): 128.

(See also sections four and nine above on Friedman, assumptions, and econometrics.)

3.2   Literature from the Philosophy of Science

3.2.1 Ackermann, Robert. 1985. "Popper and German Social Philosophy." In Gregory Currie and Alan Musgrave, eds. **Popper and the Human Sciences**. Dordrecht: Martinus Nijhoff, pp. 165-83.

3.2.2 Ackermann, Robert. 1976. **The Philosophy of Karl Popper**. Amherst: University of Massachusetts Press.

3.2.3 Adorno, Theodor W., et al. 1976. **The Positivist Dispute in German Sociology**. Trans. of **Der Positivismusstreit in der deutschen Soziologie**, 1969, by Glyn Adey and David Frisby. NY: Harper and Row.

3.2.4 Agassi, Joseph. 1975. "The Present State of the Philosophy of Science." **Philosophia** 15, No. 1: 5-20.

3.2.5 Agassi, Joseph. 1967. "Science in Flux." In Robert Cohen and Marx Wartofsky, eds. **In Memory of Norwood Russell Hanson**. Vol. 3 of **Boston Studies in the Philosophy of Science**. Dordrecht: Reidel, 1967, pp. 193-323.

3.2.6 Bartley, William Warren, III. 1982(a). "Critical Study: The Philosophy of Karl Popper Part III: Rationality, Criticism, and Logic." **Philosophia** 11, No. 1 (February): 121-21. (Parts IV and V will not appear.)

3.2.7 Bartley, William Warren, III. 1982(b). "A Popperian Harvest." In Paul Levinson, ed. **In Pursuit of Truth**. NJ: Humanities Press, 1982, pp. 249-89.

3.2.8 Bartley, William Warren, III. 1977. "Critical Study:

The Philosophy of Karl Popper Part II: Consciousness and Physics." **Philosophia** 7, No. 2 (March): 675-716.

3.2.9 Bartley, William Warren, III. 1976. "Critical Study: The Philosophy of Karl Popper Part I: Biology and Evolutionary Epistemology." **Philosophia** 6, Nos. 3-4 (September-December): 463-94.

3.2.10 Bartley, William Warren, III. 1974. "The Language and Philosophy of Science As Instruments of Educational Reform: Wittgenstein and Popper As Austrian School-teachers." In Robert Cohen and Marx Wartofsky, eds. **Methodological and Historical Essays in the Philosophy of Science.** Dordrecht: Reidel, 1974, pp. 307-337.

3.2.11 Berkson, William and John Wettersten. 1982. **Lernen aus dem Irrtum: die Bedeutung von Karl Popper's Lerntheorie für die Psychologie und Philosophie der Wissenschaft.** Hamburg: Hoffmann und Campe; Slightly revised in English as **Learning from Error.** La Salle: Open Court, 1984.

3.2.12 Bloor, David. 1974. "Popper's Mystification of Objective Knowledge." **Science Studies** 4, No. 1 (January): 65-76.

3.2.13 Braun, Gunther E. 1977. "Von Popper zu Lakatos: Das Abgrenzungsproblem zwischen Wissenschaft und Pseudo-Wissenschaft." **Conceptus** 11: 217-42.

3.2.14 Brown, Harold I. 1977. **Perception, Theory and Commitment: The New Philosophy of Science.** Chicago/London: University of Chicago Press, ch. 5.

3.2.15 Chalmers, A.F. 1982. **What Is This Thing Called Science?**, 2nd ed. St. Lucia: University of Queensland Press, Ch. 4-6.

3.2.16 Chalmers, A.F. 1973. "On Learning from Our Mistakes." **British Journal for the Philosophy of Science** 24, No. 2 (June): 164-73.

3.2.17 Frisby, David. 1972. "The Popper-Adorno Controversy: the Methododological Dispute in German Sociology." **Philosophy of the Social Sciences** 2: 105-19.

3.2.18 Grünbaum, Adolf. 1976. "Is Falsifiability the Touchstone of Scientific Rationality? Karl Popper Versus Inductivism." In Robert Cohen, Paul Feyerabend, and Marx Wartofsky, eds. **Essays in Memory of Imre Lakatos.** Vol. 39 of **Boston Studies in the Philosophy of Science.** Dordrecht: Reidel, 1967, pp. 213-52.

3.2.19 Harris, Errol E. 1972. "Epicyclic Popperism." **British Journal for the Philosophy of Science** 23: 55-67.

3.2.20 Irzik, Gürol. 1985. "Popper's Piecemeal Engineering:

What Is Good for Science Is Not Always Good for Society."
British Journal for the Philosophy of Science 36: 1-10.

3.2.21 Johansson, Ingvar. 1975. **A Critique of Karl Popper's
Methodology**. Stockholm: Scandanavian University Books.

3.2.22 Koertge,   Noretta.   1979.   "Braucht   die
Sozialwissenschaft wirklich Metaphysik?" In Hans Albert and
Kurt H. Stapf, eds. **Theorie und Erfahrung**. Stuttgart:
Klett, 1979, pp. 55-81.

3.2.23 Koertge, Noretta. 1975.   "Popper's Metaphysical
Research Program for the Human Sciences." **Inquiry** 18:
437-62.

3.2.24 Lakatos, Imre. 1974. "Popper on Demarcation and
Induction." In his **Methodology of Scientific Research
Programmes**. Vol. 1 of his **Philosophical Papers**. Ed. by John
Worrall and Gregory Currie. Cambridge: Cambridge University
Press.

3.2.25 Magee, Bryan. 1985. **Philosophy and the Real World:
An Introduction to Karl Popper**. La Salle: Open Court.

3.2.26 Mulkay, Michael and G. Nigel Gilbert. 1981. "Putting
Philosophy to Work: Karl Popper's Influence on Scientific
Practice." **Philosophy of the Social Sciences** 11: 389-407.

3.2.27 Musgrave,   Alan.   1973.   "Falsification   and   its
Critics." In Patrick Suppes, et al., eds. **Logic,
Methodology and Philosophy of Science**. Amsterdam:
North-Holland, 1973, pp. 393-406.

3.2.28 Newton-Smith, W.H. 1981. **The Rationality of Science**.
London: Routledge and Kegan Paul, ch. 3.

3.2.29 Passmore, John. 1974. "The Poverty of Historicism
Revisited." **History and Theory**, Beiheft 14: **Essays on
Historicism**. 14, No. 4: 30-47.

3.2.30 Passmore,   John.   1960.   "Popper's   Account   of
Scientific Method." **Philosophy** 35: 326-31.

3.2.31 Radnitzky, Gerard. 1976. "Popperian Philosophy of
Science As an Antidote Against Relativism." In Robert S.
Cohen, Paul Feyerabend, and Marx Wartofsky, eds. **Essays in
Memory of Imre Lakatos**. Vol. 39 of **Boston Studies in the
Philosophy of Science**. Dordrecht: Reidel, 1976, pp. 505-46.

3.2.32 Schilpp, Arthur. 1974. **The Philosophy of Karl
Popper**, 2 vols. La Salle: Open Court.

3.2.33 Schilpp, Arthur. 1963. **The Philosophy of Rudolf
Carnap**. La Salle: Open Court.

3.2.34 Stove, David C. 1982. **Popper and After: Four Modern**

Irrationalists. Oxford: Pergamon Press.

3.2.35 Urbach, Peter. 1978. "Is Any of Popper's Arguments Against Historicisim Valid?" **British Journal for the Philosophy of Science** 29: 117-30.

3.2.36 Weinheimer, Heinz. 1986. **Rationalität und Begründung: Das Grundlagenproblem in der Philosophie Karl Poppers.** Band 30: Mainzer philosophischer Forschungen. Bonn: Bouvier Verlag.

3.3   The Debate on Methodological Individualism

3.3.1 Agassi, Joseph. 1960. "Methodological Individualism." **British Journal of Sociology** 11: 244-71.

3.3.2 Brodbeck, May. 1958. "Methodological Individualisms: Definition and Reduction." **Philosophy of Science** 25, No. 1 (January): 1-22.

3.3.3 Brodbeck, May. 1954. "On the Philosophy of the Social Sciences." **Philosophy of Science** 21: 140-57.

3.3.4 Gellner, Ernest A. 1967. "Reply to Mr. Watkins." In Patrick Gardiner, ed. **Theories of History.** NY: The Free Press, 1967, pp. 514-16.

3.3.5 Gellner, Ernest A. 1956. "Explanations in History." **Proceedings of the Aristotelian Society.** Suppl. Vol. 30: 157-76; Rpt. as "Holism Versus Individualism in History and Sociology," in Patrick Gardner, ed. **Theories of History.** NY: The Free Press, 1959, pp. 489-503.

3.3.6 Goldstein, Leon J. 1958. "The Two Theses of Methodological Individualism." **British Journal for the Philosophy of Science** 9, No. 33 (May): 1-12.

3.3.7 Goldstein, Leon J. 1956. "The Inadequacy of the Principle of Methodological Individiualism." **Journal of Philosophy** 53, No. 2 (December): 801-13.

3.3.8 Lukes, Steven. 1968. "Methodological Individualism Reconsidered." **British Journal of Sociology** 19: 119-29.

3.3.9 Mandelbaum, Maurice. 1957. "Societal Laws." **British Journal for the Philosophy of Science** 8: 211-25.

3.3.10 Mandelbaum, Maurice. 1955. "Societal Facts." **British Journal of Sociology** 6: 305-17.

3.3.11 Scott, K.J. 1960-61. "Methodological and Epistemological Individualism." **British Journal for the Philosophy of Science** 11: 331-36.

3.3.12 Watkins, J.W.N. 1959. "The Two Theses of Methodological Individualism." **British Journal for the**

Philosophy of Science 9: 319-21.

3.3.13 Watkins, J.W.N. 1958. "The Alleged Inadequacy of Methodological Individualism." **Journal of Philosophy** 55: 390-95.

3.3.14 Watkins, J.W.N. 1957-58. "Historical Explanation in the Social Sciences." **British Journal for the Philosophy of Science** 8: 104-17; Rpt. in Patrick Gardner, ed. **Theories of History**. The Free Press, 1959, pp. 503-14.

3.3.15 Watkins, J.W.N. 1955. "Methodological Individualism: A Reply." **Philosophy of Science** 22: 58-63.

3.3.16 Watkins, J.W.N. 1952-53. "Ideal Types and Historical Explanation." **British Journal for the Philosophy of Science** 3: 22-24.

3.3.17 Watkins, J.W.N. 1952-53. "The Principle of Methodological Individualism." **British Journal for the Philosophy of Science** 3: 186-89.

3.3.18 Wisdom, J.O. 1970. "Situational Individualism and the Emergent Group-properties." In Robert Borger and Frank Cioffi, ed. **Explanation in the Behavioural Sciences**. Cambridge: Cambridge University Press, 1970, pp. 271-96.

3.4 Miscellaneous

3.4.1 Boyer, Alain. 1987. "Karl Popper face aux sciences sociales." **Économies et sociétés** 21, No. 10 (October): 5-24.

3.4.2 Cubeddu, Raimondo. 1987. "Popper et l'école autrichienne." **Économies et sociétés** 21, No. 10 (October): 41-62.

3.4.3 Farr, James. 1983. "Popper's Hermeneutics." **Philosophy of the Social Sciences** 13: 157-76.

3.4.4 Lieberson, Jonathan. 1982. "Karl Popper." **Social Research** 49, No. 1 (Spring): 68-115.

3.4.5 Menges, Günter. 1982. "Die statische Adäquation." **Jahrbücher für Nationalökonomie und Statistik** 197, No. 4 (July): 289-307.

3.4.6 Meyer, Willi. 1972. "Reine Wissenschaftstheorie und nationalökonomische Forschungsstrategien." **Zeitschrift für die gesamte Staatswissenschaft** 128, No. 4 (November): 713-30.

3.4.7 Mongin, Philippe. 1986. "La controverse sur l'entreprise (1940-1959) et la formation de l'irrealisme methodologique." 20, No. 3 (March): 95-151.

3.4.8 Persson, Gunnar. 1980. "Conceptual Colonialism:
Progress Or Retrogression? Issues in Labour Economics."
Economy and History 23, No. 2: 133-51.

3.4.9 Skinner, Andrew S. 1979. "Adam Smith: An Aspect of
Modern Economics?" **Scottish Journal of Political Economy**
26, No. 2 (June): 109-25.

3.4.10 Tietzel, Manfred. 1983. "Erkenntnisfortschritt und
Konjunkturtheorie." **Ifo-Studien** 29, No. 1: 11-30.

***

4

Works by Thomas Kuhn

Thomas Kuhn is chiefly an historian of science, has nonetheless made a major contribution to the philosophy of science. His **magnum opus** is **The Structure of Scientific Revolutions**, which most social scientists and historians have heard of. The "Postscript" in the second edition, his 1970(a) and (b), and some of the articles in his book **The Essential Tension** (i.e., 1977(k)) are follow-ups to the original work. **The Essential Tension** is an anthology of articles written before and after **The Structure of Scientific Revolutions** appeared.

Kuhn's **Structure of Scientific Revolutions** is chiefly concerned with the problem of scientific change. During periods of "normal science" one paradigm is refined. Revolutions occcur when the scientific community decides to stop working with the old paradigm and embrace a new paradigm. Also novel was Kuhn's emphasis on the scientific community itself (sociological factors) and on scientific theories as complex structures.

One major problem with Kuhn's work is that he used the word "paradigm" too loosely. It has led to incompatible interpretations from those using his work: these authors use any interpretation which suits their fancy. It would be best if "paradigm" were dropped. Kuhn originally meant by paradigm a theory, and specifically theories in physics.

***

4.1   Books

4.1.1   1977(b). **The Essential Tension.** Chicago: University of Chicago Press.

4.1.2   1970(c). **The Structure of Scientific Revolutions.** 2nd enlarged ed. Chicago: University of Chicago Press.

4.2   Articles

4.2.1   1977(a). "Concepts of Cause in the Development of Physics." In his 1977 (book), pp. 21-30.

4.2.2   1977(b). "The Essential Tension: Tradition and Innovation in Scientific Research." In his 1977 (book), pp. 225-39.

4.2.3   1977(c). "A Function for Thought Experiments." In his 1977(book) pp. 240-65; Rpt. in Ian Hacking, ed. **Scientific Revolutions.** Oxford: Oxford University Press, 1981, pp. 6-27.

4.2.4   1977(d). "The Function of Measurement in Modern Physical Science." In his 1977 (book), pp. 178-224.

4.2.5   1977(e). "The Historical Structure of Scientific Discovery." In his 1977 (book), pp. 165-77.

4.2.6   1977(f). "The History of Science." In his 1977 (book), pp. 105-26; Rpt. from **International Encyclopedia of the Social Sciences,** 1968 ed.

4.2.7   1977(g). "Mathematical Versus Experimental Traditions in the Development of Physical Science." In his 1977 (book), pp. 31-65.

4.2.8   1977(h). "Objectivity, Value Judgement, and Theory Choice." In his 1977 (book), pp. 320-39.

4.2.9   1977(i). "The Relations Between History and the History of Science." In his 1977 (book), pp. 127-61.

4.2.10   1977(j). "The Relations Between the History and the Philosophy of Science." In his 1977 (book), pp. 3-20.

4.2.11   1977(k). "Second Thoughts on Paradigms." In his 1977(b), pp. 293-319; Rpt. from Suppe, 1977 (book), pp. 459-82.

4.2.12   1971. "Notes on Lakatos." In Roger C. Buck and Robert S. Cohen, eds. **PSA 1970 in Memory of Rudulf Carnap.** Vol. 8 of **Boston Studies in the Philosophy of Science.** Dordrecht: Reidel, 1971, pp. 137-46.

4.2.13   1970(a). "Logic of Discovery Or Psychology of Research?" In Imre Lakatos and Alan Musgrave. **Criticism and the Growth of Knowledge.** London: Cambridge University Press, 1970, pp. 1-23; Rpt. in his 1977 (book), pp. 266-92.

4.2.14   1970(b). "Reflections on My Critics." In Imre Lakatos and Alan Musgrave, eds. **Criticism and the Growth of Knowledge.** London: Cambridge University Press, 1970, pp. 231-78.

4.2.15 1963. "The   Function   of   Dogma   in   Scientific
Research."   In   A.C.   Crombie,   ed. **Scientific   Change:
Historical   Studies   in   the   Intellectual,   Social   and
Technical Conditions for Scientific Discovery and Technical
Invention, from Antiquity to Present.** London: Heinemann,
1963, pp. 347-69.

4.2.16 Kuhn,   Thomas,   et   al.   1977.   "Discussion."   In
Frederick Suppe, ed. **The Structure of Scientific Theories,**
2nd ed. Urbana: University of Illinois Press, pp. 500-17.

***

5

On Kuhn

Kuhn's philosophy was a big hit among social scientists. His philosophy was widely applied to economics. Ward applied his philosophy perhaps most successfully in his book **What's Wrong with Economics?**. Most of the authors in § 5.1 simply assume that Kuhn's philosophy is useful to economists. Two who do not are Baumberger and Rousseas.

§ 5.2. treats not only Kuhnian revolutions, but the concept revolution in general. Revolutions are not foreign to economists. Well before Kuhn's philosophy became popular, economists spoke of revolutions: marginal revolutions, the Keynesian revolution, the monetarist revolution, etc. See, e.g., Kaysen referring to game theory, and Johnson.

Cohen (1985 in book form and 1976 in more digestable article form) discusses all aspects of revolution in science: the origin of the word and its evolution, and its uses in the natural and social sciences.

In § 5.3. one finds the critics of Kuhn's work. These philosophers of science cover a wide range of issues discussed by Kuhn. Gutting's work has a bibliography of all of Kuhn's works and applications of Kuhn's philosophy to other disciplines. Hacking collects some of the key articles on revolutions. Most of the works in § 5.3. are highly critical of Kuhn's work, which has great problems indeed.

***

5.1   Applications of Kuhnian Paradigms to Economics

5.1.1 Abele, Hanns. 1971. "From One-Dimensional to Multidimensional Economics: 'Paradigm' Lost." **Zeitschrift für Nationalökonomie** 31: 45-62.

5.1.2 Aeppli, Roland. 1980. "Ökonomie als multiparadigmatische Wissenschaft." **Kyklos** 33, No. 4: 682-708.

5.1.3 Baumberger, Jörg. 1977. "No Kuhnian Revolutions in Economics." **Journal of Economic Issues** 11 (March): 1-20; Rpt. in Warren Samuels, ed. **The Methodology of Economic Thought: Critical Papers from the Journal of Economic Issues.** New Brunswick, NJ: Transaction Books, 1977, pp. 322-41.

5.1.4 Bliss, Christopher. 1986. "Progress and Anti-Progress in Economic Science." In Mauro Baranzini and Roberto Scazzieri, eds. **Foundations of Economics.** Oxford: Basil Blackwell, 1986, pp. 363-76.

5.1.5 Canterbery, E. Ray and Robert J. Burkhardt. 1983. "What Do We Mean by Asking Whether Economics Is a Science?" In Alfred S. Eichner, ed. **Why Economics Is Not Yet a Science.** London: Macmillan, 1983, pp. 15-40.

5.1.6 Chase, Richard X. 1983. "Adolf Lowe's Paradigm Shift for a Scientific Economics: An Interpretive Perspective." **American Journal of Economics and Sociology** 42, No. 2 (April): 167-77.

5.1.7 Coats, A.W. 1969. "Is There a 'Structure of Scientific Revolutions' in Economics?" **Kyklos** 22, No. 2: 289-96.

5.1.8 Dillard, Dudley. 1978. "Revolutions in Economic Theory." **Southern Economic Journal** 44, No. 4 (April): 705-24.

5.1.9 Dow, Sheila C. 1980. "Methodological Morality in the Cambridge Controversies." **Journal of Post Keynesian Economics** 2, No. 3 (Spring): 368-80.

5.1.10 Eichner, Alfred S. and S.A. Kregel. 1975. "An Essay on Post Keynesian Theory: A New Paradigm in Economics." **Journal of Economic Literature** 13, No. 4 (December): 1293-1314.

5.1.11 Gordon, Donald F. 1965. "The Role of the History of Economic Thought in the Understanding of Modern Economic Theory." **American Economic Review: Supplement** 55 (May): 119-27.

5.1.12 Hennings, Klaus H. 1986. "The Exchange Paradigm and the Theory of Production and Distribution." In Mauro Baranzini and Roberto Scazzieri, eds. **Foundations of Economics.** Oxford: Basil Blackwell, 1986, pp. 91-101.

5.1.13 Hutchison, T.W. 1978. **On Revolutions and Progress in Economic Knowledge.** Cambridge: Cambridge University Press.

5.1.14 Jalladeau, Joel. 1978. "Research Program Versus Paradigm in the Development of Economics." **Journal of Economic Issues** 12, No. 3 (September): 583-608.

5.1.15 Johnson, L.E. 1983. "Economic Paradigms: A Missing Dimension." **Journal of Economic Issues** 17, No. 4 (December): 1097-1111.

5.1.16 Johnson, L.E. 1980. "A Neo-Paradigmatic Model for Studying the Development of Economic Reasoning." **Atlantic Economic Journal** 8, No. 4 (December): 52-61.

5.1.17 Katouzian, Homa. 1980. **Ideology and Method in Economics.** NY: New York University Press, chapter 4.

5.1.18 Kunin, Leonard and F. Stirton Weaver. 1971. "On the Structure of Scientific Revolutions in Economics." **History of Political Economy** 3, No. 2 (Fall): 391-97.

5.1.19 Meier, Alfred and Daniel Mettler. 1985. "Auf der Suche nach einem neuen Paradigma der Wirtschaftspolitik." **Kyklos** 38, No. 2: 171-99.

5.1.20 Pasinetti, Luigi L. 1986. "Theory of Value--A Source of Alternative Paradigms in Economic Analysis." In Mauro Baranzini and Roberto Scazzieri, eds. **Foundations of Economics.** Oxford: Basil Blackwell, 1986, pp. 409-31.

5.1.21 Peabody, Gerald E. 1971. "Scientific Paradigms and Economics: An Introduction." **Review of Radical Economics** 3, No. 2 (July): 1-16.

5.1.22 Rousseas, Stephen. 1973. "Paradigm Polishing Versus Critical Thought in Economics." **American Economist** 17 (Fall): 72-78.

5.1.23 Routh, Guy. 1975. **The Origin of Economic Ideas.** London: Macmillan.

5.1.24 Stanfield, J. Ron. 1979. **Economic Thought and Social Change.** Carbondale and Edwardsville: Southern Illinois University Press.

5.1.25 Stanfield, J. Ron. 1974. "Kuhnian Scientific Revolutions and the Keynesian Revolution." **Journal of Economic Issues** 8 (March): 97-109.

5.1.26 *Stigler, George J. 1969. "Does Economics Have a Useful Past?" **History of Political Economy** 1, No. 2 (Fall): 217-30. (applies the concept with reservation)

5.1.27 Sweezy, Paul M. 1971. "Toward a Critique of Economics." **Review of Radical Political Economics** 3, No. 2 (July): 59-66.

5.1.28 Vroey, Michel de. 1975. "The Transition from

Classical to Neoclassical Economics: A Scientific Revolution." **Journal of Economic Issues** 9: 415ff; Rpt. in Warren Samuels, ed. **The Methodology of Economic Thought: Critical Papers from the Journal of Economic Issues.** New Brunswick, NJ: Transaction Books, 1980, pp. 297-321.

5.1.29 Ward, Benjamin. 1972. **What's Wrong with Economics?** London: Macmillan.

5.1.30 Worland, Stephen T. 1972. "Radical Political Economy As a Scientific Revolution." **Southern Economic Journal** 39, No. 2 (October): 274-84.

5.1.31 Zinam, Oleg. 1978. "Search for a Logic of Change in Economic Theories: Evolution, Revolutions, Paradigmatic Shifts and Dialectic." **Revista Internazionale di Scienze Economiche e Commercialle** 25 (February): 156-88.

5.1.32 Zweig, Michael. 1971. "Bourgeois and Radical Paradigms in Economics." **Review of Radical Political Economics** 3, No. 2 (July): 43-58.

5.2   On Revolutions, Kuhnian and Other

5.2.1 Blaug, Mark. 1973. "Was There a Marginal Revolution?" In R.D.C. Black, A.W. Coats, and Craufurd D.W. Goodwin, eds. **The Marginal Revolution in Economics: Interpretation and Evaluation.** Durham, North Carolina: Duke University Press, 1973, pp. 3-14.

5.2.2 Bowley, Marion. 1972. "The Predecessors of Jevons--The Revolution That Wasn't." **Manchester School of Economic and Social Studies** 40, No. 1 (March): 9-29.

5.2.3 Bronfenbrenner, Martin. 1971. "The 'Structure of Revolutions' in Economic Thought." **History of Political Economy** 3, No. 1 (Spring): 136-51.

5.2.4 Coats, A.W. 1969. "Is There a 'Structure of Scientific Revolutions' in Economics?" **Kyklos** 22, No. 2: 289-96.

5.2.5 Cohen, I. Bernard. 1985. **Revolution in Science.** Cambridge, MA: Belknap Press of Harvard University Press.

5.2.6 Cohen, I. Bernard. 1976. "The Eighteenth-Century Origins of the Concept of Scientific Revolution." **Journal of the History of Ideas** 37: 257-88.

5.2.7 Dillard, Dudley. 1978. "Revolutions in Economic Theory." **Southern Economic Journal** 44, No. 4 (April): 705-24.

5.2.8 *Hicks, Sir John. 1976. "'Revolutions' in Economics." In Spiro J. Latsis, ed. **Method and Appraisal in Economics.** Cambridge: Cambridge University Press, 1976, pp.

207-18; Rpt. in his **Classics and Moderns**. Oxford: Oxford University Press, 1983, pp. 3-16.

5.2.9 Hutchison, T.W. 1978. **On Revolutions and Progress in Economic Knowledge**. Cambridge: Cambridge University Press.

5.2.10 Hutchison, T.W. 1972. "The 'Marginal Revolution' and the Decline of English Classical Political Economy." **History of Political Economy** 4 (Fall): 442-68; Rpt. in R.D. Collison Black, A.W. Coats, and Craufurd D.W. Goodwin, eds. **The Marginal Revolution in Economics: Interpretation and Evaluation**. Durham, N. Ca.: Duke University Press, 1972, pp. 176-202.

5.2.11 Johnson, H.G. 1971. "Revolution and Counter-Revolution in Economics." **Encounter** 36, No. 4 (April): 23-33.

5.2.12 Kaysen, Carl. 1945-46. "A Revolution in Economic Theory?" **Review of Economic Studies** 14: 1-15.

5.2.13 Kunin, Leonard and F. Stirton Weaver. 1971. "On the Structure of Scientific Revolutions in Economics." **History of Political Economy** 3, No. 2 (Fall): 391-97.

5.2.14 Leijonhufvud, Axel. 1976. "Schools, 'Revolutions', and Research Programs in Economic Theory." In Spiro J. Latsis. **Method and Appraisal in Economics**. Cambridge: Cambridge University Press, 1976, pp. 65-108.

5.2.15 Mirowski, Philip. 1984. "Physics and the 'Marginalist Revolution.'" **Cambridge Journal of Economics** 8: 361-79.

5.2.16 Reynolds, L. 1976. "The Nature of Revolutions in Economics." **Intermountain Economic Review** 7, No. 1 (Spring): 25-33.

5.2.17 Skinner, Andrew S. 1965. "Economics and History--The Scottish Enlightenment." **Scottish Journal of Political Economy** 12 (February): 1-22.

5.2.18 Spengler, Joseph J. 1968. "Economics: Its History, Themes, Approaches." **Journal of Economic Issues** 2, No. 1 (March): 42-49.

5.2.19 Toulmin, Stephen E. 1967. "Conceptual Revolutions in Science." In Robert S. Cohen and Marx Wartofsky, eds. **In Memory of Norwood Russell Hanson**. Vol. 3 of **Boston Studies in the Philosophy of Science**. Dordrecht: Reidel, 1967, pp. 331-47.

5.2.20 Wieland, Bernhard. 1985. "Towards an Economic Theory of Scientific Revolutions--A Cynical View." **Erkenntnis** 23 (May): 79-96.

5.2.21 Vroey, Michel de. 1975. "The Transition from Classical to Neoclassical Economics: A Scientific Revolution." **Journal of Economic Issues** 9: 415ff.

5.2.22 Zinam, Oleg. 1978. "Search for a Logic of Change in Economic Theories: Evolution, Revolutions, Paradigmatic Shifts and Dialectic." **Revista Internazionale di Scienze Economiche e Commerciale** 25 (February): 156-88.

5.3   Literature from the Philosophy of Science

5.3.1 Barnes, Barry. 1982. **T.S. Kuhn and Social Science.** NY: Columbia University Press.

5.3.2 Ben-David, Joseph. 1964. "Scientific Growth: A Sociological View." **Minerva** 2, No. 2 (Summer): 455-76.

5.3.3 Böhler, Dietrich. 1972. "Paradigmawechsel in analytischer Wissenschaftstheorie." **Zeitschrift für allgemeine Wissenschaftstheorie** 3, No. 2: 219-42.

5.3.4 Brown, Harold I. 1983. "Incommensurability." **Inquiry** 26, No. 1 (March): 3-30.

5.3.5 Brown, Harold I. 1977. **Perception, Theory and Commitment: The New Philosophy of Science.** Chicago/London: University of Chicago Press, ch. 7-8.

5.3.6 Chalmers, A.F. 1982. **What Is This Thing Called Science?**, 2nd ed. St. Lucia: University of Queensland Press, ch. 8.

5.3.7 Diederich, Werner. 1986. "What Is Revolutionary About the Copernican Revolution?" In **Essays on Creativity and Science.** Papers Delivered at a Conference Held in Honolulu, Hawaii, March 23-24, 1985. Hawaii Council of Teachers of English, 1986, pp. 31-42.

5.3.8 Diederich, Werner, ed. 1974. **Theorien der Wissenschaftsgeschichte: Beiträge zur diachronischen Wissenschaftstheorie.** Frankfurt am Main: Suhrkamp.

5.3.9 Glymour, Clark. 1980. **Theory and Evidence.** Princeton: Princeton University Press, ch. 4.

5.3.10 Grünfeld, Joseph. 1979. "Progress in Science." **Logique et analyse** 85-86 (March-June): 208-21

5.3.11 Gutting, Gary, ed. 1980. **Paradigms and Revolutions: Appraisals and Applications of Thomas Kuhn's Philosophy of Science.** Notre Dame: University of Notre Dame Press.

5.3.12 Hacking, Ian, ed. 1981. **Scientific Revolutions.** Oxford: Oxford University Press.

5.3.13 Kockelmans, Joseph J. 1972. "On the Meaning of

228 Philosophy of Science

Scientific Revolutions." **Philosophy Forum** 11 (September): 243-64.

5.3.14 Krüger, Lorenz. 1974. "Die systematische Bedeutung wissenschaftlicher Revolutionen, pro und contra Thomas Kuhn." In Diederich, 1974, pp. 210-46.

5.3.15 Lakatos, Imre and Alan Musgrave, eds. 1970. **Criticism and the Growth of Knowledge.** London: Cambridge University Press.

5.3.16 Newton-Smith, W.H. 1981. **The Rationality of Science.** London: Routledge and Kegan Paul, ch. 5, 7.

5.3.17 Scharnberg, Max. 1984. **The Myth of Paradigm-Shift, Or How to Lie with Methodology.** No. 20 of **Uppsala Studies in Education.** Stockholm: Almquist and Wiksell International.

5.3.18 Scheffler, Israel. 1972. "Vision and Revolution: A Postscript on Kuhn." **Philosophy of Science** 39, No. 3: 366-74.

5.3.19 Shapere, Dudley. 1971. "The Paradigm Concept." **Science** 172, No. 3984 (14 May): 706-09.

5.3.20 Shapere, Dudley. 1964. "The Structure of Scientific Revolutions." **Philosophical Review** 73 (July): 383-94.

5.3.21 Shapin, Steven. 1982. "History of Science and Its Sociological Reconstructions." **History of Science** 20, No. 49 (September): 157-211.

5.3.22 Stegmüller, Wolfgang. 1978/1987. **Hauptströmungen der Gegenwartsphilosophie. Eine kritische Einführung.** 3 vols: Vol. I (6th ed.) 1978; Vol. II (8th ed.) 1987; Vol. III (8th ed.) 1987. Stuttgart: Kröner, III: chap. 2-3.

5.3.23 Stove, David C. 1982. **Popper and After: Four Modern Irrationalists.** Oxford: Pergamon Press.

5.3.24 Suppe, Frederick. 1977. "Exemplars, Theories and Disciplinary Matrixes." In his **The Structure of Scientific Theories,** 2nd ed. Urbana: University of Illinois Press, 1977, pp. 483-99.

5.3.25 Toulmin, Stephen. 1972. **Human Understanding,** Vol. I. Princeton: Princeton University Press, pp. 98-130.

***

6

Works by Imre Lakatos

Lakatos never wrote a book. Upon his death in 1974, most of his works were collected and published by John Worrall and Gregory Currie in two volumes of philosophical papers (1978(a) and (b)). Lakatos was schooled as a philosopher of mathematics, won his fame however as a philosopher of science. He is associated with the Popper school of critical rationalism.

The work which made Lakatos famous is his "Falsification and the Methodology of Scientific Research Programmes." His "History of Science and Its Rational Reconstructions" (1971(a)) should also be mentioned.

The thrust of Lakatos' work is that Popper's theory of falsification can be corrected by shifting the problem of appraising theories to that of appraising historical series of theories, i.e., "research programmes." In addition, he denies that the falsification rule of theory rejection is actually practised by scientists.

Each research programme has a "positive" and "negative" heuristic," "hard core," and "protective belt." The positive heuristic provides guidelines for the development of the research programme. The hard core contains the basic assumptions of the research programme. The negative heuristic does not allow these assumptions to be rejected or modified. Thus the negative heuristic renders the hard core of the programme unfalsifiable. The protective belt contains the auxiliary hypotheses and initial conditions, etc. which may be modified. Research programmes are "degenerating" if they fail to predict novel phenomena, "progressive" if they predict novel phenomena. A degenerating programme may, nonetheless, never be rejected conclusively because a change in the protective belt may lead to a novel discovery, suddenly rendering the programme progressive.

***

* *
Lakatos, Imre. 1970. "Falsification and the
Methodology of Scientific Research Programmes."
In Lakatos and Musgrave, 1970, pp. 91-196
and in Vol. 1 of his **Philosophical Papers**,
1978(b), pp. 8-101.
* *

6.1 1978(a). **Mathematics, Science and Epistemology.**
Vol. 2 of his **Philosophical Papers.** Ed. by John Worrall and
Gregory Currie. Cambridge: Cambridge University Press.

6.2 1978(b). **The Methodology of Scientific Research
Programmes.** Vol. 1 of his **Philosophical Papers.** Ed. by John
Worrall and Gregory Currie. Cambridge: Cambridge University
Press.

6.3 1978(c). "The Problem of Appraising Scientific
Theories: Three Approaches." In his 1978(b), pp. 107-20.

6.4 1978(d). "Understanding Toulmin." In his 1978(b),
pp. 224-43.

6.5 1974(a). "Popper on Demarcation and Induction." In
his 1978(b), pp. 139-67; Rpt. from Paul Arthur Schilpp, ed.
The Philosophy of Karl Popper, 2 vols. La Salle: Open
Court, 1974, Vol. I, pp. 241-73.

6.6 1974(b). "The Role of Crucial Experiments in
Science." **Studies in History and Philosophy of Science** 4:
309-25.

6.7 1974(c). "Science and Pseudoscience." **Conceptus** 8:
5-9.

6.8 1971(a). "History of Science and Its Rational
Reconstructions." In Roger C. Buck and Robert S. Cohen,
eds. **PSA 1970 in Memory of Rudolf Carnap.** Vol. 8 of **Boston
Studies in the Philosophy of Science.** Dordrecht: Reidel,
1971, pp. 91-136; Rpt. in Ian Hacking, ed. **Scientific
Revolutions.** Oxford: Oxford University Press, 1981, pp.
107-25.

6.9 1971(b). "Replies to Critics." In Roger C. Buck,
Robert S. Cohen, eds. **PSA 1970 in Memory of Rudolf Carnap.**
Vol. 8 of **Boston Studies in the Philosophy of Science.**
Dordrecht: Reidel, 1971, pp. 174-82.

6.10 1970. "Falsification and the Methodology of
Scientific Research Programmes." In Lakatos and Musgrave,
1970, pp. 91-196; Rpt. in Vol. 1 of his **Philosophical
Papers**, 1978(b), pp. 8-101.

6.11 Lakatos, Imre and Alan Musgrave, eds. 1970.
Criticism and the Growth of Knowledge. London: Cambridge

University Press.

6.12 Lakatos, Imre and Alan Musgrave, eds. 1968.
Problems in the Philosophy of Science. Vol. 3 of the
**Proceedings of the International Colloquium in the
Philosophy of Science, London, 1965.** Amsterdam:
North-Holland.

***

7

On Lakatos

In section 7.1. a list of applications of Lakatosian research programmes to economics appears. Mark Blaug is probably the most prolific writer to have applied Lakatos' philosophy to economics. As is somewhat clear from the titles of his 1983 and 1980(a), Blaug appraises Marxian economics and concludes that the Marxian programme is degenerating. Hands and Rosenberg do not find Lakatos' methodology useful for economists.

The Latsis volume, **Method and Appraisal in Economics**, is devoted to economics and the methodology of scientific research programmes. That Lakatos' philosophy did not hold up to criticism is not mentioned in that volume. But the literature from the philosophy of science in § 7.2. confirms this. The **Boston Studies in the Philosophy of Science** volume edited by Cohen, Feyerabend, and Wartofsky is dedicated to Lakatos' legacy. See Agassi (1976), Bartley, Koertge (1976), Musgrave, and Worrall therein.

***

7.1   Applications of Lakatosian Research Programmes to Economics

7.1.1 Blaug, Mark. 1983. "A Methodological Appraisal of Radical Economics." In A.W. Coats. **Methodological Controversy in Economics: Historical Essays in Honor of T.W. Hutchison.** Greenwich, CT: Jai Press, 1983, pp. 211-46.

7.1.2 Blaug, Mark. 1980(a). **A Methodological Appraisal of Marxian Economics.** Amsterdam: North-Holland.

7.1.3 Blaug, Mark. 1980(b). **The Methodology of Economics Or How Economists Explain.** Cambridge: Cambridge University Press.

7.1.4 Blaug, Mark. 1978. **Economic Theory in Retrospect,**

3rd ed. Cambridge: Cambridge University Press.

7.1.5   Blaug, Mark. 1976. "Kuhn Versus Lakatos **Or** Paradigms Versus Research Programmes in the History of Economics." In Spiro J. Latsis, ed. **Method and Appraisal in Economics.** Cambridge: Cambridge University Press, 1976, pp. 149-80; Rpt. from **History of Political Economy** 7, No. 4 (Winter 1975): 339-433.

7.1.6   Brown,   Elba   K.   1981.   "The   Neoclassical   and Post-Keynesian   Research   Programmes: The   Methodological Issues." **Review of Social Economy** 39, No. 2 (October): 111-32.

7.1.7   Coats, A.W. 1976. "Economics and Psychology: the Death and Resurrection of a Research Programme." In Latsis, 1976(a), pp. 43-64.

7.1.8   Dagum, Camilo. 1986. "Economic Model, System and Structure, Philosophy of Science and Lakatos' Methodology of Scientific Research Programmes." **Revista Internazionale di Scienze Economiche e Commerciale.** 33, No. 9 (September): 859-86.

7.1.9   de Marchi, Neil. 1976. "Anomaly and the Development of Economics: the Case of the Leontief Paradox." In Latsis, 1976(a), pp. 109-27.

7.1.10 Fisher,   Robert   M.   1986. **The   Logic   of   Economic Discovery: Neoclassical   Economics   and   the   Marginal Revolution.** Brighton: Wheatsheaf.

7.1.11 Fulton, G. 1984. "Research Programmes in Economics." **History of Political Economy** 16, No. 2 (Summer): 187-205.

7.1.12 Goodwin, Craufurd. 1980. "Toward a Theory of the History of Economics." **History of Political Economics** 12, No. 4 (Winter): 610-19.

7.1.13 Green,   Edward   J.   1977.   "Review   of **Method   and Appraisal in Economics** by S. Latsis." **Philosophy of Science** 44: 663-66.

7.1.14 Hands,   Douglas   W.   1985.   "Second   Thoughts   on Lakatos." **History of Political Economy** 17, No. 1: 1-16.

7.1.15 Hands, Douglas W. 1979. "The Methodology of Economic Research Programmes." **Philosophy of the Social Sciences** 9, No. 3 (September): 293-303.

7.1.16 *Hicks,   Sir   John.   1976.   "'Revolutions'   in Economics." In Latsis, 1976(a), pp. 207-18.

7.1.17 Khalil, Elias. 1987. "Kuhn, Lakatos, and the History of   Economic   Thought." **International   Journal   of   Social Economics** 14, Nos. 3/4/5: 118-31.

7.1.18 Langlois, Richard N. 1982. "Austrian Economics As Affirmative Science: Comment on Rizzo." In Israel M. Kirzner, ed. **Method, Process, and Austrian Economics.** Lexington, MA/ Toronto: Lexington/D.C. Heath, 1982, pp. 75-84.

7.1.19 Latsis, Spiro J., ed. 1976(a). **Method and Appraisal in Economics.** Cambridge: Cambridge University Press.

7.1.20 Latsis, Spiro J. 1976(b). "A Research Programme in Economics." In Latsis, 1976(a), pp. 1-42.

7.1.21 Laudan, Larry. 1985. "Kuhn's Critique of Methodology." In Joseph C. Pitt, ed. **Philosophy in Economics.** Dordrecht: Reidel, 1981, pp. 283-99.

7.1.22 Leijonhufvud, Axel. 1976. "Schools, 'Revolutions', and Research Programmes in Economic Theory." In Latsis, 1976(a), pp. 65-108.

7.1.23 O'Brien, D.P. 1976. "The Longevity of Adam Smith's Vision: Paradigms, Research Programmes and Falsifiability in the History of Economic Thought." **Scottish Journal of Political Economy** 23, No. 2 (June): 133-51.

7.1.24 Rizzo, Mario J. 1982. "Mises and Lakatos: A Reformulation of Austrian Methodology." In Israel M. Kirzner, ed. **Method, Process, and Austrian Economics.** Lexington, MA/Toronto: Lexington/D.C. Heath, 1982, pp. 53-73.

7.1.25 Robbins, Lionel. 1983. "On Latsis's 'Method and Appraisal in Economics': A Review Essay." In A.W. Coats. **Methodological Controversy in Economics: Historical Essays in Honor of T.W. Hutchison.** Greenwich, CT: Jai Press, 1983, pp. 43-54 and in **Journal of Economic Literature** 17, No. 3 (September): 996-1003.

7.1.26 Rosenberg, Alexander. 1986. "Lakatosian Consolations for Economics." **Economics and Philosophy** 2, No. 1 (April): 127-39.

7.1.27 Shionoya, Yuichi. 1986. "The Science and Ideology of Schumpeter." **Revista Internazionale di Scienze Economiche e Commerciali** 33, No. 8 (August): 729-62.

7.1.28 Weintraub, E. Roy. 1987. "Rosenberg's 'Lakatosian Consolations for Economists.'" **Economics and Philosophy** 3, No. 1 (April): 139-42.

7.1.29 Weintraub, E. Roy. 1985. **General Equilibrium Analysis.** Cambridge: Cambridge University Press.

7.2   Literature from the Philosophy of Science

7.2.1 Agassi, Joseph. 1986. "Lakatos: An Exchange."
Philosophia 16: 209-38.

7.2.2 Agassi, Joseph. 1979. "The Legacy of Lakatos."
Philosophy of Social Science 9, No. 3 (September): 316-26.

7.2.3 Agassi, Joseph. 1976. "The Lakatosian Revolution."
In Cohen, Feyerabend, and Wartofsky, eds., 1976, pp. 9-21.

7.2.4 Andersson, Gunnar. 1986. "Lakatos and Progress and
Rationality in Science: A Reply to Agassi." **Philosophia** 16:
239-43.

7.2.5 Bartley, William W. 1976. "On Imre Lakatos." In
Cohen, Feyerabend, and Wartofsky, 1976, pp. 37-38.

7.2.6 Chalmers, A.F. 1982. **What Is This Thing Called
Science?**, 2nd ed. St. Lucia: University of Queensland
Press, ch. 7.

7.2.7 Cohen, Robert S., Paul K. Feyerabend, and Marx W.
Wartofsky, eds. 1976. **Essays in Memory of Imre Lakatos.**
Vol. 39 of **Boston Studies in the Philosophy of Science.**
Dordrecht: Reidel.

7.2.8 Feigl, Herbert. 1971. "Research Programmes and
Induction." In Roger C. Buck and Robert S. Cohen, eds. **PSA
1970 in Memory of Rudolf Carnap.** Vol. 8 of **Boston Studies
in the Philosophy of Science.** Dordrecht: Reidel, 1971, pp.
147-82.

7.2.9 Feyerabend, Paul K. 1975. "Imre Lakatos." **British
Journal for the Philosophy of Science** 26, No. 1 (March):
1-18.

7.2.10 Feyerabend, Paul K. 1970. "Consolations for the
Specialist." In Lakatos and Musgrave, 1970, pp. 197-230.

7.2.11 Gähde, Ulrich. forthcoming. "Bridge Structures and
the Borderline Between the Internal and External History of
Science." Special edition of **Boston Studies in the
Philosophy of Science.**

7.2.12 Hacking, Ian. 1981. "Lakatos's Philosophy of
Science." In his **Scientific Revolutions.** Oxford: Oxford
University Press, 1981, pp. 128-43.

7.2.13 Hall, Richard. 1971. "Can We Use the History of
Science to Decide Between Competing Methodologies?" In
Roger Buck and Robert Cohen, eds. **PSA 1970 in Memory of
Rudolf Carnap.** Vol. 8 of **Boston Studies in the Philosophy
of Science.** Dordrecht: Reidel, 1971, pp. 151-59.

7.2.14 Koertge,   Noretta.   1979.   "Braucht   die

Sozialwissenschaft wirklich Metaphysik?" In **Theorie und Erfahrung**. Ed. by Hans Albert and Kurt Staph. Stuttgart: Klett, 1979, pp. 55–81.

7.2.15 Koertge, Noretta. 1976. "Rational Reconstructions." In Cohen, Feyerabend, and Wartofsky, 1976, pp. 359–69.

7.2.16 Koertge, Noretta. 1971. "Inter–Theoretic Criticism and the Growth of Science." In Roger Buck and Robert Cohen, eds. **PSA 1970 in Memory of Rudolf Carnap**. Vol. 8 of **Boston Studies in the Philosophy of Science**. Dordrecht: Reidel, 1971, pp. 160–73.

7.2.17 Kuhn, Thomas S. 1971. "Notes on Lakatos." In Roger Buck and Robert Cohen, eds. **PSA 1970 in Memory of Rudolf Carnap**. Vol. 8 of **Boston Studies in the Philosophy of Science**. Dordrecht: Reidel, 1971, pp. 137–46.

7.2.18 Lakatos, Imre and Alan Musgrave, eds. 1970. **Criticism and the Growth of Knowledge**. London: Cambridge University Press.

7.2.19 Lakatos, Imre and Alan Musgrave, eds. 1968. **Problems in the Philosophy of Science**. Vol. 3 of the **Proceedings of the International Colloquium in the Philosophy of Science, London, 1965**. Amsterdam: North–Holland.

7.2.20 McMullin, Ernan. 1976. "The Fertility of Theory and the Unit for Appraisal in Science." In Cohen, Feyerabend, and Wartofsky, 1976, pp. 395–432.

7.2.21 Musgrave, Alan. 1976. "Method Or Madness?" In Cohen, Feyerabend, and Wartofsky, 1976, pp. 457–91.

7.2.22 Newton–Smith, W.H. 1981. **The Rationality of Science**. London: Routledge and Kegan Paul, ch. 4.

7.2.23 Radnitzky, Gerard and Gunnar Andersson, eds. 1978. **Progress and Rationality in Science**. Vol. 58 of **Boston Studies in the Philosophy of Science**. Dordrecht: Reidel.

7.2.24 Sakar, Husain. 1980. "Imre Lakatos's 'Meta–Methodology': An Appraisal." **Philosophy of the Social Sciences** 10: 397–416.

7.2.25 Schramm, Alfred. 1974. "Demarkation und rationale Rekonstruktion bei Imre Lakatos." **Conceptus** 8: 10–16.

7.2.26 Stove, David C. 1982. **Popper and After: Four Modern Irrationalists**. Oxford: Pergamon Press.

7.2.27 Worrall, John. 1976. "Imre Lakatos (1922–1974): Philosopher of Mathematics and Philosopher of Science." In Cohen, Feyerabend, and Wartofsky, 1976, pp. 1–8.

***

8

From and on
Paul K. Feyerabend

Feyerabend must be the most colourful personality in the discipline. He is a lively writer, but tends to exaggerate, as is clear from his **Against Method**, which should really be entitled **Against One Universal Method**, or alternatively, **For Tolerance and a Pluralism of Methods**. These are two major themes of his philosophy of science.

The books in § 8.1.1. have been annotated. The articles in § 8.1.2. mirror the substance of his books. His 1975(a), "How to Defend Society Against Science" and his 1970(a) "Consolations for the Specialist" contain the core of his philosophy.

Section 8.2. is a list of critiques of Feyerabend's work. There has been very little written about Feyerabend which has much substance. The Duerr anthologies are an exception, but have only appeared in German so far. Chalmers and Newton-Smith can also be recommended. McCloskey is one of the few economists to have spoken out in favour of Feyerabend's philosophy, or at least one version of it.

***

8.1   From Feyerabend

8.1.1 Books

8.1.1.1   1983 (1976). **Wider den Methodenzwang. Skizze einer anarchistischen Erkenntnistheorie** (teils gekürzt, teils ergänzt, teils umgeschrieben). Frankfurt am Main: Suhrkamp. In English as **Against Method**. London: Verso, 1978 (1975).

> This is Feyerabend's **magnum opus**. Here he argues against the use of any set method in science and for the proliferation of theories. Feyerabend's style is

rather lively and entertaining. The German edition has been revised beyond the English version.

8.1.1.2   1981(a). **Problems of Empiricism**. Vol. 2 of **Philosophical Papers**. Cambridge: Cambridge University Press.

This volume, and the first volume, are a collection of Feyerabend's works centering on proliferation, criticism, and reality. In this volume Feyerabend discusses the decay of modern philosophy of science, classical empiricism, the philosophies of Mill, Hegel, Mach, Einstein, Lakatos, Popper, Laudan, and more.

8.1.1.3   1981(b). **Realism, Rationalism, and Scientific Method**. Vol. 1 of **Philosophical Papers**. Cambridge University Press.

In this volume Feyerabend discusses realism, the interpretation of scientific theories, the meaning of scientific terms, induction, Bohm's philosophy of nature, Bohr's Weltanschauung, and other topics.

8.1.1.4   1979. **Erkenntnis für freie Menschen**. Frankfurt am Main: Suhrkamp; Rev. German version of his **Science in a Free Society**. London: NLB, 1978.

Here Feyerabend further develops the arguments in **Against Method**. He stresses that rationality is one tradition among many other. A free society is one in which all traditions have equal rights. The German version has been revised beyond the English and includes replies to the critics.

8.1.1.5   1978. **Der wissenschaftstheoretische Realismus und die Autorität der Wissenschaften**. Braunschweig: Vieweg.

This work collects Feyerabend's essays in German. All essays discuss some aspect of science in our society. Some of the articles are translations of works in his **Philosophical Papers**; ca. one-half have only appeared in German.

8.1.2   Articles

8.1.2.1   1982. "Academic Ratiofascism: Comments on Tibor Machan's Review." **Philosophy of the Social Sciences** 12, No. 2 (June): 191-95.

8.1.2.2   1980. "Democracy, Elitism, and Scientific Method." **Inquiry** 23, No. 1 (March): 3-18.

8.1.2.3   1977(a). "Changing Patterns of Reconstruction." **British Journal for the Philosophy of Science** 28: 351-82.

8.1.2.4   1977(b). "Rationalism, Relativism and Scientific

Method." **Philosophy in Context** 6: 7-19.

8.1.2.5   1976. "On the Critique of Scientific Reason." In
Robert S. Cohen, Paul K. Feyerabend, and Marx W. Wartofsky,
eds. **Essays in Memory of Imre Lakatos.** Vol. 39 of **Boston
Studies in the Philosophy of Science.** Dordrecht: D. Reidel,
pp. 109-43.

8.1.2.6   1975(a). "How to Defend Society Against Science."
Radical Philosophy 11: 3-8; Rpt. in Ian Hacking, ed.
Scientific Revolutions. Oxford: Oxford University Press,
1981, pp. 156-67.

8.1.2.7   1975(b). "Imre Lakatos." **British Journal for the
Philosophy of Science** 26, No. 1 (March): 1-18.

8.1.2.8   1975(c). "'Science.' The Myth and Its Role in
Society." **Inquiry** 18, No. 2 (Summer): 167-81.

8.1.2.9   1974. "Popper's **Objective Knowledge.**" Inquiry 17,
No. 4 (Winter): 475-507.

8.1.2.10 1972.   "Von   der   beschränkten   Gültigkeit
methodologischer Regeln." **Neue Hefte für Philosophie** 2/3:
124-71.

8.1.2.11 1970(a). "Consolations for the Specialist." In
Imre Lakatos and Alan Musgrave, eds. **Criticism and the
Growth of Knowledge.** London: Cambridge University Press,
1970, pp. 197-230.

8.1.2.12 1970(b). "Philosophy of Science: A Subject with a
Great Past." In Roger H. Stuewer, ed. **Historical and
Philosophical Perspectives of Science.** Vol. 5 of **Minnesota
Studies   in   the   Philosophy   of   Science.**   Minneapolis:
University of Minnesota Press, 1970, pp. 172-83.

8.1.2.13 1969. "Science Without Experience." **Journal of
Philosophy** 66, No. 22 (November): 791-94.

8.1.2.14 1968. "Science, Freedom, and the Good Life."
Philosophical Forum 1, No. 2 (Winter): 127-35.

8.1.2.15 1967. "On the Improvement of the Sciences and the
Arts, and the Possible Identity of the Two." In Robert S.
Cohen and Marx W. Wartofsky, eds. **In Memory of Norwood
Russell Hanson.** Vol. 3 of **Boston Studies in the Philosophy
of Science.** Dordrecht: Reidel, 1967, pp. 307-415.

8.1.2.16 1965. "Problems of Empiricism." In Robert G.
Colodny, ed. **Beyond the Edge of Uncertainty.** Vol 2 of the
**University of Pittsburgh Series in the Philosophy of
Science.** Englewood Cliffs, NJ: Prentice-Hall.

8.1.2.17 1964. "Realism and Instrumentalism." In **The
Critical Approach to Science and Philosophy.** Ed. by Mario

Bunge. NY: Free Press, 1964, pp. 280-308.

8.1.2.18 1962. "Explanation, Reduction, and Empiricism." In Herbert Feigl and Grover Maxwell, eds. **Scientific Explanation, Space and Time.** Vol. 3 of **Minnesota Studies in the Philosophy of Science.** Minneapolis: University of Minnesota Press, pp. 28-97.

8.1.2.19 1961(a). "Comments on Hanson's 'Is There a Logic of Scientific Discovery.'" In Herbert Feigl and Grover Maxwell, eds. **Scientific Explanation, Space and Time.** Vol. 3 of **Minnesota Studies in the Philosophy of Science.** Minneapolis: University of Minnesota Press, 1961, pp. 35-39.

8.1.2.20 1961(b). "Knowledge Without Foundations." The Nellie Heldt Lectures, VIII. Oberlin College.

8.1.2.21 Feyerabend, Paul K. and Martin Gardner. 1983. "Feyerabend Vs. Gardner: Sciences, Church Or Instrument of Research?" **Free Inquiry** 3 (Summer): 58-60.

8.2 On Feyerabend

8.2.1   Baskar, Roy. 1975. "Feyerabend and Bachelard: Two Philosophies of Science." **New Left Review** 94 (November-December): 3155.

8.2.2   Broad, William J. 1979. "Paul Feyerabend: Science and the Anarchist." **Science** 209, No. 4418 (2 November): 534-37.

8.2.3   Chalmers, A.F. 1982. **What Is This Thing Called Science?**, 2nd ed. St. Lucia: University of Queensland Press, ch. 12.

8.2.4   Duerr, Hans Peter. 1980/1981. **Versuchungen, Aufsätze zur Philosophie Paul Feyerabends.** 2 Vols. Frankfurt am Main.

8.2.5   Crittenden, P.J. 1983. "Anarchistic Epistemology and Education." **Methodology and Science** 16: 211-29.

8.2.6   Gardner, Martin. 1982/83. "Anti-Science: The Strange Case of Paul Feyerabend." **Free Inquiry** 3 (Winter): 32-35.

8.2.7   Machan, Tibor R. 1982(a). "Anarchosurrealism Revisited: Reply to Feyerabend's Comments." **Philosophy of the Social Sciences** 12, No. 2 (June): 197-99.

8.2.8   Machan, Tibor R. 1982(b). "The Politics of Medicinal Anarchism." **Philosophy of the Social Sciences** 12, No. 2 (June): 183-89.

8.2.9   McCloskey, Donald. 1983. "The Rhetoric of

Economics." **Journal of Economic Literature** 21 (June): 481–517.

8.2.10   McEvoy, John G. 1975. "A 'Revolutionary' Philosophy of Science: Feyerabend and the Degeneration of Critical Rationalism into Skeptical Fallibilism." **Philosophy of Science** 42, No. 1 (March): 49–66.

8.2.11   Newton–Smith, W.H. 1981. **The Rationality of Science**. London: Routledge and Kegan Paul, ch. 6.

8.2.12   Steedman, P.H. 1982. "Should Debbie Do Shale? A Playful Polemic in Honor of Paul Feyerabend." **Educational Studies** 13, No. 2 (Summer): 240–51.

***

9

On (German) Structuralism

German structuralism is perhaps the newest approach in the philosophy of science. The attribute German is used in order to distinguish this form of structuralism from French structuralism. Associated with Joseph Sneed and Wolfgang Stegmüller, this group of philosophers has, unlike most other schools of philosophy of science, applied their methods directly to economics, especially to general equilibrium theory.

Joseph Sneed's book on the scientific structure and theory dynamics of mathematical physics, which appeared in 1971, marks the birth of German structuralism. Stegmüller further develops Sneed's work in various books and articles, some of which appear below.

The crucial idea behind structuralism is that scientific theories be viewed as structures and not statements. The structures are related to empirical claims by logical relationships. The structuralist philosopher's goal is to specify these logical relationships. To do this, the theory is axiomatized, and thus put into its simplest, most concise form. This school advocates set-theoretic axiomatization, following Patrick Suppes. Thus the scientific theories appraised must be quite formal; in economics the only theories which the structuralists could analyze are Debreu's general equilibrium theory and Sraffa's Marxist models. (See Balzer, Diederich, Garcia de la Sienra, Händler, Hamminga, Haslinger, Kötter, Pearce and Tucci, and Sneed.) This, of course, is a great drawback of the philosophy. Analysis of revolutionary theories and the evolution of theories (an adaption of Kuhn's work) is also an important part of the philosophy. Falsification, by the way, is considered to be meaningless by the German structuralists: an empirical hypothesis may be falsified (rejected), but not a theory.

Hands (1985(b)) provides an excellent short

introduction to German structuralism and its significance for economics. He concludes that German structuralism has as its subject mathematical physics and is thus simply not suited for appraisal of <u>economic</u> theories because

> the economic theories that are formally amenable to structuralist axiomatization are simply **not empirical in the same way that structuralist authors argue that physical theories are empirical** (p. 332).

Diederich, et al. (1989), have compiled a complete bibliography on the structuralist philosophy from its inception in 1971 to 1988.

***

9.1   The Structuralists and Their Philosophy

9.1.1   Balzer, Wolfgang, C. Ulises Moulines, and Joseph Sneed. 1987. **An Architecture for Science.** Dordrecht: Reidel.

> This is the school's most recent book. The work is about the structure of knowledge. Empirical science is the paradigm example of knowledge. The work presupposes a knowledge of set theory, classical particle mechanics, and more; in other words, it is not light reading. The authors treat models and structures, theory elements and nets, the diachronic structure of theories, intertheoretical relations, approximation, and the global structure of science.

9.1.2   Diederich, Werner, Andoni Ibarra and Thomas Mormann. 1989. "The Development of Structuralism" (with a comprehesive Bibliography attached as appendix). **Erkenntnis** (forthcoming).

> The bibliography attached as appendix is arranged by year and contains all of the works of the German structuralists, as well as those on the structuralist philosophy, starting with the original work of Sneed's in 1971 (see below) and finishing with the year 1988.

9.1.3   Sneed, Joseph D. 1979 (1971). **The Logical Structure of Mathematical Physics**, 2nd rev. ed. Vol. 35 of the Synthese Library. Dordrecht: Reidel.

> This work marks the beginning of German structuralism as a school. It is about theories of mathematical physics. The focus of the work is logical theory structure and axiomatization. Sneed acknowledges that the intellectual foundations of the work are built upon the works of Ramsey and Suppes. This work presupposes a sophisticated knowledge of physics and mathematics.

9.1.4 Stegmüller, Wolfgang. 1986. **Theorie und Erfahrung**, 3. Teilband. **Die Entwicklung des neuen Strukturalismus seit 1973.** Berlin: Springer-Verlag.

> This book discusses the developments of structuralism since 1973. Discussed are evolution of theories, the structuralist interpretation of Kuhn, reduction, T-theoricity, holism, the Duhem-Quine thesis, approximation, incommensurability, realism, Sneed's work, and applications outside of physics. Stegmüller provides an excellent list of sources on structuralism in his bibliography and on pp. 15-18. (This work brings the structuralist philosophy up-to-date, is however, only available in German.)

9.1.5 Stegmüller, Wolfgang. 1979. **The Structuralist View of Theories.** Berlin/ Heidelberg/NY: Springer-Verlag.

> In this slim volume Stegmüller attempts to answer critics, especially the critique of Feyerabend. This work provides a good, short introduction to the philosophy and its problems.

9.1.6 Stegmüller, Wolfgang. 1976. **The Structure and Dynamics of Theories.** NY/Heidelberg/Berlin: Springer-Verlag; Trans. of his **Theorie und Erfahrung**, Part 2: **Theorienstrukturen und Theoriendynamik.** Berlin: Springer, 1973.

> Stegmüller develops a metascientific reconstruction of Kuhn's philosophy of science. Sneed's original work is treated in readable fashion. Part II is dedicated to a reconsideration of Kuhn's philosophy.

9.2 Structuralism Applied to Economics

9.2.1 Balzer, W. 1985. "The Proper Reconstruction of Exchange Economics." **Erkenntnis** 23 (August): 185-200.

9.2.2 Balzer, W. 1982. "Empirical Claims in Exchange Economics." In Stegmüller, et al., 1982, pp. 16-40.

9.2.3 Diederich, Werner. 1982. "A Structuralist Reconstruction of Marx's Economics." In Stegmüller, et al., 1982, pp. 145-60.

9.2.4 Garcia de la Sienra, Adolfo. 1982. "The Basic Core of the Marxian Economic Theory." In Stegmüller, et al., 1982, pp. 118-44.

9.2.5 Händler, Ernst W. 1984. "Measurement of Preference and Utility." **Erkenntnis** 21: 319-48.

9.2.6 Händler, Ernst W. 1982(a). "The Evolution of Economic Theories: A Formal Approach." **Erkenntnis** 18:

65-96.

9.2.7 Händler, Ernst W. 1982(b). "Ramsey-Elimination of Utility in Utility Maximizing Regression Approaches." In Stegmüller, 1982, pp. 41-62.

9.2.8 Händler, Ernst W. 1980(a). "The Logical Structure of Modern Neoclassical Static Microeconomic Equilibrium Theory." **Erkenntnis** 15: 33-53.

9.2.9 Händler, Ernst W. 1980(b). "The Role of Utility and of Statistical Concepts in Empirical Economic Theories." **Erkenntnis** 15: 129-57.

9.2.10 Hamminga, Bert. 1983. **Neoclassical Theory Structure and Theory Development**. Berlin: Springer.

9.2.11 Hamminga, Bert. 1982. "Neoclassical Theory Structure and Theory Development: The Ohlin Samuelson Programme in the Theory of International Trade." In Stegmüller, 1982, pp. 1-15.

9.2.12 Hamminga, B. and W. Balzer. 1986. "The Basic Structure of Neo-Classical General Equilibrium Theory." **Erkenntnis** 25: 31-46.

9.2.13 Hands, Douglas W. 1985(a). "The Logical Reconstruction of Pure Exchange Economics: Another Alternative." **Theory and Decision** 19 (November): 259-78.

9.2.14 Hands, Douglas W. 1985(b). "The Structuralist View of Economic Theories: A Review Essay." **Economics and Philosophy** 1: 303-35.

9.2.15 Haslinger, Franz. 1983. "'A Logical Reconstruction of Pure Exchange Economics': An Alternative View." **Erkenntnis** 20 (July): 115-29.

9.2.16 Haslinger, Franz. 1982. "Structure and Problems of Equilibrium and Disequilibrium Theory." In Stegmüller, et al., 1982, pp. 63-84.

9.2.17 Kötter, Rudolf. 1982. "General Equilibrium Theory--An Empirical Theory." In Stegmüller, et al., 1982, pp. 103-117.

9.2.18 Pearce, David and Michele Tucci. 1982. "A General Net Structure for Theoretical Economics." In Stegmüller, et al., 1982, pp. 85-102.

9.2.19 Sneed, Joseph D. 1982. "The Logical Structure of Bayesian Decision Theory." In Stegmüller, et al., 1982, pp. 201-22.

9.2.20 Stegmüller, Wolfgang, W. Balzer, and W. Spohn, eds. 1982. **Philosophy of Economics**. Berlin: Springer Verlag.

(The follow-up to this volume, the proceedings of the
Tilburg conference of 1987, is forthcoming in an **Erkenntnis
Sonderheft.**)

***

10

Holism and the
Duhem Thesis

Holism has been a thorn in the side of philosophers of
science from the very beginning. The Duhem thesis
considers the problem of the theory as a whole. No
scientific theory is made up of one single statement.
Because "controlled experience," i.e., testing of
scientific hypotheses, is the basis for distinguishing
between acceptable and unacceptable theories in science,
the problem that only the whole theory and not an
isolated hypothesis can be tested poses a major problem for
some philosophers. This means that unambiguous
falsification or verification does not exist. Almost all
philosophers of science, from Karl Popper on, address this
problem.

Duhem's work is the key source, but Poincaré and
Quine have also formulated similar views. Quine's thesis
is considered to be a stronger version of the Duhem thesis.
Cross and Boland have discussed Duhem's problem within the
context of economics. Harding provides an excellent
introduction to the Duhem thesis and collects some of the
most important works on the subject.

***

* *
Duhem, Pierre. 1962. **The Aim and Structure
of Physical Theory**. Trans. Philip P. Wiener.
NY: Atheneum.
* *

10.1 Alexander, Peter. 1967(a). "Conventionalism."
Encyclopedia of Philosophy. 1967 ed.

10.2 Alexander, Peter. 1967(b). "Duhem, Pierre Maurice
Marie." **Encyclopedia of Philosophy**. 1967 ed.

10.3 Boland, Lawrence A. 1970. "Conventionalism and

Economic Theory." **Philosophy of Science** 37, No. 2 (June): 239-48.

10.4   Cross, Rod. 1984. "Monetarism and Duhem Thesis." In Peter Wiles and Guy Routh, eds. **Economics in Disarray.** Oxford: Basil Blackwell, 1984, pp. 78-99.

10.5   Cross, Rod. 1982. "The Duhem-Quine Thesis, Lakatos and the Appraisal of Theories." **Economic Record** 92 (June): 320-40.

10.6   Duhem,   Pierre,   1976.   "Physical   Theory   and Experiment." In Harding, 1976, pp. 1-40; Originally chapter VI of his **The Aim and Structure of Physical Theory**, 1954 (1906).

10.7   Duhem, Pierre. 1962. **The Aim and Structure of Physical Theory.** Trans. Philip P. Wiener. NY: Atheneum.

10.8   Feyerabend, Paul K. 1976. "The Rationality of Science" (From 'Against Method'). In Harding, 1976, pp. 289-318; Originally as § 11- § 15 of "Against Method: Outline of an Anarchistic Theory of Knowledge." In **Minnesota Studies in the Philosophy of Science,** Vol. 4. Ed. by Michael Radner and Stephen Winokur, 1970, pp. 17-130.

10.9   Giannoni, Carlo. 1976. "Quine, Grünbaum, and the Duhemian Thesis." In Harding, 1976, pp. 162-75; Originally in **Nous** 1 (1967): 283-97.

10.10 Grünbaum, Adolf. 1976(a). "The Duhemian Argument." In Harding, 1976, pp. 116-31; Originally in **Philosophy of Science** 27, No. 1 (January 1960): 75-87.

10.11 Grünbaum, Adolf. 1976(b). "Is It **Never** Possible to Falsify a Hypothesis Irrevocably?" In Harding, 1976, pp. 260-88; Originally as chapter 17 of **Philosophical Problems of Space and Time,** 2nd, enl. ed. Vol. 12 of **Boston Studies in the Philosophy of Science.** Ed. by R.S. Cohen and M. Wartofsky, Dordrecht: Reidel, 1974, pp. 585-629.

10.12 Harding, Sandra G., ed. 1976. **Can Theories Be Refuted? Essays on the Duhem-Quine Thesis.** Dordrecht: Reidel.

10.13 Hempel, Carl G. 1976. "Empiricist Criteria of Cognitive Significance: Problems and Changes." In Harding, 1976, pp. 65-88; Originally in his **Aspects of Scientific Explanation.** The Free Press, 1965.

10.14 Hesse, Mary. 1976. "Duhem, Quine and a New Empiricism." In Harding, 1976, pp. 184-204; Originally from the Royal Institute of Philosophy Lectures. **Knowledge and Necessity,** 1970.

10.15 Hodgson,   Geoff.   1986.   "Behind   Methodological

Individualism." **Cambridge Journal of Economics** 10, No. 3 (September): 211-24.

10.16 Kuhn, Thomas S. 1976. "Scientific Revolutions As Changes of World View." In Harding, 1976, pp. 135-54; Originally chapter X of his **The Structure of Scientific Revolutions** (1979).

10.17 Lakatos, Imre. 1976. "Falsification and the Methodology of Scientific Research Programmes." In Harding, 1976, pp. 205-59; Originally in **Criticism and the Growth of Knowledge**. Ed. by Lakatos and Musgrave (1970).

10.18 Laudan, Laurens. 1976. "Grünbaum on 'The Duhemian Argument'." In Harding, 1976, pp. 155-61; Originally in **Philosophy of Science** 32, No. 3 (July 1965): 295-99.

10.19 Popper, Karl R. 1976(a). "Some Fundamental Problems in the Logic of Scientific Discovery." In Harding, 1976, pp. 89-112; Originally as chapter 1 of his **The Logic of Scientific Scientific Discovery** (1959).

10.20 Popper, Karl R. 1976(b). "Background Knowledge and Scientific Growth." In Harding, 1976, pp. 113-15; Originally as "Truth, Rationality, and the Growth of Knowledge," of his **Conjectures and Refutations** (1969), pp. 238-39.

10.21 Quine, Willard van Orman. 1976(a). "A Comment on Grünbaum's Claim." In Harding, 1976, p. 132.

10.22 Quine, W.O. 1976(b). "Two Dogmas of Empiricism." In Harding, 1976, pp. 41-64; Originally in his **From a Logical Point of View**. Cambridge, Mass.: Harvard University Press, 1953.

10.23 Ramstad, Yngve. 1986. "A Pragmatist's Quest for Holistic Knowledge: The Scientific Methodology of John R. Commons." **Journal of Economic Issues** 20, No. 4 (December): 1067-105.

10.24 Wedeking, Gary. 1976. "Duhem, Quine and Grünbaum on Falsification." In Harding, 1976, pp. 176-83; Originally in **Philosophy of Science** 36 (December 1969): 375-80.

***

On the Relationship Between the History and Philosophy of Science

A major controversy about the relationship between the history and the philosophy of science raged in the philosophy of science journals in the 1970's and early 1980's. The fifth volume of **Minnesota Studies in the Philosophy of Science,** 1970, was dedicated to exploring this relationship. The literature seems to have arrived at the conclusion that the history and philosophy of science definitely belong together; how great the role for history should be is still debatable. Giere does not believe the relationship is very intimate. Burian, Brown, Hanson, Kuhn, McMullin, Moulines, and Wartofsky deem it to be a close or inextricable relationship.

This section has been included because this debate parallels the one in economics, i.e., economics and its relationship with history (whether it be history of economic analysis or economic history). See part I, § 17.

***

11.1 Brown, James Robert. 1980. "History and the Norms of Science." In Peter Asquith and Ronald Giere, eds. **PSA 1980,** Vol. 1. East Lansing, MI: Philosophy of Science Association, 1980, pp. 236-48.

11.2 Burian, Richard M. 1977. "More Than a Marriage of Convenience: On the Inextricability of History and Philosophy of Science." **Philosophy of Science** 44, No. 1 (March): 1-42.

11.3 Cohen, I. Bernard. 1977. "History and the Philosopher of Science." In Frederick Suppe, ed. **The Structure of Scientific Theories,** 2nd ed. Urbana: University of Illinois Press, 1977, pp. 308-49.

11.4 Hanson, Norwood Russell. 1971. "The Irrelevance of History of Science to Philosophy of Science." In his **What I**

Do Not Believe, and Other Essays. Ed. by Stephen Toulmin and Harry Woolf. Dordrecht: Reidel, 1971, pp. 274-87.

11.5 Kuhn, Thomas. 1977. "The Relations Between History and the Philosophy of Science." In his **The Essential Tension**. Chicago: University of Chicago Press, 1977, pp. 3-20.

11.6 Losee, John. 1983. "Whewell and Mill on the Relation Between Philosophy of Science and History of Science." **Studies in History and the Philosophy of Science** 14, No. 2 (June): 113-26.

11.7 McMullin, Ernan. 1976. "History and Philosophy of Science: A Marriage of Convenience?" In R.S. Cohen, C.A. Hooker, et al., eds. **PSA 1974**. Vol. 32 of **Boston Studies in the Philosophy of Science**. Dordrecht: Reidel, 1976, pp. 585-601.

11.8 McMullin, Ernan. 1970. "The History and Philosophy of Science: A Taxonomy." In Roger H. Stuewer, ed. **Historical and Philosophical Perspectives of Science**. Vol. 5 of the **Minnesota Studies in the Philosophy of Science**. Minneapolis: University of Minnesota Press, 1970, pp. 12-67.

11.9 Moulines, C. Ulises. 1983. "On How the Distinction Between History and Philosophy of Science Should Not Be Drawn." **Erkenntnis** 19 (May): 285-96.

11.10 Thackray, Arnold. 1985. "The Historian and the Progress of Science." **Science, Technology, and Human Values** 10, No. 1 (Winter): pp. 17-27.

11.11 Toulmin, Stephen. 1977. "From Form to Function: Philosophy and History of Science in the 1950's and Now." **Daedalus** 106, No. 3 (Summer): 143-62.

11.12 Toulmin, Stephen. 1971. "Rediscovering History." **Encounter** 36, No. 1 (January): 53-64.

11.13 Wartofsky, Marx W. 1976. "The Relation Between Philosophy of Science and History of Science." In Robert S. Cohen, Paul Feyerabend, and Marx Wartofsky, eds. **Essays in Memory of Imre Lakatos**. Vol. 39 of **Boston Studies in the Philosophy of Science**. Dordrecht: Reidel, 1976, pp. 717-37.

***

12

Miscellaneous Works in the Philosophy of Science

This is a mixed bag of works which do not fit anywhere else. Here one finds additional members of the Popper school: Joseph Agassi, Hans Albert, William Bartley, Noretta Koertge, Gerard Radnitzky, and Gunnar Andersson. In addition to Feyerabend and Kuhn, who rate as historically-minded philosophers, there are Stephen Toulmin, Michael Polanyi, Ludwik Fleck, Russell Hanson, and Laurens Laudan. Polanyi and Fleck inspired Thomas Kuhn and thereby won themselves a revival. Laudan has further extended Kuhn's philosophy. Baker provides an overview of Polanyi; Robert Cohen has edited a volume **In Memory of Norwood Russell Hanson**. Whereas Polanyi, Fleck, and Kuhn stress sociological factors, Hanson does not. Hanson originated discussions on the theory-ladenness of observation and attempted to develop a logic of discovery.

The following authors provide background information about the philosophy of science: Peter Alexander, Bernard Barber, Arthur C. Danto, Rom Harré, Patrick Heelen, Theodore Kisiel and G. Johnson, Laurens Laudan (1968), Milton Munitz, and Jerome Ravetz.

In addition, Rudolf Carnap's classic should be mentioned, as well as the **PSA** volume **in Memory of Carnap**, edited by Roger C. Buck and Robert Cohen. Herbert Simon has contributed to the pure philosophy of science as well as to economic methodology.

Immanuel Kant's **Critique of Pure Reason**, in which he discusses the analytic-synthetic distinction, and Hans Reichenbach's **Experience and Prediction**, in which he argues that the "context of discovery" belongs to psychology and the "context of justification" to philosophy of science, are both classics.

***

12.1 Agassi, Joseph. 1971. "The Standard Misinterpretation of Skepticism." **Philosophical Studies** 22, No. 4 (June): 49-50.

12.2 Agassi, Joseph. 1963. **Towards an Historiography of Science. History and Theory**, Beiheft 2. n.p.: Wesleyan University Press.

12.3 Albert, Hans. 1980. **Traktat über kritische Vernunft**, 4th rev. ed. Tübingen: Mohr.

12.4 Albert, Hans. 1965. "Tradition und Kritik." **Club Voltaire II: Jahrbuch für kritische Aufklärung**. München: Szczesny Verlag, pp. 156-66.

12.5 Albert, Hans. 1964. "Die Idee der kritischen Vernunft." **Club Voltaire I: Jahrbuch für kritische Aufklärung**. München: Szczesny Verlag, pp. 17-30.

12.6 Alexander, Peter. 1964. "The Philosophy of Science, 1850-1910." In **A Critical History of Western Philosophy**. Ed. by D.J. O'Connor. NY: The Free Press, 1964, pp. 402-25.

12.7 Amsterdamski, Stephen. 1975. **Between Experience and Metaphysics**. Vol. 35 of **Boston Studies in the Philosophy of Science**. Ed. by Robert S. Cohen and Marx W. Wartofsky. Dordrecht: Reidel.

12.8 Andersson, Gunnar, ed. 1984. **Rationality in Science and Politics**. Vol. 79 of **Boston Studies in the Philosophy of Science**. Dordrecht: Reidel.

12.9 Asquith, Peter D. and Ronald N. Giere, eds. 1980. **PSA 1980**, Vol. 1. East Lansing, MI: Philosophy of Science Association.

12.10 Asquith, Peter D. and P. Kitcher, eds. 1984. **PSA 1984**, Vol. 2. East Lansing, MI: Philosophy of Science Association.

12.11 Asquith, Peter D. and Henry E. Kyburg, eds. 1979. **Current Research in Philosophy of Science**. East Lansing, MI: Philosophy of Science Association.

12.12 Baker, John R. 1979. "In the Cause of Freedom of Science." **New Scientist** 83, No. 1163 (12 July): 108-09.

12.13 Barber, Bernard. 1968. "Science: The Sociology of Science." In the **International Encyclopedia of the Social Sciences**. 1968 ed.

12.14 Bartley, William Warren, III. 1987. "A Refutation of the Alleged Refutation of Comprehensively Critical Rationalism." In Radnitzky and Bartley, 1987, pp. 314-41.

12.15 Bartley, William Warren, III. 1984(a). "Logical

Strength and Demarcation." In Andersson, 1984, pp. 69-93.

12.16 Bartley, William Warren, III. 1984(b) (1962). **The Retreat to Commitment**, 2nd. rev. enl. ed. La Salle: Open Court.

12.17 Bartley, William Warren, III. 1975. "Wissenschaft und Glaube: Die Notwendigkeit des Engagements." **Neue Anthropologie**, Vol. 7. Ed. by Hans-Georg Godamer and Paul Vogler. Stuttgart: n.p., 1975, pp. 64-102.

12.18 Bartley, William Warren, III. 1969. "Approaches to Science and Skepticism." **Philosophical Forum** 1, No. 3 (Spring): 318-31.

12.19 Bartley, William W., III. 1965. "Das Haus der Wissenschaft." In **Club Voltaire II: Jahrbuch für kritische Aufklärung**. München: Szczesnay Verlag, 1965, pp. 118-34.

12.20 Bartley, William W., III. 1964. "Rationality Versus the Theory of Rationality." In Mario Bunge, ed. **The Critical Approach to Science and Philosophy**. Glencoe: The Free Press, 1964, pp. 3-31.

12.21 Bartley, W.W., III. 1962. "Achilles, the Tortoise, and Explanation in Science and History." **British Journal for the Philosophy of Science** 13 (May 1962-February 1963): 15-33.

12.22 Berlin, Sir Isaiah. 1978. **Concepts and Categories**. London: The Hogarth Press.

12.23 Black, Max. 1967. "Induction." **Encyclopedia of Philosophy**. 1967 ed.

12.24 Bohm, David. 1961. "On the Relationship Between the Methodology in Scientific Research and the Content of Scientific Knowledge." **British Journal for the Philosophy of Science** 12, No. 46 (August): 103-16.

12.25 Buck, Roger C. and Robert S. Cohen, eds. 1971. **PSA in Memory of Rudolf Carnap**. Vol. 8 of the **Boston Studies in the Philosophy of Science**. Dordrecht: Reidel.

12.26 Butts, Robert. E. and Jaako Hintikka, eds. 1977. **Historical and Philosophical Dimensions of Logic, Methodology, and Philosophy of Science**. Vol. 12 of the **University of Western Ontario Series in Philosophy of Science**. Dordrecht: Reidel.

12.27 Carnap, Rudolf. 1966. **The Philosophy of Science**. Ed. by Martin Gardner. NY: Basic Books.

12.28 Cartwright, Nancy. 1983. **How the Laws of Physics Lie**. Oxford: Oxford University Press.

12.29 Cohen, Robert S. and Marx W. Wartofsky, eds. 1974. **Methodological and Historical Essays in the Philosophy of Science.** Dordrecht: Reidel.

12.30 Cohen, Robert S. and Marx W. Wartofsky, eds. 1967. **In Memory of Norwood Russell Hanson.** Vol. 3 of **Boston Studies in the Philosophical of Science.** Dordrecht: Reidel.

12.31 Danto, Arthur C. 1967. "Philosophy of Science, Problems of." In the **Encyclopedia of Philosophy.** 1967 ed.

12.32 Dewey, John. 1966 (1939). **Theory of Valuation. International Encyclopedia of Unified Science.** Vol. II, No. 4 of **Foundations of the Unity of Science.** Chicago: University of Chicago Press.

12.33 Fearnside, W. Ward and William B. Holther. 1959. **Fallacy: The Counterfeit of Argument.** Englewood Cliffs: Prentice-Hall.

12.34 Feigl, Herbert. 1970. "The 'Orthodox' View of Theories: Remarks in Defense As Well As Critique." In Michael Radner and Stephen Winokur, eds. **Minnesota Studies in the Philosophy of Science,** Vol. IV. Minneapolis: University of Minnesota Press.

12.35 Fire, Arthur and Peter Machamer, eds. 1986. **PSA 1986,** Vol. 1. East Lansing, MI: Philosophy of Science Association.

12.36 Fleck, Ludwik. 1980 (1935). **Entstehung und Entwicklung einer wissenschaftlichen Tatsache.** Ed. by Lothar Schäfer and Thomas Schnelle. Frankfurt am Main: Suhrkamp.

12.37 Gutting, Gary. 1979. "Continental Philosophy of Science." In Asquith and Kyburg, 1979, pp. 94-117.

12.38 Hanson, Norwood Russell. 1971(a). **Observation and Explanation: A Guide to Philosophy of Science.** NY: Harper and Row.

12.39 Hanson, Norwood Russell. 1971(b). **What I Do Not Believe, and Other Essays.** Ed. by Stephen Toulmin and Harry Woolf. Dordrecht: Reidel.

12.40 Hanson, Norwood Russell. 1969(a). "Logical Positivism and the Interpretation of Scientific Theories." In Peter Achinstein and Stephen Barker, eds. **The Legacy of Logical Positivism.** Baltimore, MD: John Hopkins University Press.

12.41 Hanson, Norwood Russell. 1969(b). **Perception and Discovery.** San Francisco: Freeman, Cooper and Company.

12.42 Hanson, Norwood Russell. 1961(a). "Is There a Logic of Discovery?" In Herbert Feigl and Grover Maxwell, eds.

Current Issues in the Philosophy of Science. NY: Holt, Rinehart and Winston.

12.43 Hanson, Norwood Russell. 1960. "More on 'The Logic of Discovery'." **Journal of Philosophy** 57 (March):182-88.

12.44 Hanson, Norwood Russell. 1958(a). "The Logic of Discovery." **Journal of Philosophy** 60, No. 25 (December): 1073-89.

12.45 Hanson, Norwood Russell. 1958(b). **Patterns of Discovery.** Cambridge: Cambridge University Press.

12.46 Harré, Rom. 1967. "Philosophy of Science, History of." In the **Encyclopedia of Philosophy.** 1967 ed.

12.47 Heelan, Patrick A. 1979. "Continental Philosophy and the Philosophy of Science." In Asquith and Kyburg, 1979, pp. 84-93.

12.48 Hempel, Carl G. 1973. "The Meaning of Theoretical Terms: A Critique of a Critique of the Standard Empiricist Construal." In Patrick Suppes, et al., eds. **Logic, Methodology and Philosophy of Science.** Amsterdam: North-Holland, 1973, 367-78.

12.49 Hesse, Mary. 1980. **Revolutions and Reconstructions in the Philosophy of Science.** Brighton: The Harvester Press.

12.50 Holton, Gerald. 1973. **Thematic Origins of Scientific Thought.** Cambridge, MA: Harvard University Press.

12.51 Kant, Immanuel. 1983 (1781). **Kant's Critique of Pure Reason: An Introductory Text.** Ed. (abridged and simplified) by Humphrey Palmer. Cardiff: University College Cardiff Press.

12.52 Kisiel, Theodore with Galen Johnson. 1974. "New Philosophies of Science in the USA; A Selective Survey." **Zeitschrift für allgemeine Wissenschaftstheorie** 5, No. 1: 138-91.

12.53 Koertge, Noretta. 1979. "The Problem of Appraising Scientific Theories." In Asquith and Kyburg, eds. 1979, pp. 228-51.

12.54 Koertge, Noretta. 1978. "Toward a New Theory of Scientific Inquiry." In Radnitzky and Andersson, 1978, pp. 253-78.

12.55 Koertge, Noretta. 1974. "Bartley's Theory of Rationality." **Philosophy of the Social Sciences** 4: 75-81.

12.56 Koertge, Noretta. 1971. "Inter-Theoretic Criticism and the Growth of Science." In Buck and Cohen, 1971, pp. 160-73.

12.57 Koyré, Alexandre. 1961. "Influence of Philosophic Trends on the Formation of Scientific Theories." In **The Validation of Scientific Theories**. Ed. by Philipp Frank. NY: Collier, 1961, pp. 177-87.

12.58 Laudan, Laurens. 1981. "A Problem-Solving Approach to Scientific Progress." In Ian Hacking, ed. **Scientific Revolutions**. Oxford: Oxford University Press, pp. 144-55.

12.59 Laudan, Laurens. 1979. "Historical Methodologies: An Overview and Manifesto." In Asquith and Kyburg, 1979, pp. 40-54.

12.60 Laudan, Laurens. 1977(a). **Progress and Its Problems**. Berkeley/Los Angeles: University of California Press.

12.61 Laudan, Laurens. 1977(b). "The Sources of Modern Methodology." In Butts and Hintakka, 1977, pp. 3-19.

12.62 Laudan, Laurens. 1976. "Two Dogmas of Methodology." **Philosophy of Science** 43, No. 4 (December): 585-97.

12.63 Laudan, Laurens. 1968. "Theories of Scientific Method from Plato to Mach: A Bibliographical Review." **History of Science** 7: 1-63.

12.64 Lugg, Andrew. 1978. "Disagreement in Science." **Zeitschrift für allgemeine Wissenschaftstheorie** 9, No. 2: 276-92.

12.65 McMullin, Ernan. 1976. "The Fertility of Theory and the Unit for Appraisal in Science." In Robert S. Cohen, Paul K. Feyerabend, and Marx W. Wartofsky, eds. 1976. **Essays in Memory of Imre Lakatos**. Vol. 39 of **Boston Studies in the Philosophy of Science**. Dordrecht: Reidel, 1976, pp. 395-432.

12.66 McMullin, Ernan. 1969. "Philosophies of Nature." **New Scholasticism** 43, No. 1 (Winter): 29-74.

12.67 Munitz, Milton K. 1981. **Contemporary Analytic Philosophy**. NY: Macmillan.

12.68 Musgrave, Alan. 1974. "Logical Versus Historical Theories of Confirmation." **British Journal for the Philosophy of Science** 25, No. 1 (March): 1-23.

12.69 Pitt, Joseph C., ed. 1985. **Change and Progress in Modern Science: Papers Relating to and Arising from the Fourth International Conference on History and Philosophy of Science, Blacksburg, Virginia, November, 1982**. Vol. 27 of the **University of Western Ontario Series in the Philosophy of Science**. Dordrecht: Boston.

12.70 Pitt, Joseph C. and Marcello Pera, eds. 1987.

Rational   Changes   in   Science: Essays   on   Scientific
Reasoning. Vol. 98 of **Boston Studies in the Philosophy of
Science**. Dordrecht: Reidel.

12.71 Polanyi, Michael. 1969. **Knowing and Being.** Chicago:
University of Chicago Press.

12.72 Polanyi, Michael. 1967 (1966). **The Tacit Dimension.**
NY: Anchor Books.

12.73 Polanyi, Michael. 1963. "The   Potential   Theory   of
Adsorption." **Science** 141, No. 3585 (13 September): 1010-13.

12.74 Polanyi, Michael. 1962. "The Unaccountable Element in
Science." **Philosophy** 37, No. 139 (January): 1-14.

12.75 Polanyi,   Michael.   1957.   "Scientific   Outlook: Its
Sickness   and   Cure."   **Science**   125,   No.   3245   (8   March):
480-84.

12.76 Polanyi, Michael. 1958. **Personal Knowledge: Towards a
Post-Critical Philosophy.** Chicago: University of Chicago
Press.

12.77 Polanyi,   Michael.   1955.   "Words,   Conceptions   and
Science." **The   Twentieth   Century** 158 (July-December):
256-67.

12.78 Polanyi, Michael. 1952. "The   Stability   of   Beliefs."
British Journal for the Philosophy of Science 3, No. 2
(November): 218-19.

12.79 Polanyi, Michael and Harry Prosch. 1975. **Meaning.**
Chicago: University of Chicgo Press.

12.80 Radnitzky,   Gerard   and   Gunnar   Andersson.   1978.
Progress and Rationality in Science. Vol. 58 of **Boston
Studies in the Philosophy of Science.** Dordrecht: Reidel.

12.81 Radnitzky, Gerard and William Bartley, eds. 1987.
**Evolutionary Epistemology, Rationality, and the Sociology
of Knowledge.** La Salle/London: Open Court.

12.82 Ravetz, Jerome. 1985. "The History of Science." In
the **Encyclopedia Britannica.** 1985 ed.

12.83 Reichenbach, Hans. 1938. **Experience and Prediction:
An Analysis of the Foundations and the Structure.**
Chicago/London: University of Chicago Press.

12.84 Salmon, Wesley C. 1966. **The Foundations of Scientific
Inference.** Pittsburgh: University of Pittsburgh Press.

12.85 *Simon, Herbert A. 1977. **Models of Discovery and
Other Topics in the the Methods of Science.** Dordrecht:
Reidel/Pallas Paperbacks.

12.86 Suppe,   Frederick.   1979.   "Theory   Structure."   In
Asquith and Kyburg, 1979, pp. 317-38.

12.87 Suppe,   Frederick.   1976.   "Theoretical   Laws."   In
Marion Prezelecki, Klemens Szaniawski and Ryszard Wojcicki,
eds. **Formal Methods in the Methodology of Empirical
Science: Proceedings of the Conference for Formal Methods
in the Methodology of Empirical Sciences, Warshaw, June
17-21, 1974.** Dordrecht: Reidel, 1976, pp. 247-67.

12.88 Suppes, Patrick. 1979. "The Role of Formal Methods in
the Philosophy of Science." In Asquith and Kyburg, 1979,
pp. 16-27.

12.89 Toulmin,   Stephen   E.   1985.   "Pluralism   and
Responsibility   in   Post-Modern   Science."   **Science,
Technology, and Human Values** 10, No. 1 (Winter): 28-37.

12.90 Toulmin, Stephen E. 1982. "The Construal of Reality:
Criticism in Modern and Postmodern Science." **Critical
Inquiry** 9, No. 1 (Autumn): 93-110.

12.91 Toulmin,   Stephen   E.   1972(a).   "The   Historical
Background to the Anti-Science Movement." In **Civilization
and Science in Conflict Or Collaboration?** Amsterdam: Ciba
Foundation, 1972, pp. 23-32.

12.92 Toulmin, Stephen E. 1972(b). **Human Understanding,**
Vol. 1. Princeton: Princeton University Press. (Vols. II &
III unlikely to appear).

12.93 Toulmin, Stephen E. 1969. "From Logical Analysis to
Conceptual History." In Peter Achinstein and Stephen
Barker, eds. **The Legacy of Logical Positivism.** Baltimore,
MD: John Hopkins University Press.

12.94 Toulmin,   Stephen   E.   1961.   **Foresight   and
Understanding.** NY: Harper and Row.

12.95 Toulmin, Stephen E. 1960. **The Philosophy of Science.**
London: Hutchinson Co.

(See also the single volumes in the following series: (1)
the **Boston Studies in the Philosophy of Science,** (2) the
Foundations of the Unity of Science, (3) the **Minnesota
Studies in the Philosophy of Science,** (4) the **PSA,** and (5)
the **University of Western Ontario Series in the Philosophy
of Science.**

***

Author Index

Authors in Part I are indicated by normal type,
Authors in Part II by bold face.

Subject Index

Subjects in Part I are indicated by normal type,
Subjects in Part II by bold face. (Chapter
Subjects are not repeated.)

About the Compiler

DEBORAH A. REDMAN is a freelance bibliographer and translator.